THE REVOLUTIONARY ORATOR

Treatise on the art of oratory and parliamentary debate

By

André Blondel Tonleu Mendou

DEDICATION

To Hadrien Élie and Noémie Sabine:

May this booklet illuminate your future challenges!

ALSO BY ANDRE BLONDEL

Pacific Verses

They have forgotten that politics is a priesthood!
That politics is above all a commitment,
A priestly commitment!
That politics is nothing but a priesthood!
And nothing but a priesthood!
They have forgotten that the politician
Is not an economic operator!
And that in his role as a political opponent,
He has a historical responsibility!
Because he is invested with a particular mission,
At a very particular moment,
And in a very particular era,
They have forgotten!

Table of Contents

PROLOGUE

Dignus est intrare. You, dear readers, who are embarking on the reading of my friend André's work, who wish to learn or perfect the art of oratory, have proven yourselves worthy of joining the fellowship of orators and debaters—a private circle that you are now part of and one that André aspires to democratize.

In this book, André will rigorously and methodically outline the structure of debate, its techniques, its strategies, and many other topics. For my part, I want to dedicate this preface to what I consider the most important aspects of the debate and the art of oratory: the friendships you will forge, the freedom of expression, and the joy it brings.

I met André during a tournament at McGill University around 2011 or 2012 when our respective teams faced each other in a preliminary round early in the weekend. We were two enthusiastic young people with ideas and a passion for debating but with almost no knowledge of the structure of Canadian parliamentary debate. Perhaps we should have attended practice sessions more regularly before the tournament, but you'll agree with me that tournaments are far more exciting. The first piece of advice: Attend practice sessions. You'll meet the members of your college or university debate team, make friends, and find mentors.

The motion was about the celibacy of Catholic priests. I can't recall who argued in favour of priestly celibacy and who defended the opposing position. As you know,

it is the organizers who decide who represents the government and who represents the opposition. What I do remember, however, is that running out of arguments, one of us ended up inventing a Gospel passage to support their position. The other, sensing the bluff, in turn, began fabricating Gospel passages that said the opposite. The whole situation was hilariously absurd, with each new "quotation" more outrageous than the last. I don't recall who won that debate, and we didn't score well in the round since our arguments were weak. Yet, I still look back on that debate with great fondness.

It was during that weekend that I became friends with André. We each recognized in the other the joy of arguing, of passionately discussing—even rambling—about any topic, with humour whenever possible.

What also allowed us to embrace the adrenaline of debating fully was our shared understanding that the opinions expressed during debates were solely for the purpose of the debate and did not reflect the personal beliefs of those presenting them. However, over the past ten years, I have noticed a troubling trend in academia: a narrowing of freedom of expression. This shift has led to restrictions on debate topics and arguments, often under the guise of "equity" and to avoid offending anyone.

Taking the example of the McGill debate on priestly celibacy, it's possible that a practicing Catholic who heard us spouting nonsense about the Bible might have felt offended, whether rightly or wrongly. However, it would be a grave mistake to impose a debate rule that prohibits inventing words in the Holy Scriptures. Without this, would André and I have been able to develop our friendship?

To further the discussion, I would say that debaters should not be forbidden from presenting misogynistic, homophobic, or racist arguments. Indeed, these are often weak arguments, easy to refute, and ultimately, they cast a shadow over the entire speech of the speaker. In this sense, the debater would already be penalized with points for their arguments and the overall impression their performance left; no need to add anything more.

Moreover, by saying "it is forbidden to forbid," we leave open the entire spectrum of the debater's thoughts. The periods to prepare arguments or rebuttals are already limited enough, so please, let's not ask them to think with blinders on.

Returning to our university debating years, from 2011 to 2014, André and I participated in about fifteen tournaments in Quebec, including the Canadian championships, each representing the colours of our respective universities. Neither of us won one of these tournaments. The second piece of advice: learn to lose. Within a tournament, the closer you get to the finish line, the harder the defeat becomes. Moreover, if you lose several tournaments, it can start to affect your self-confidence, but be resilient. Even if you enter the tournament with the intention to win, know that regardless of the outcome, you'll see your debate friends again and share great moments with them.

At the beginning of 2014, André and I were among the top ten French-speaking debaters in Canada. We were approached to represent Canada at the World Francophone Debate Championship in Paris. André asked me if I wanted to partner with him, as our university teams no longer bound us. I had to decline, as my partner for the past three years, Gabrielle was also among the Canadian representatives, and it was largely thanks to her that we had come so close to winning several times.

In May 2014, André, Gabrielle, and the Canadian delegation spent a very enjoyable week in Paris debating against teams from all over the world. It was fascinating not only to compete with opponents from French-speaking countries, each with their own rich background and worldview but also to encounter very different approaches to debate. Once again, I made friends in Paris. Some of them came to do student exchanges in Montreal, and we stayed in touch. It's wonderful to know privileged witnesses to the significant moments of your life and revisit youthful memories when chance brings you back together. I thank André for allowing me to write his preface, as it gives me the chance to dive back into these memories with tenderness and nostalgia.

Furthermore, André and Élisabeth's team won the world championship, while my team was eliminated in the semifinals. There is a rumour that the organizers didn't want two of the four teams in the final to be from Quebec... Joking aside, André ultimately won the most important debate of 2014, and you stand to gain much by reading his work on doctrine. I wish you wonderful careers as speakers and hope you experience much joy throughout all of this. You will never regret the time you've invested in becoming a speaker. We are not born speakers; we become them!

Barrister Gabriel Meunier

Lawyer at the Quebec Bar

Semi-finalist at the World Debate Championship

FOREWORD

Before starting the reading, it seems essential to emphasize that the practice of the art of oratory is not limited to simply speaking in public. It is a transversal skill that plays a crucial role in many aspects of your professional and personal life. Whether it's to present an idea, gain support, engage people in a cause, influence opinions, advocate for claims, or simply make your voice heard, oratory proves to be an undeniable asset.

For those working in the community sector, who are called to defend the rights of a population, represent marginalized voices, and mobilize community members to address societal issues, mastery of the art of oratory is indispensable. The revolutionary orator is presented as a practical and inspiring guide designed to help you improve your verbal communication, adapt your speeches to your audience, and develop advanced techniques such as rhetoric, improvisation, and storytelling to influence and mobilize your community. With this work as your companion, you will be able to embody an inspiring leader capable of rallying your community and advancing a cause that is close to your heart.

By exploring the fundamental principles of oratory, this work invites you to understand how to structure a compelling speech, captivate your audience, and use advanced techniques such as rhetoric, improvisation, and storytelling to inspire and engage your community for social and community development. It will guide you in understanding these key elements, allowing you to develop an effective speech and master these powerful tools that will open the doors to inspiration and mobilization.

Community sector workers are frequently called upon to voice the concerns of their users, defend their rights and interests, and sometimes take on the role of representatives for their members or partners in front of various bodies, whether governmental, funders, elected officials, or citizens. To carry out this mission successfully, they must be able to communicate clearly, persuasively, and in a way that mobilizes their audience. Eloquence thus becomes an indispensable tool for community workers who strive to mobilize their community and advance a cause.

Moreover, community workers are often entrusted with the responsibility of speaking on behalf of vulnerable or marginalized individuals who have limited access to public platforms. In this context, they assume a special responsibility to amplify their voices, defend their rights, and provide them with a platform for expression.

In a context where social and political issues are becoming increasingly complex and intertwined, community workers must have the ability to collaborate with other stakeholders and engage in concerted efforts to achieve their goals; this requires effective communication with people who have different perspectives, the ability to negotiate compromises and find innovative solutions. The revolutionary orator responds to this need by providing practical tools and advice aimed at improving oral communication and strengthening speaking skills, thus enabling fruitful collaboration and building effective coordination to achieve common goals.

The revolutionary orator transcends the simple nature of a practical guide. It is truly a call to action for all those who aspire to strengthen their speaking skills and become influential agents of change within their community. I sincerely hope that this book will be a source of inspiration for all those who are agents of change because together, we have the power to build more just, equitable, and flourishing societies.

Sabrina Fauteux-A

Executive Director of Saint-Léonard Coordination

INTRODUCTION

More than two millennia ago, the masters of rhetoric were already questioning the rules of an art that would guarantee every speaker the ability to "mobilize all that is proper to persuade[1]" an audience. Speech is undoubtedly an art that has marked the history of humanity. Encompassed by sacred powers, it can change the course of the world or ruin its destiny. Indeed, all it takes is for a speech to be well-crafted to trigger a war, a genocide, save an innocent, condemn a guilty person, or bring about peace. Cicero did not mince words when making this known in an anthology work: "... if I consider the evils that have torn our homeland, if I recall the disasters that once shook the most flourishing cities, everywhere I see the greatest part of these misfortunes caused by eloquent men.

But when I want, with the help of history, to go back to earlier times, I see wisdom. Even more so eloquence, founding cities, extinguishing wars, establishing lasting alliances, and binding the ties of holy friendship[2]." Since Greco-Roman antiquity, rhetoric has been elevated to the level of "the primary field of education." It has been the origin of great democratic revolutions and various revolutionary movements that have punctuated the history of societies and the future of communities[3]. Its pedagogical dimension gives rise to a new type of intellectuals, called to become the elite of tomorrow.

From the Greek rhetorike, meaning "the art of speech," rhetoric is none other than the art of discourse aimed at convincing an audience. In work with a memorable title, Quintilian defines rhetoric as: "the power to persuade" (Uis persuadendi). This Quintilian conception of the art of well-saying places the speaker at the center of the art of persuasion, with speeches that electrify audiences, hanging on their every word during public addresses on various issues. Specifically, political, civic, legal, or economic questions. The tribune, through his magical words, is convinced of the righteousness of his cause. Rhetoric would actually be: "the science of speaking.[4]" In other words, the art of expressing oneself in a distinguished manner, with ease, presence, and skill. It would, therefore, be difficult to mention the word "rhetoric" without referring to the art of speaking well, but also, and above all, to the ability to persuade. It is, broadly speaking, "a phenomenon that involves leading someone, without apparent coercion, to think something they had not thought before (...) It is an art that aims to understand, produce, and regulate persuasion.[5]" In this logic, rhetoric appears as a technique, a method, an art aimed at producing persuasive discourse based on know-how and magical formulas that every citizen in a rule-of-law state should master.

The art of oratory has experienced moments of glory since Greco-Roman antiquity. It was an elite field of education, both in primary schools where children were trained to read and write, and in secondary schools where it was taught by grammarians, and even in universities where it was taught by "rhetoricians.[6]" Rhetoric at that time was the most valued and sought-after training. Beyond preparing for advocacy, it also prepared young people for roles as officials, administrators, and politicians, and even to become exemplary citizens capable of seasoning the democratic process. Most of the dignitaries of the empire were graduates of rhetoric schools. Thus, rhetoric was indispensable and acted as a vehicle for social ascent. Its teaching was centred around preparatory exercises and declamation. The preparatory exercises focused on fables, storytelling, description, prosopopoeia, praise, thesis, reading, listening, paraphrasing, and contradiction, to name just a few. It was a glorious time for the art of verbal magic, which was at the heart of society and various democratic revolutions. An influential art, presiding over the distribution of power and influence in society. An art that stood as the alpha and omega of the political system, public life, or the economic microcosm.

At some point, people began to distrust orators. Many claimed that the Athenians' great speeches were too difficult to understand. Rhetoric began to be fiercely criticized, both by comedians and the courts, the sanctuary par excellence of oratory. Plato,[7] in the same vein, called orators "false specialists of false values[8]."

Even in contemporary times, the name or adjective "rhetoric" still refers, in a popular or populist conception, to words lacking objective foundations. Many express deep fears regarding the omnipotence of speech. Speech plays a key role in a nation's democracy, as it can calm fears, bring joy, or evoke pity. However, it's important to explore the nuances of this art that have benefited human societies for thousands of years. It is probably these fears that pronounce the funeral oration of oratory, which disappeared like a magic spell from the school curriculum starting in 1902 in France.

The art of the spoken word was harshly vilified. Its critics argued that it was an art of deception institutionalized in education. Therefore, it would not lead to truth but rather divert the youth from good values.

From then on, the control of linguistic abilities was no longer based on the invention of speeches by students. They would, however, have to prove this competence through writing exercises and, more specifically, the essay. We witness, almost extraordinarily, the collapse of the oral aspect of learning, which had been so glorified in the past. The student would no longer admire or identify with a Cicero, a Quintilian, or a Demosthenes... They would now be required to exercise their critical thinking by analyzing a topic or commenting on a literary text submitted for their assessment. More concerning, the art of oratory soon deserted law schools. The pleading no longer became a major subject but rather a trivial one. In this regard, Hélène Tronc asserts that lawyers "sometimes engage in eloquence competitions for fun, delivering ceremonial speeches, but they have no true oral training.[9]

The scientific and technical aspects of trials have increased, and judges form their opinions more from the case file, while the relative importance of the lawyer's plea has declined.[10]" This deplorable and almost macabre situation clearly explains the precedence of written culture over oral culture and the tendency to view rhetoric as a set of superfluous techniques.[11] Starting in 1902, we witnessed the downfall of the strong oratory tradition, which became only a shadow of itself. Rhetoric certainly fell into disfavor, but it remains present in other social spheres, such as politics, advertising, marketing, and the media. The tradition of speeches survives only on occasions of certain celebrations and commemorations.[12]

At the dawn of the third millennium, we are fortunately witnessing a timid but progressive resurrection of rhetoric in various universities, cultures, and countries. Debate societies and oratory clubs are emerging in major American, European, Asian, and African schools, although in many countries, rhetoric still hasn't been integrated into the official education system. Oratory is becoming the favorite sport of many committed students, ready to face the challenges of tomorrow. Major social revolutions highlight the need to make persuasion techniques accessible to everyone. The goal is to inspire revolutionary orators who can awaken the people and lead movements filled with hope for humanity.

Both in international plea competitions and in the debate practices during our civil law studies at the University of Montreal, the Sorbonne, or Sciences Po in Paris, the practice of revolutionary debate could be conducted without being judged or despised. The orator, like a scout, now has the historical responsibility to enlighten society with innovative ideas, the strength of their arguments, and their social commitment, or their rhetorical talent. Speech thus plays an essential role in public life, and hoping to change the world requires that the revolutionary knows how to wield words, which is by no means an obstacle to action but a prerequisite. How is it possible to consider action before discussion sheds light on the path?[13] This, in truth, is difficult. One might discover that contrary to certain opinions, mastering the art of oratory develops critical thinking and allows for a dialectical journey toward knowledge through a contradictory debate. Rhetoric, as taught by its great ancient masters, can shape a new kind of leader—one who is aware of social issues and equipped to address society's challenges. Oratory undeniably plays a fundamental role in the process of building our societies, especially when its beauty and power are dedicated to noble causes, thus leaving an indelible mark on history. Through their speech, the orator expresses their ideas, motivations, and deep convictions. Their social action contributes to the materialization of these convictions. Albert Camus was, therefore, not wrong when he said, in this perspective, "I understood that it was not enough to denounce injustice; one had to give one's life to fight it."[14] Rhetoric is an incitement to objective reflection and community engagement, a mould in which the leaders who will shake the world of tomorrow are forged. In a world where tyrannical, despotic regimes continue to exist, disguised in democratic colors and shells, it is clear that only contradictory debate and the clash of ideas could lead these societies toward a democratic ideal. Rhetoric would thus in this context, would serve the democratic revolution. Born in Athens, the birthplace of democracy, it is no coincidence that it found a fertile ground there for its emergence. Power should always limit power in the arrangement of things;[15] it is under this condition that the clash of ideas, which produces change, could take place.

We should, therefore, not fear rhetoric or orators, for they embody noble and republican values that help build societies distinguished by the strength of their institutions, not by strongmen and providential figures who have established the sanctification, divinization of power, and even perpetual governance as a mode of rule. The orator is inevitably a good person who embodies the values of peace, justice, equality, coexistence, and tolerance.

This is especially true given that Cicero, the Roman lawyer, famously said during a plea, "Let arms yield to the toga." Jacques Amyot, a Renaissance humanist, recommended using "the sharpness of the tongue" instead of the sword.[16] The revolutionary orator is a distinguished citizen who feels invested in a very particular social mission at a very specific moment. While it is true that the orator is an ambassador of free speech, this freedom of speech is so well embodied through their speeches. However, it remains true that there is a limit to the statements they can make in a speech.

Hate speech, therefore, does not receive any legal protection, and the orator who resorts to it is certainly a pseudo-orator, useless to society. They will have to face the extreme rigours of the law and the judgment of history.

As can be easily seen, rhetoric allows for logical and scientific demonstrations. Above all, it allows for the successful execution of the necessary revolutions that guarantee the advent of the rule of law, democracy, economic stability, and social progress. It is wrong to believe that the art of speech is just empty words and that orators are manipulators using speech to deceive people.

Oratory is rather a technique, a method that, when properly followed, leads to scientific truth while fostering a certain social commitment from the speaker, now ready for the great revolutions to come, great revolutions during which they will champion their convictions with rhetorical methods and emphasize the weight of ideas, the strength of arguments, to the great benefit of the sovereign people.

In this context, it becomes urgent to democratize the techniques of oratory to give every citizen the opportunity to highlight the revolutionary impulse that still slumbers within them, constantly waiting for the oratorical spark to take flight. Therefore, oratory should not be reserved for a certain elite, which is why it is more than wise for rhetoric to regain its nobility by reappearing in official school curricula, lawyer training, and the education of dignitaries at various levels of the nations. One should be trained in rhetoric to allow the emergence of tomorrow's young leaders, who will serve the people, the republic, democracy, the economy, and diplomacy. Oratory remains a cultural mode of expression, and it is urgent to master the language through this art to savour the fragrance of words in osmosis of conviviality. When we know the stakes involved in mastering a language for the socio-professional integration of a citizen, we can only be happy to practice this noble art, which rises above the fray.

As Cicero already said, "One is born a poet, one becomes an orator." It is through daily effort that the budding orator strives for perfection and thus becomes the orator of tomorrow. Not everything will happen overnight. Far from being essentially an artist, the orator is a methodical person who will follow the techniques of the great masters to express themselves in a distinguished manner. For thousands of years, the principles of rhetoric have remained largely relevant. To help our orators become better, the techniques and methods of oratory must be popularized and mastered before venturing into parliamentary debate, a form of rhetorical training that takes contemporary realities into account. In this journey toward this atypical world, there will be a back-and-forth between antiquity, which holds the ancient secrets of an art that has hardly aged, and the present. Don't we say that the oldest pots make the best soups? But it remains urgent not to stay in a past that may already be outdated. The world has changed, and it's important to recognize the rhetorical realities of today while still valuing the Greco-Roman principles.

Eloquence would thus play an essential role in public life. It's clear that our orator must know how to persuade an audience, present their ideas confidently, and counter opponents' arguments while following the rules of the art. Since the orator cannot say whatever they want, a journey or exploration of legal issues and the ethics of speech prove essential to frame this verbal jungle, sometimes worthy of great battles.

The revolutionary orator will follow the proper practices to speak with distinction, taking on the role of a teacher when addressing others. They will captivate their audience through various techniques and must know how to move their listeners in order to lead them to victory gently.

Structured parliamentary debate, being a very effective contemporary mode of training in revolutionary rhetoric, requires the orator also to know the techniques of parliamentary debate and their implications in Canada, France, and Africa and their practical applications.

This will allow them to easily make a comparative study to draw the necessary lessons for the development of their oratory skills in a world strongly marked by globalization and multiculturalism. Finally, our orator must be aware of the limits of their speech and the legal rules that punish those who give speeches that fail to uphold the nobility of oratory.

Through continuous training in rhetoric, like an apprentice blacksmith learning to forge, like a chick learning to sing, through practicing preparatory exercises and declamations as in antiquity, the budding orator will undoubtedly become the orator of tomorrow, capable of leading the great revolutions that will be imposed on their society, now invested with a special mission they must accomplish in the sense of Frantz Fanon in *The Wretched of the Earth*.[17] *They will no longer be just the poet of today but will surely become the orator of tomorrow: "Nascuntur poetas fiunt oratores.[18]"*

FIRST PART:
THE LOGOS19

When the orator speaks in public, they have duties[20] and missions toward their audience. They must instruct, teach, and inform (probare), please, charm (conciliare), and finally move (flectere).[21] The role of teaching and instruction is what is commonly called logos, the rational part of the speech in which the orator speaks to the reason of the listeners, using a dialectical and logical approach that methodically leads to the truth. As a lover of wisdom, the orator will aim to have the intellectual skills needed in every speech, using a logical approach that leads directly to clear, understandable knowledge. They will employ multiple mental operations to prove the validity of their arguments, provide tangible evidence, palpable facts, and, if necessary, relevant statistics that will show how, from a scientific and methodical point of view, their plea remains primarily rational. They will make strong logical connections and use the most respected authorities to back up the ideas they are defending. Before pleasing and moving, the orator must first be able to develop a subject "interesting for a cultured audience.[22] It would, in truth, be dishonourable to agree to speak on a subject when one does not know its background or its outcomes. In order to make the ideas that are close to their heart triumph, the orator must have reasoning that is both scientific and logical, making full use of various argumentative methodologies, both in their outlines and in their detours. The debater must demonstrate exceptional research skills, knowing how to find the best arguments in service of their cause, but also show discernment when faced with the results of the research they have gathered after a laborious process. Only by doing this will they be able to identify the argument that best supports their main point. It is imperative that they master the art of construction, the structure of the speech, as well as the art of arranging the arguments.

Only under these conditions can they truly fulfill their role as a teacher, guiding an audience eager to absorb knowledge, which they convey clearly and effectively through their speech. Above all, the distinguished orator must demonstrate realism to make their speech interesting for the audience listening. In this regard, Cicero says about Pericles: "Like Pericles, whom I mentioned earlier, I would like him also to know physics; he would be all the greater and nobler for it. When he transitions from celestial matters to the affairs of mortals, all his language and his thinking will have gained in grandeur and elevation, there is no doubt about that.[23]"

Thus, it becomes necessary in this logic to analyze in turn what their reasoning should be (Chapter I), the invention or techniques of research and argumentative categorization (Chapter II), and finally, the art of construction, the structure of the speech (Chapter III). Thus, we will be able to understand better the strategies that the orator uses to conquer the mind of the audience, the reason of the judges and juries, with the goal of making the cause for which they plead and deliver their speech triumph.

CHAPTER I:
OF ORATORICAL REASONING

The orator is a permanent thinker engaging in a contradictory debate with a neutral arbiter, which is the reason. They methodically move toward knowledge, establishing not only the weight of their ideas but also the strength of their arguments, which they highlight with a certain mastery. In their position as a friend of wisdom and ethical values, they stand apart from the common citizens and, by the same token, rise above the fray through the mastery of a reasoning methodology unique to the distinguished intellectuals of prestigious forums and courts. The oratory method here refers to a pursuit, a search, or an effort to achieve an end. It is, in fact, according to André Lalande: "a definable direction, regularly followed in a mental operation."[24] In this context, argumentative reasoning is the set of rules to follow in order to find the most convincing arguments that support a given thesis.

Many researchers from different fields, especially psychology, have studied how reasoning works in the mind. While acknowledging the value of contributions from modern psychology specialists, it must also be recognized that Aristotle did commendable foundational work in the 4th century BC when he first conceived two categories of reasoning: "Analytical reasoning," which, starting from necessary or indisputable premises, leads to certain conclusions, and "dialectical reasoning," which, by contrast, is based on elements that are apparent to all.[25] Argumentation is the main part of dialectical reasoning. It relies on statements that can be debated, even if everyone doesn't agree on them.

From the Latin verb *arguere*, which in its original sense meant "To illuminate," and from the Latin word *argumentatio*, argumentation is "The set of discursive techniques aimed at provoking or increasing the interlocutor's agreement with the theses presented to them."[26] The orator, in their argument, must clearly show the thesis they are supporting. Beyond using images, they need to present their ideas clearly. As can clearly be seen, the orator is not just a charmer or a rhetor. The art of oratory has codes, methods, and sacred rites that have governed its practice since time immemorial. In order to decode in detail this method specific to great communicators, it would undoubtedly be necessary, before addressing the issues related to paralogism (III), to first raise the veil on what exactly constitutes the architecture of argumentative reasoning (I), the reasoning par excellence of revolutionary orators. After this overview of oratory reasoning, we will certainly realize why it is more than important to think before speaking one's thoughts. We will see how this method has been the foundation for orators for thousands of years and how it remains an essential tool for future orators.

The Architecture of The Speech

Like any good leader, the orator should follow a method, codes, and a dialectical path toward the truth. This approach appears to be the condition without which they would not be able to convince adversaries or an audience to recognize the validity of the cause to which they have devoted themselves. A speech is not a random collection of ideas. It is like a house, with a foundation, walls, a structure, openings, and a roof. These seem to us to be the steps that the exceptional communicator must respect in order to hope to express themselves abundantly and majestically. Thus, the speech and argumentative reasoning have, in fact, an architecture, a structure, or better yet, a methodical progression that every tribune, driven by the desire to convince through the weight of ideas and the strength of arguments, should follow. In this case, the orator is no longer just an artist of speech wishing, beyond ideas and arguments, to charm and move their audience through various rhetorical strategies; they are also, above all, a methodist who must follow a certain protocol to say what they have to say. The method established for centuries by the great masters thus allows for a little more readability, clarity, and, above all, scientificity in the oration. This objectivity gives the speech great educational value, allowing it to influence the listeners' reasoning and help convince them of the speech's validity. It is therefore important to specify here that the argumentative speech should follow two major steps: the premise, which constitutes the first phase (A), and the inference, which is the logical conclusion that naturally follows from the premise (B).

A - The Premise

Every argumentative speech begins with a premise, which in strictly logical terms means: "Each of the two initial propositions of a syllogism from which the conclusion is drawn."[27] Even though some authors believe that the premise is an explicit or implicit thesis put forward by the one who argues, based on reasoning[28], the orator must have a high-quality premise with the aim of persuading and seeing their thesis gain some prominence. Hence, the urgency of putting forward, or simply giving priority to, the most widely shared, most accepted, and most praised premises. In any case, the premises must be acceptable (1), relevant (2), and, of course, present general guarantees to justify a conclusion (3).[29] The orator who adheres to this triptych ensures a certain strength to the arguments they present.

1 - The Acceptability of The Premise

Very few arguments are based on obvious premises. Ideally, however, one would want to have true premises. This situation could partly be explained by the uncertainty that accompanies us during our times and moments of argumentation. The uncertainty is more based on ignorance of the facts than on aspects of theoretical and empirical knowledge that would allow us to clearly distinguish between the true and the false, the useful and the pleasant. Hence the urgency of placing more importance not on the truth of the premise, but on its acceptability. This means that not only do premises (the statements or ideas that form the basis of an argument) need to be true, but they also need to seem reasonable or believable to the audience. If a premise is plausible—meaning it makes sense or fits with what people expect or understand—it becomes easier for them to accept, even if it's not 100% proven. When premises are based on a credible source, they are acceptable.[30] Information from Radio-Canada, CNN, or Africa24 about a major international current event on which a premise is based would be more credible than a premise based on the statement of an amateur in the field of information. Similarly, the testimony of a trusted person on which a premise is based can make that premise acceptable. Finally, the acceptability of the premise can be grounded in its plausibility, as it aligns with our knowledge and is not questioned by the data we possess.[31] As we have seen, the acceptability of the premise should not lead the orator to place primary importance on its relevance.

1- The Relevance of the Premise

The premise must certainly be acceptable, but it must also be relevant. Otherwise, the orator would struggle to present their ideas and arguments with strength when the chance comes. Therefore, an acceptable but irrelevant premise would have no place, either because it would be of no interest to the issue at the heart of the argument or because it would lead the orator to commit "hara-kiri" by consolidating a conclusion that is the opposite of the one developed in the argument. "Plausible" here means what is "rightfully considered true" (Robert). In his manual *A Practical Study of Argument*, on pages 128 to 135 of the 2010 edition, Govier proposes to orators a set of questions to ask themselves in order to verify the acceptability of a premise:"1: the premise is true! 2: Is the premise classically accepted by competent persons or institutions? 3: Is the premise the conclusion of a solid argument? 4: Is the premise stated by an authoritative source? 5: Has the premise been stated by a trustworthy witness?"

The premise must, therefore, contribute to justifying the conclusion that will naturally follow from the argument. However, it may happen that a premise causes the conclusion to be rejected. In this case, we are dealing with a rebuttal.

Practical Case:

Ariane: People with low income do not get involved enough in community events. There is no need to invite them to said events.

Sorel: In reality, it is precisely because they do not get involved in the community that it becomes more urgent than ever to invite them and, as much as possible, offer them accommodation measures.

In fact, Sorel challenged the argument, agreeing that Ariane's premise was acceptable, but pointing out that it led to a conclusion nearly the opposite of his own. The orator has the responsibility to verify several parameters to ensure that the premise is relevant. Does it relate to the conclusion? Does it help strengthen the conclusion of the argument? Is it off-topic? Can it support a conclusion opposite to the one in the argument? These are all critical questions the orator must ask to validate the relevance of their premise. While the relevance of the premise is crucial, it is also important that it provides enough evidence to support the conclusion.

2 - Sufficient Guarantees to Justify the Conclusion

Acceptable and relevant premises may prove insufficient to justify the conclusion. Arguments based on insufficient evidence would thus struggle to thrive.[32] Similarly, clues do not constitute proof, just as arguments based solely on emotions remain insufficient.[33]

The orator must, therefore, ask themselves whether the premise is acceptable. If so, is it relevant? If yes, are there reasons to believe that it could lead to a conclusion that opposes the one put forward in the argument? Are there, in truth, other acceptable and relevant premises that would lead to a conclusion opposing the argument presented? It is only through an objective response to this set of questions that one can be sure to have a premise that meets the standards of argumentative reasoning.

As can be clearly seen, the premise constitutes the first phase of the speech delivered by the orator. But reasoning is not limited to a simple premise unless it is partial, biased, or otherwise completely fragmented. Therefore, it becomes important to develop the next phase, which is realized in the inference (B), materializing in the process of concluding the premise through logical steps and: "Indicators of strength"[34] such as: "therefore," "hence," "consequently," "that's why," "the reason why," "accordingly"[35]...

B - The Inference

Inference refers to the operation by which one moves from a set of premises to a justified conclusion, made legitimate by those premises.[36] It is, in reality, the backbone of all reasoning, although it is not always logical, nor does it always ensure theoretical and empirical validity for the conclusion. Inference can take several forms: it can be immediate, mediated (1), or simply inductive or deductive (2).

1 - Immediate Or Mediated Inference

Immediate inference consists of two terms: a premise and a conclusion. In contrast, mediated inference is made up of at least two premises and a conclusion.

Practical Case:

P1: Barthélemy is a man,

P2: All men are mortal,

C: Therefore, Barthélemy is mortal.

1 - Deductive Or Inductive Inference

Deductive inference is one that follows a path that guarantees the truth of its conclusion. In this case, when the premises are true, it follows that the conclusions can also be true. Such an inference is, therefore, valid because it conforms to a certain logic, a certain method. In contrast, if one of the premises is false, the conclusion will undoubtedly be false as well.

Practical Case:

P1: Barthélemy is a man (true),

P2: All men are mortal (true),

C: Therefore, Barthélemy is mortal (true).

Contrary to deductive inferences, inductive inferences do not guarantee any transfer of truth between the premises and the conclusion. Therefore, the premises can be true and the conclusion false.

Practical Case:

P1: This river floods every May,

C: Therefore, it will flood again this May.

The fact that the river has always flooded during this time of year does not necessarily guarantee that it will do so again this year at the same time. This inference may make the conclusion plausible or probable but not necessarily true. Inference is, therefore, an essential element of argumentative discourse. The question remains, however, how to determine if the discourse beyond the premises is logically acceptable and logically correct.

1 - Methodology Of Oratory Reasoning

The orator is a strategist, a methodist who places great importance on method in order to convince more, to persuade, and to stir passions. From "Socratic maieutics[37]" to "Socratic irony[38]," from "doubt" to "Cartesian doubt," the orator has many tricks to deliver a speech that leaves a lasting impression. However, for a long time, those who possess verbal magic have used reasoning through syllogism (A), reasoning through induction (B), or reasoning through hypothesis and abduction. These four methods appear as classics whose relevance has not lost its significance in this third millennium.

A - Reasoning Through Syllogism

The syllogism is, without a doubt, one of the major tools at the orator's disposal. They must use it with a certain mastery. Presented by Aristotle more than two thousand years ago, it remains highly relevant and has lost none of its flavour, depth, or significance. From *syllogimos*, syllogism is a "discourse in which, certain things having been posited, something else necessarily follows from these posited things because it is thus.[39]" This definition, at least general, allows us to get an overview of what the budding orator should know about the syllogism. The one proposed by Maritain[40] in his work seems to shed more light on our understanding. A syllogism is a form of argument where, from a premise that relates two terms to a third, the speaker draws a conclusion that links the two terms directly.

Practical Case:

All men are mortal,

Now, Joseph is a man,

Therefore, Joseph is mortal.

The first two propositions of the syllogism are called premises. The more general one, and most often the first, is the major premise (All men are mortal). The less general and usually the second is called the minor premise (Now, Joseph is a man). Finally, the third proposition, which derives from the other two by consequence, is the conclusion (Therefore, Joseph is mortal).

Practical Case:

Every accused person is presumed innocent (major premise),

Now, Dominique is accused (minor premise),

Therefore, Dominique is presumed innocent (conclusion).

When well-constructed, syllogism allows one to formulate non-contradictory judgments with exceptional logical vigor, even if the judgment is not always true, as the truth of substance depends on the premises. There are several types of syllogisms: the "demonstrative.[41]"

The "dialectic,[42]" the "eristic,[43]" and the most dangerous: the "paralogism," built on premises that are not necessarily true and prone to lead astray. However, the orator should not ignore that the syllogism cannot go beyond the implicit in the context of a premise. In light of this observation, Aristotle found it wise to explore a new type of reasoning to address this gap, which could strip the word magician of a highly important aspect of their relevance. This is why inductive reasoning is needed to fix the flaws of the syllogism. While many orators see it as the foundation of reasoning, it still has its limits.

Reasoning Through Induction

Induction is undoubtedly one of the logical tools at the orator's disposal. It generally consists of starting from a certain number of facts to assert a general truth, which will be called an empirical law or, if based on experience, an "experiential maxim[44]." Through the inductive approach, the orator seeks not to explain but to establish a universal truth, a universal maxim. Moreover, a truth that is more accepted by all and more universally recognized than that carried by other forms of logical thought. Unlike syllogism, where the orator moves from general to specific, induction starts with specific cases or examples and then uses them to create a general principle or rule.[45]

Practical Case:

César is mortal, Aristotle is mortal, Mussolini is mortal, I am mortal,

We are all men,

Therefore, all men are mortal.

Practical Case:

Jonathan killed Patrice for money, Jonathan killed Patrice out of betrayal, Jonathan killed Patrice out of anger,

Therefore, homicides involve a motive (experiential maxim).

However, the orator must always remember that, like syllogism, induction is not a flawless method of reasoning and has its own limitations. It would still be necessary to verify the universal through all the particular cases: "virtually experimental.[46]" A situation that is almost utopian. Therefore, there is no guarantee that the generalization is not abusive. This is, in fact, the same point made by Karl Marx when he asserts: "[...] induction, that is, an inference based on a multitude of observations, is a myth. It is neither a psychological given, nor an expensive life fact, nor a phenomenon that falls under the scientific approach." This is one of the reasons why the orator, in addition to induction, has every interest in resorting to the logical procedure model of hypothesis and abduction (C). In this way, they would have several "logical tools" at their disposal to support their ideas and, by using them wisely, ensure their arguments succeed in any situation.

A - Reasoning Through Hypothesis and Abduction

From the Latin *hypothesis*, borrowed from ancient Greek *hupothesis*, the hypothesis is a supposition, a conjecture made without affirming or denying the consequences derived from it.[47] In this logic, the orator, in order to conform to this system of reasoning and thought, must present a supposition not validated by real data but which may be true if experimentation confirms it or if previously established truths support it. At the core of every original idea, there is always a hypothesis, which serves as one of the best ways to question and explore the truth. Naville did not hesitate to assert without reservation that "there is not a single law in science that was not born in the form of a supposition." This is even more true

26

because any mental exercise with innovative tendencies must submit to the triptych: "observation," "supposition," and "verification."[48] This is certainly an approach that the orator must follow if they wish to give themselves an objective channel for argumentation and demonstration. The hypothesis is certainly the best way of thinking to "bring forth minds"[49] and scientific data that are truly original and new. It provides a strong foundation for creative and groundbreaking ideas. This system of reasoning was the guiding thread for the great scientific discoveries of the 17th century. Furthermore, hypothetical reasoning seems most suitable. The hypothesis is the channel par excellence that allows for demonstrating an accusatory theorem, building a plea of guilt or innocence, a defense speech, or a plea. When we understand how necessary it is to convince an audience today in various places and contexts, there is no doubt that this mode of reasoning is an absolute necessity for the distinguished orator! Although on its own and in specific contexts or pretexts, there may be some shortcomings. Hence, the urgency of verifying the ammunition that reasoning through abduction could offer us can prove to be a lifesaver in certain circumstances.

Abduction is a type of reasoning where the orator starts by considering several possible explanations for a phenomenon and then narrows them down to find the most likely one.[50] This process helps focus on the most plausible explanation. Also called "abductive reasoning," it closely resembles reasoning through hypothesis. While abduction can be effective in certain investigations and many situations, it is a difficultly admissible argumentative system, as it could lead to an argumentative trick of bad taste. The orator, being by nature a man of honour, should limit such an option, which, although allowing them always to be right, can make them a person of questionable morality. Even though, after all, the most important thing is to be right! All means are good when they are effective.[51]

I - Paralogism and Argumentative Fallacies

Argumentative falsehood, also known as "sophism," is considered "a formally false inference of reason, although it has the appearance of a correct inference.[52]" In this special structure of reasoning, we can see a truth with plausible characteristics, granting the reasoning almost certain persuasive power but with an error lurking in the shadows, leading to an incorrect conclusion. Beyond sophism, the orator may invoke various strategies always to be right[53], even when everything suggests that they are mistaken or simply wrong. From exaggeration[54] to *ad personam*[55] *argumentation, through ad hominem* argumentation, it is clear that the orator could have an inexhaustible source of resources in their arsenal. Through a game of questions and answers, they could still mislead an interlocutor and lead them to provide an answer desired by the questioner.[56] Verbal traps and argumentative[57] fallacies, like sophism or paralogism, are tricks developed by some orators always to be right. Normand Baillargeon, in his *Petit cours d'auto-défense intellectuelle*, has listed about seventeen sophisms:

The False Dilemma[58], Hasty Generalization[59], Appeal to Authority, Smokescreen, Slippery Slope, Appeal to Fear[60], False Analogy, Suppression of Relevant Data, Straw Man, *Ad Populum*[61]... *More than ever, the orator must grasp both the contours and the detours of maneuvers that, in truth, can determine the outcome of a debate, even if supported by highly questionable ethical foundations. This is the case with argumentum ad hominem (A), argumentum ad ignorantiam (B), and argumentum ad misericordiam (C).*

A - Argumentum Ad Hominem62

The orator must be skilled in using various rhetorical techniques, including sophisms like the ad hominem argument. This is one of the most common sophisms, and it often works in many situations, though it may not always be the most ethical approach. It is a rhetorical approach that involves attacking the character or personal aspects of the opponent rather than addressing the idea or argument presented by that orator. It is an argument based on the person who expresses an idea rather than on the weight of the ideas and the strength of the arguments put forward by them. Thus, the orator, by using this strategy, aims to shift the Debate from Ideas to the Characteristics of One's Opponent in order to erroneously conclude that there is a certain similarity between the traits and characteristics of the orator and the arguments they present. This mechanism ultimately allows for discrediting the proposed idea by discrediting the orator who states it and creating an effect known as the "poisoning the well.[63]"

As we can see, the sophistic orator uses ad hominem in certain situations, depending on the context, the audience, and the stakes of the argument. The approach may change based on what is at play and what the orator aims to achieve. In certain times and places, the word "anarchist" or "communist" is largely sufficient to discredit an opponent! In other places, these terms can be seen as a guarantee of credibility.[64] In other contexts, any word or expression referring to sexual orientation, nationality, gender, religion, race, ethnicity, or physical appearance, among others, can be used to either discredit or praise an orator, depending on whether one appreciates or despises them.[65]

Argumentum ad hominem can prove effective in political jousts and other forms of discourse that do not necessarily rely on logic. But from a strictly ethical and scientific standpoint, this sophism is not recommended for distinguished orators—those who believe in the weight of ideas, the strength of arguments, and a certain scientific approach to public debate.

B - Argumentum Ad Ignorantiam66

The orator uses *argumentum ad ignorantiam* when, in the absence of relevant facts and valid reasons, they still take the risk of concluding the truth or falsehood of the proposition or motion being analyzed.[67] On the one hand, this approach allows an orator to conclude despite not being able to demonstrate the validity of the conclusion or, better yet, the intellectual gymnastics that would naturally and logically lead to it. On the other hand, using the same rhetorical method, the orator allows themselves to conclude even though they cannot prove such a conclusion. In reality, this is a shortcut in reasoning that removes any scientific rigour or dialectical flavour from the orator's approach. One of the best examples illustrating this paralogism comes directly from *Petit cours d'autodéfense intellectuelle* by Normand Baillargeon.[68]

However, it remains difficult to detect this form of sophism. We are more likely to hastily conclude what we firmly believe for one reason or another. For example, an orator who believes extraterrestrials exist might be tempted to conclude, disregarding the necessary epistemological process, that "after all, it has never been proven that they don't exist. There's probably something true about it." This process, although limited in the objective sense of the term, can have certain relevance in some circumstances, particularly in cases that legitimize concluding in the absence of tangible data.

C - Argumentum Ad Misericordiam69

It is undeniable that the ideal[70] orator should, in all circumstances, give precedence to the weight of ideas and the strength of arguments in a completely objective manner. The appeal to pity goes beyond this recommendation from the Roman orator. It emphasizes special circumstances that would evoke sympathy for a cause or a person. It invites the conclusion that, based on this reason, one should depart from the usual criteria of evaluation or at least refrain from applying them with full rigor.

Practical Cases:

Before condemning the head of state, let us consider his high responsibilities and the weight of his presidential task above the fray. Therefore...

If you make me fail this exam, I will have to retake it this summer! Yet, I absolutely must work in order to survive.

However, it must be acknowledged that in normal reasoning, it is indeed possible to invoke particular circumstances to justify a decision without... As long as they are based on sympathy or feelings devoid of any logic. However, argumentum and misericordia arise when illegitimate circumstances are invoked to provoke sympathy that should not be part of the argumentative and dialectical process.

The Orator Is a Dialectical Thinker

As we have seen throughout this chapter, the ideal orator, in developing their speech, should not speak for the sake of speaking or speak just for the pleasure of speaking. They should follow the nomenclature developed over millennia by the pioneers of rhetoric and dialectic. The orator "thinks their words before speaking their thoughts,[71]" an architect of words who strives daily to build an original path without completely abandoning the well-trodden ones. They can make their ideas and arguments succeed by using different methods of thinking and reasoning, carefully selecting the most effective strategies to strengthen their points and persuade their audience. It is, however, up to them to determine which mechanism of thought seems appropriate in a particular context. Sophisms and argumentative fallacies have a place within the overall oratorical architecture. Although this strategy may flourish more in political or political-jousting debates, it is important to recognize that because they do not always respect the process of contradictory debate and the dialectical path toward knowledge that is required of any orator adorned with the bright colors of logic and objectivity, they remain problematic, both in their meaning, relevance, and consistency, as well as in the process that allows the weight of ideas and the strength of arguments to prevail. Finally, the orator is...

An orator is always seen as a person of honour and integrity, someone who understands the importance of good morals, aesthetics, and ethics in their words and actions. They aim to inspire respect and trust through their principles. However, it is undeniable, and regrettable, that paralogism is often supported by low values, closer to Machiavellian logic than to the intellectual honesty embodied by those entrusted with the responsibility of addressing social ills through the power of words. Nevertheless, beyond this debate on the values of discourse, it seems rather urgent that the orator masters these mechanisms in order to know when their opponent uses them to divert their attention or that of the audience from the meaning and essence of a joust or if, by extraordinary circumstances, they deem it wise to use them to save a noble cause.

CHAPTER II:
ON ORATORICAL INVENTION72

The orator is similar to Hegel's owl of Minerva, which only takes flight at dusk. This symbolizes that wisdom and understanding often come after reflection when the situation is clearer, and the orator is ready to speak with insight. With the historical responsibility of returning to the sensible world, shining their beacons and flashlights of wisdom into areas that, as if by extraordinary circumstances, sometimes slumber in ignorance without even knowing it. Possessing an almost encyclopedic knowledge, the source from which emanate the "seven rivers of the liberal[73] arts," they are by nature a dialectician,[74] in that they affirm or deny a given based on the question or response of an interlocutor. However, it is still necessary that the argument they present supports their thesis, convincing a jury. That is why, beyond their immense general knowledge, it is more than prudent to proceed with *the invention,* that is, the search for arguments that can support the thesis they intend to defend.[75]

The search for relevant arguments is unquestionably the most delicate phase in the construction[76] of a speech. It's important to clarify that in this context, *inventio* is not about creating something new, but rather the process of searching and discovering within one's broad knowledge and wisdom. It involves finding the most suitable arguments to support the validity of a thesis and strengthen the overall argument. It is an operation where the orator, in their preparation, must extract from their rivers of wisdom the most solid arguments related to the thesis they defend, much like a miner extracting minerals from the ground. In the process of preparing for a debate or speech, the orator must logically find the arguments that are closest to their thesis, exercising discernment.[77] For a given cause or a particular debate, there would thus be a kind of "deposit," in other words, specific places the orator, like the miner, must orient themselves toward in order to "extract[78]" the necessary arguments for their cause. The key question to ask when undertaking argumentative research is, of course, where to find the most relevant arguments to bring the thesis to light. What are the most appropriate places the orator should explore, like the miner, in order to make the truth triumph? After gathering the arguments, the next step is to consider how they can be organized based on the logical approach the orator wants to follow. This classification helps in presenting the arguments in a clear and effective way to support their position.

That is why, more than ever, it is wise to first consider an analysis of the most appropriate places for the orator to explore when seeking ideas and arguments to reveal the truth through a logical approach (I). On the other hand To analyze the classification of arguments obtained as a result of the aforementioned research (II).

I - Argumentative Exploration

Argumentative exploration consists of the orator searching for the most relevant arguments for a given topic or subject, which are likely to lead to victory. They will, therefore, resort to specific "argumentative places[79]." Cicero argues that the argumentative place, also called "*loci*," "is where the arguments[80] are hidden." But before this, the orator must put into practice their research skills, a scientific attitude that allows the orator, like the miner seeking mines, to search for arguments in specific places. Before any in-depth debate, the orator is strongly encouraged to ask the following general questions, identified by Hermagoras of Temnos and then Cicero: "Is it?" "Why?" "Where?" "When?" "How?" "With what means?[81]" The answer to any of these questions could give rise to an argument[82]. It could also be extremely useful for determining the places to search for arguments, which Cicero classifies into "common" (A) and "special" or specific (B) places. In exploring common places, the orator seeks very general arguments that can be used, regardless of the field of knowledge.

Special places allow one to find arguments specific to a particular field of knowledge or a specific genre of oratory. The orator will carefully examine the arguments and select the most relevant ones for each situation, understanding that not all arguments hold the same weight or importance.

This ensures that the chosen arguments are the most effective for supporting their message in the given context. Therefore, he must also weigh the arguments, for as Cicero notes: "Nothing is more fertile than the mind, especially when cultivated by study. But the rich and fertile land produces both the harvest and the weeds that harm it."[83]

A - Exploration of Common Places

Through the exploration of common places, the orator seeks general arguments that may be valid in any field of knowledge.

They could explore the places of quantity[84], which highlight how one thing can be greater than another for reasons related to quantity. When it comes to arguments, having strong and relevant ones is always important. An orator who presents more solid evidence on a specific issue will have a greater chance of convincing their audience and winning their case compared to someone who relies on only a few points or weak evidence. The strength and quantity of arguments often make a significant difference in achieving success. This can be concretely demonstrated in testimonial evidence when proving the precedence of one factual version over another. The number of witnesses called can further support an opinion formed about the case. The more witnesses align with a version of events, the more credit that version will receive.

Conversely, the fewer witnesses identify with a version, the less it will be praised. The orator may, however, choose to focus more on the "places of quality," which emphasize not the number of arguments converging in the same direction but their value... and the probative strength of the arguments highlighted. The place of quality indeed presents itself as the antidote to the place of quantity, which is essentially based on the number of arguments.[85]

As Cicero says, it is not only about finding arguments but also about discerning and weighing them, as "the cultivated mind, just like the land with its richness and fertility, can produce both the harvest and the weeds that harm it."[86] Places of quality stand in contrast to the places of quantity, adhering to a logic that gives precedence to the probative strength of an argument over the number of arguments. Is it because you have so many arguments that they are necessarily relevant? The orator should always focus on this key question as they carefully search for arguments rooted in quality. It is this process of thoughtful exploration that allows them to find the most effective points to strengthen their case and persuade their audience. It is the quality of the argument from this place that allows an orator to prove that the majority can be wrong, that the declarations of various witnesses, despite their striking unanimity, may stand in opposition to legal and even logical truth. In exploring the "place of comparison," the orator relies on the idea that every element of a trial or debate is comparable to similar facts, affecting judgments between like facts.

This is one of the basic rules of reasoning for common law jurists, who conclude based on *stare decisis.*[87] *It is the comparative argument that allows an orator or pleader to find elements in a previous court decision or past facts that relate to the subject they are working on and thus draw inspiration from them. It is finally the comparative argument that allows the orator to construct certain argumentative forms, such as the argument by analogy, the argument by contrast, and the argument by a fortiori, which we will explore in more detail a little later. In their journey toward exploring arguments in service of their cause, the orator cannot ignore the existence of "places of probability,"[88] "places of possibilities,"[89] and "places of suppositions."[90]*

The exploration of common places allows one to find arguments that can be used in various fields of wisdom and various domains of knowledge. The argument here is similar to minerals found in the common places of a mine that can be exploited for various uses in the mining industry. However, there are aspects of the mining industry that require specific, atypical mines. The orator, like the miner, should not limit themselves to common places. To uncover arguments tailored to specific areas of knowledge or unique speaking styles (B), the orator must be willing to step outside the usual paths and explore less conventional ideas or sources. By searching these atypical places, they increase their chances of finding arguments that truly stand out and resonate with their audience.

B - Exploration of Atypical Places

Beyond the common places of exploration, the orator is more than ever required to explore specific places in order to find particular solutions to specific problems and at specific times. They must, therefore, explore what Cicero called "proper places.[91]" The exploration of atypical places allows the orator to answer questions that require a certain level of knowledge or a particular type of expertise, as common places alone may not provide an effective answer to the question posed. This is the case of the criminal defense attorney who, in the context of a trial, finds a certain category of arguments only by examining the case facts, the consequences of the action[92], and the circumstances of time and place.

Similarly, *ad persona* arguments are generally deduced from the person of the accused, the witnesses, and other subjects present at the trial. In this context of argument research based on the person, the orator will verify elements of the accused such as gender, age, nationality, education level, and others[93]. When dealing with topics like maritime law, armed conflicts, international trade, education, or philosophy, the orator must make an effort to study works by respected experts in those fields. By doing so, they can speak with confidence, accuracy, and clarity, ensuring their arguments are well-informed and credible. It cannot be stressed enough: "What is well conceived is clearly expressed, and the words to say it come easily.[94]"

It's clear that, as Cicero points out, mastering specific topics is essential for any orator who wants to stand out and speak with authority. When addressing a sensitive issue that demands expertise, the orator must rely on accurate knowledge and express themselves with authenticity and confidence. This specific knowledge generally escapes the common person. These specific arguments, the atypical places themselves, provide the necessary deposit that can feed the orator with more rationality and objectivity, helping them reach their highest level of oratorical reasoning.

Thus, in his speech to the United Nations Security Council on February 14, 2003, on the disarmament of Iraq, Dominique De Villepin, beyond common places, certainly explored the proper places related to diplomacy and international law in order to request, on behalf of France, the continuation of inspections.[95]

A speech so precise and perfectly suited to the diplomatic context of the time could not have been achieved with general arguments alone. It was the career diplomat's ability to focus on specific, well-chosen points that allowed the speech to stand out and meet the demands of the moment.[96] A similar case can be seen in the speech by Patrice Lumumba on June 30, 1960, during the independence ceremony of the Congo. The speech highlights an exceptional orator speaking with a certain virtuosity on the colonial history of the Congo. Orator Lumumba explored the important dates in the country's history and notable facts from the past to give the speech the authenticity it had at that time.[97] We discover an orator who knows his subject, his facts, a historian keen on presenting the history not from the perspective of the hunters... but from the perspective of the lions, that is, the perspective of the victors. This is the case for many other great Orators who, through their speeches, highlight the specific places of their argumentative research.

As we have observed, the orator is primarily a rational researcher who, in intense dialectical gymnastics, must systematically move back and forth between the "common" and "specific" places when confronted with a particular speech or oratorical genre. Their history almost merges with that of a miner who must extract specific minerals from certain places in a mine for particular needs. After this exercise of argumentative extraction, they will certainly have a collection of arguments. Could they then directly place them into an argumentation without discernment?[98] At this stage of research, it becomes crucial to carefully organize and classify the arguments that have been gathered. Without doing so, the speech risks losing one of its most important aspects—effectively addressing the core of the issue. Taking time to weigh and prioritize these arguments ensures the speech remains clear, persuasive, and impactful.

I - Argumentative Categorization

Once the orator has gathered all the necessary arguments, both general and specific, they must take on the role of a careful strategist. To make the speech or plea as clear and effective as possible, the orator needs to organize these arguments in a structured way. This process involves using time-tested, traditional methods of classification, which continue to be just as valuable and relevant today. They may use the argument of authority, which involves presenting, for a specific thesis, the position of authors renowned for their mastery of the subject and their scientific authority in the matter.

A method used so methodically would lead to the audience's agreement and acceptance[99]. The authority presented in this context must be unquestionable and uncontested. A controversial authority would not serve the cause at all. As brilliantly pointed out by the lawyer Alessandro Traversi, the orator could just as well use arguments and draw examples[100] to demonstrate points analogous to the cause they represent, the cause they defend. They must recognize in the argumentative toolkit at their disposal arguments of contradiction[101], arguments dividing the whole into parts and including the part in the whole, and the argument of identity[102]. But even more, they must pay particular attention to arguments by analogy, *by contrast* (A), and double hierarchy arguments (B), on which we will deeply analyze the dialectical mechanics involved.

A - The Analogical Category

Once the orator has completed the process of gathering arguments, their next task is to carefully review the results of their research. In this step, they should focus on identifying arguments that can be used by analogy. By drawing meaningful comparisons, the orator can strengthen their speech and make complex ideas easier for the audience to understand. This category of argument and reasoning is based on the idea that similar situations should be treated in the same way.[103]

In the interpretation of laws, the orator uses it to extend the application of a legislative norm to a situation similar to the one expressly targeted by the law. They can use it to prevent a legal gap or ensure the coherence of the law.[104] As shown in many methodology guides, analogical arguments are especially powerful in legal cases or when pleading before the courts. This type of reasoning has been proven to be effective for thousands of years, and its relevance remains just as strong today. By drawing comparisons between similar situations, the orator can make their point more persuasive and relatable to the audience. It draws its persuasive power from a legal rule that requires the application of the same treatment to subjects or factual elements belonging to the same category, or differentiated treatments a contrario. In light of this dialectical maneuver, the orator has the possibility of using two types of arguments that have long inspired various indictments, pleadings, or revolutionary speeches: the argument à *pari* and the à *contrario* *argument.*

The à pari[105] argument involves presenting a case similar to the one in question and considering that the law, jurisprudence, or rule applied to the first must necessarily be applied to the second. The stronger the similarities between the two cases, the more persuasive this approach becomes. When the points of coincidence are clear and obvious, the argument gains even more strength. By emphasizing these connections, the orator can make a much more convincing case to their audience. It, therefore, becomes quite logical for the orator to verify and ensure that the situations highlighted are not too different. Otherwise, it would be cutting the branch they are sitting on by invoking this category, which in certain circumstances could certainly prove detrimental to both themselves and the credibility they are supposed to represent. Cicero, in his emblematic work *De oratore*, provides one of the best uses[106] of the *à pari* argument: "Spending the state's money against the public interest is as criminal as stealing it."[107]

In his argumentation process, the orator must also be able to discern *à pari* arguments for special use, notably the "reciprocity argument," which allows the same treatment to be applied to symmetrical situations, as well as the *transitivity argument[108]*. The orator, in their classification, cannot ignore the *à contrario* argument, which is a comparison between two facts. However, unlike the *à pari* argument, it aims to demonstrate that the principle applied to one specific case cannot be applied to another, based on the fact that the other cases function differently. This could provide a significant persuasive force. This is especially true when the case or fact that inspires it constitutes an exception to a given rule. The orator will typically invoke the *à contrario* argument in legal situations to oppose the application of a rule to a particular case. They will demonstrate *à contrario* that different principles govern cases similar to the one highlighted.

Practical Case:

Dogs must be kept on a leash on beaches.

À contrario: Leopards, which are not dogs, do not have to be kept on a leash on the beach.

B - The Category of Double Hierarchy

After exploring the common and specific places, the orator must pay particular attention to the arguments of double hierarchy or a fortiori. These are arguments based on a double hierarchy of value, drawing truth from another already accepted with even greater strength, using similar arguments that are stronger and more numerous than those legitimizing the first. Specifically, the orator uses a premise by making it a universally recognized hierarchy of values and deduces from the comparison between two terms that belong to the same system of different values. Whatever is considered applicable to one must, a fortiori, be valid for the other.

One of the prominent examples highlighting this category is emphasized by Aristotle: "If even the gods do not know all things, men will know them even more difficultly."[109]

The orator could use this category in various situations, both legal and non-legal. It can be applied from the greater to the lesser, as the Greeks understood it years ago, and as the Romans used it in *comparatio a minore ad maius, and in the medieval era, as ductus obliques*[110]. One of the best examples can be drawn from the Holy Scriptures as an extraordinary case. Indeed, Jesus uses this technique and category to exhort men not to worry about material goods[111]. As mentioned above, the speaker will invoke these arguments when confronted with a normative situation, for essentially factual issues, or to highlight a number of rebuttals.

The Speaker Is a Researcher.

Faced with a verbal duel opposing them to tough adversaries, Eugène Afarin and Eugenie Kotelnikova from Russia prepared arguments against their opponent. After researching the most appropriate rebuttals, the two debaters proceeded to categorize them to have a greater impact on the opponent. It was a real delight for the audience, who had filled the Louis Liard amphitheatre at the Sorbonne with enthusiasm, to witness the dialectic unfold through these speakers, now world debate champions. Before taking the floor, the speaker should ensure the quality of their research, the strength of their ideas, and the weight of their arguments.

The speaker, like the miner, is, first and foremost, a researcher. Every opportunity to speak is a chance for research, which is, in reality, the essential element of any speech, reasoning, or argument. A speech without tangible arguments would be odourless, colourless, or simply tasteless. The relevant argument thus becomes the foundation of the verbal magic held by the speaker, which should refrain from turning into generalized verbiage soaked in inflated vocabulary and semantic convolutions.

This is why, when confronted with a debate, exploring the "commonplaces" for general arguments is more than essential. Likewise, exploring the "specialized places" for debates, which bring particular domains of knowledge into focus, is more crucial than ever. The speaker must not only master research skills, but also act as a strategist. After gathering their arguments, they need to organize them carefully. This organization helps ensure that the arguments are used effectively in a debate.

The debate, being dialectical, depends on the weight of ideas and the strength of arguments to persuade the audience. Invention appears to be the most important phase in the speaker's preparatory process, as it aims to identify arguments capable of convincing an audience, persuading a judge, and overcoming and triumphing over an opponent. Sometimes, despite thorough research, the speaker may not find any strong arguments. They might only come across weaker arguments than those their opponent has presented.

This situation can be frustrating, as it limits the speaker's ability to counter the opposing arguments. In such cases, the speaker must adapt their strategy to address the challenge effectively. What to do in such a situation? Cicero believes there is only one solution: to focus on areas of the debate where one feels stronger.

Otherwise, one risks losing all credibility in the eyes of the judge or the audience, who are simply hanging on one's every word[113]. The construction of the speech is similar to the construction of a building: when the orator completes the research and categorization of arguments, they must weigh them to determine which will be most useful in making the case they are defending succeed. The speaker must not only find arguments but also organize them carefully. It is crucial to arrange each argument in a way that maximizes its effectiveness in persuading the audience. This organization ensures that every argument has its proper place in the speech. Therefore, it becomes essential to structure the arguments carefully, making sure they are positioned for the strongest impact.

It is similar to the construction of a building: when the orator completes the research and categorization of arguments, they must weigh them to determine which will be most useful in making the case they are defending succeed. But most importantly, they must organize them to ensure each argument is placed in a way that maximizes its use in the persuasive speech. Hence, the urgency of arranging the arguments arising from the research.

Chapter III:
OF THE ARGUMENTATIVE DISPOSITION

The speaker who finalizes their research must proceed with the arrangement of the arguments derived from their findings, with the aim of highlighting their maximum strength. This is what Cicero, in an epistolary treatise written at the request of Brutus, already recognized when he stated: "The speaker must appeal to his judgment to make a rigorous selection... But how will he arrange what he has found? ... The speaker will compose his introduction like a beautiful vestibule leading to the cause with clear access points.

Once he has captured the audience's attention from the first assault, he will establish his position, refute, and sidestep his opponent's objections. He will place the strongest arguments at the beginning and end and put the weaker ones in the middle." The arrangement of arguments in a speech is a phase that is far from being a negligible technique, as it is essential for the coherence of the speech, preventing the accumulation and crystallization of arguments without logical support.

While the search for arguments makes the orator primarily a researcher, akin to a miner in a mine, the arrangement of arguments is more a matter of strategy, a technique of rhetorical construction for persuasive purposes.

In this regard, Quintilian, in his memorably titled work, considers the building of a speech to be, in several ways similar to that of a building.[114] One can read: "Just as it is not enough for those who build buildings to gather stones, materials, and everything necessary for a builder if they do not implement a technical knowledge in arranging and placing everything in order, similarly, in the art of speaking, the wealth of arguments would mean only a jumble and a pile of elements unless a single criterion organizes them once collected and united."[115]

The orator must make an effort to select, thus eliminating arguments that, in their understanding, seem superfluous, confusing, or simply counterproductive, potentially compromising their cause. Insignificant arguments and those that appear useful but are actually not beneficial should not be highlighted, as Cicero clearly advises: "When I collect the arguments of a case, I am more accustomed to weighing them than counting them."[116]

The choice of arguments should be guided purely by their significance and the strength of their reasoning. This ensures that the most compelling ideas take center stage. However, unlike Cicero's approach, where the arrangement of arguments might prioritize their logical impact, presenting them in the order they occurred could also be useful, depending on the situation. This alternative approach can provide clarity or context that might otherwise be overlooked.

The orator is an architect of speech who, beyond research, should master technical and strategic mechanisms that, when well executed and well organized, would give strength, impact, and power to the speech they deliver. Therefore, it becomes crucial to pay attention to the codes of rhetorical arrangement. In this vein, before analyzing the order of presentation and the weight of the arguments (II), it would be prudent first to understand the process of constructing and structuring the speech (I).

I - Construction and Structure of The Speech

For over 2,500 years, from 46 BCE to the present day, the construction and structure of a speech has followed an identical approach. These principles, developed by great masters like Demosthenes and Cicero, form the empirical foundation of rhetorical construction. Their methods emphasized the careful arrangement of arguments and the strategic use of emotional appeals to captivate audiences.

Additionally, these techniques demonstrated how the art of persuasion could transcend cultural and historical boundaries, remaining relevant across generations. It must be acknowledged, has not lost its vitality, and we are its worthy heirs. The orator must always begin the speech with clear[117], strategic access points through the exordium (A), which serves not only to introduce the subject but also to capture the audience's attention while gaining their goodwill. Logically, after this step, the orator must proceed with the *narratio* (the narrative), persuasively presenting the facts that have occurred or are presumed to have occurred[118] (B). Following the brief story of the facts, the orator will establish their position through argumentation. Naturally, they will refute and avoid any objections from the opponent (C). The orator will close the speech with the peroratio(D), described by Cicero as "the end and the culmination of the entire speech" (exitus et determinatio tortius orationis). Carefully examining these stages is crucial to understanding how an orator builds and structures their speech. This is especially important for anyone who wants to convince, persuade, and effectively engage an audience, keeping their attention and influencing their thoughts step by step.

A - The Exordium

The exordium is the opening part of a speech and plays a crucial role in setting the tone. This phase requires a careful and thoughtful approach, emphasizing its importance. Through the exordium, the speaker builds a connection with the audience, laying the foundation for their engagement and attention throughout the speech. The speaker will take various measures to ensure that the audience is receptive, attentive, and favorably disposed. In other words, this is what the Romans called Captatio benevolentiae. Like the prologue in theater or the prelude for flutists, the exordium is an "introduction to the course of the oration."

Beyond its stylistic and rhetorical appearances, the exordium primarily aims to break the silence and, in another sense, to "break the ice" before delving into the main debate. However, there are occasions when, for the sake of greater objectivity—such as avoiding off-topic distractions or sidetracking the judges or audience—the speaker may choose to skip the exordium to allocate more space to the substance of the argument.

Every speech or case is unique, shaped by its specific context and circumstances. For this reason, the speaker needs to craft an exordium that fits the particular situation, ensuring it is tailored to the purpose and audience of that speech.

Cicero, the orator of orators, believes that the speaker must certainly tackle these challenges with mastery: "The exordium, indeed, should not be influenced by external factors but must emerge from the very core of the cause itself." The speaker may start with a major idea derived from the speech itself, highlighting the strong points of the case he is advocating. He could also start with an idea advanced by his opponent or simply address points or ideas that would undoubtedly attract the goodwill and sympathy of the judges. A situation that the author of De *oratore* believes should be achieved more through the persuasive power of the cause and the defense of the case than through sometimes overly flattering appeals to the sagacity of the judges.[119] Sometimes, the orator may face a difficult audience, especially when the audience harbors hostility toward the people the orator is defending or disagrees with the facts being presented. In these cases, it becomes even more important for the skilled orator to work on making the audience attentive, open-minded, and receptive to their message.

But how can this be achieved? It is understood that the orator must avoid offending his audience, thereby ruining his case forever!

The orator should focus on building a sense of trust and credibility, ensuring the audience feels respected and valued from the very beginning. Once again, Cicero gives the answer and recommends the use of insinuation, which consists of trying to subtly make a way into the mind of each listener without them noticing, whether by talking about oneself, the opponents, the judges, or the subject of the case.

Finally, the orator must establish a bond of sympathy with the audience, so that the audience, hanging on his every word, can, without realizing it, identify with the orator. One of the techniques used since antiquity is for the orator to apologize for his shortcomings by showing apparent timidity and a few difficulties. In his first speech against Philip, the King of Macedon, who is threatening Athens, Demosthenes justifies speaking before others. He does not want to appear presumptuous by speaking before the more experienced orators.

By beginning his speech with this careful approach, Demosthenes ensures he doesn't anger the audience, while also preparing the Athenians to listen with attention, openness, and a willingness to be persuaded. The speech by Mark Antony in Shakespeare's *Julius Caesar* is a notable example of this strategy.[120] A similar effect can be observed in the opening words of President John F. Kennedy's address, where he announces to the Americans the launch of a space exploration program.

He expresses his pleasure at being in such great company, flattering his audience by emphasizing the unity of the American people before presenting a challenge that will mobilize enormous resources in the country.[121] In an exordium, the orator may also seek to create an element of surprise to shock, disturb, or simply engage the audience. The beginning of Cicero's first speech against Catiline (108-62 BC) before the Roman Senate is a vivid example. Instead of addressing the senators according to traditional oral customs, Cicero directly confronts Catiline, who is conspiring against Rome: "How long, Catiline, will you abuse our patience? How much longer will your madness evade our blows?"

In this historical context, the conspirator is among the senators. This bold directness not only shocks the audience but also signals Cicero's control over the situation, demonstrating his command of the moment. By addressing him directly, Cicero not only intends to frighten him but also to alert the senators to the impending danger.

Through this confrontation, Cicero challenges the senators to recognize their responsibility and act decisively, strengthening the urgency of his message. This approach demonstrates the strategic use of the exordium to create an immediate connection with the audience, establish authority, and set the tone for the rest of the speech, whether through flattery, surprise, or confrontation.

B - The Narration

Narration is a real power that every orator should possess. It allows the speaker to engage the audience emotionally and intellectually, making the message more relatable and memorable. This power has been widely demonstrated by Adrien Rivierre in a memorable[122] work, in which, among other things, he reveals the richness and utility of storytelling and its use in discourse[123]. Rivierre's work emphasizes how effective narration can captivate an audience, turning abstract arguments into vivid, compelling narratives that resonate with listeners.

Narration consists of persuasively presenting events that have happened or are assumed to happen in a matter or speech. Through this narrative approach, the orator presents the facts, all the facts, but only the facts that have occurred, in order to prepare to develop an argument that naturally follows.

There is no doubt that narration, for the orator, is a preparatory phase in the process of bringing forth the arguments, as it is part of the reconstruction of relevant facts that logically connect to the arguments the orator will present later.

To maximize the impact of his narration, the orator must ensure its brevity, clarity, and of course, its benevolence.[124] The orator should focus on the main points of the story, leaving out any unnecessary details that don't support his cause or might even weaken it. Above all, he must ensure that his message is clear and easy to follow. This means he must not only respect the chronology of the facts but also demonstrate mastery over the facts so that the judges or the audience can confirm that he is well-versed in his subject. The narration must flow smoothly, like a long, tranquil river. The facts highlighted by the orator must be probable, meaning they should align with reality, but also, they should not contradict the truth.[125]

The narration, as we will see, is a prominent part of the judicial oratory art, where, in general, the speaker recalls the facts of the case in order to justify the arguments being presented. This allows the orator to frame the facts in a way that supports their position, making the case more compelling and credible. However, when the speaker believes that the narration will not aid the case they are trying to defend, they may choose to skip this step. In some situations, omitting the narration can prevent the introduction of harmful details that might undermine the speaker's argument.

Indeed, the description of unfavorable facts could have negative consequences. In some circumstances, however, narration is unavoidable. This is the case with the defense of Milo or the narration of the events on the day of Clodius's assassination. By carefully choosing which details to emphasize, the orator can steer the narrative in a direction that benefits their case, influencing how the audience perceives the facts.

The facts as narrated demonstrate the power that narration can have in a speech, whether judicial or political in nature. In doing so, the orator can create a vivid and persuasive image of events that supports their argument, making the message resonate more deeply with the audience.

Setting such a stage creates a clear argumentative path for the speaker, who, seizing the opportunity, will address the related logical arguments with greater clarity and grandeur.

C - Argumentation

What would a speech be without solid argumentation? What would a speech be without ideas and substantial content? Of course, without consistency or substance, it would be nothing more than airy verbiage with no real scientific support. That is why the distinguished orator must first and foremost think about the arguments they intend to present when they decide to take the stage and savor the fragrance of words. It's not enough to merely appreciate the beauty of words; the speaker must use their speech to address societal problems with precision and impact. Therefore, in the third part of the speech, the orator must clearly present the arguments that back up their main point.

The argument must respond to the problem or question raised at the beginning of the speech. This ensures that the audience remains focused on the central issue, guiding the speech in a clear direction. It will be supported by a main idea and secondary ideas that explain the reasoning behind the argument put forth to make their case succeed. The secondary arguments should not only clarify the main point but also strengthen its credibility by providing additional perspectives.

The main argument must be clearly distinguished from the secondary arguments, which serve to support the main one. To reinforce their thesis or position, it would be wise for the orator to invoke authorities who are recognized in the field being discussed, after explaining the mechanics of their reasoning. For example, if the topic concerns the law, a legal precedent, a relevant law article, applicable doctrine, or relevant legal custom would strengthen the orator's defense of their case. Similarly, any subject relating to other fields of knowledge requires the orator to reference reputable authors, specialists, or experts in the area to further demonstrate the validity of their claims. A factual example highlighting the real-world application of the topic could be raised after invoking the relevant authorities to add more weight to the orator's argument.

The example serves the advantage of creating a vivid image in the mind of the audience or jury, making the argument clearer and more impactful. The orator should then conclude their argument by following the logical and argumentative principles discussed earlier. In doing so, they can also incorporate rhetorical figures and other stylistic techniques to enhance the argument, making it more engaging, impactful, and memorable for the audience.

It may happen that the orator proceeds with the refutation either before or after their argumentation, depending on the context dictated by the circumstances of the debate. In some cases, refuting the opponent's argument first may disarm them, creating a stronger foundation for the speaker's own case. The refutation consists of demonstrating the lack of foundation in the arguments of the opponent or the thesis opposing the one they are firmly defending.

This requires careful analysis to identify logical weaknesses or inconsistencies in the opposing argument, allowing the orator to challenge its validity effectively. In this approach, the orator, following this contesting strategy, need only be guided by the very ancient Aristotelian principle, which simply asserts: "either the fact does not exist, or no harm was done, or the extent of the damage is not as claimed, or one acted justly.[126]" One of the exemplary instances of refutation is Cicero's oration during the defense of Marcus Caelius.

D - The Peroration

The final words of a speech are as delicate and decisive as the first ones. They are important to ensure a certain persuasive force and a real impact on the audience. As Cicero already said in *Rhetorici qui vocantur de interventione*, it is "the crowning of the entire speech." The peroration, defined by Hélène Tronc as "the end of the speech which summarizes and heightens the emotions,[127]" appears to the orator as a final opportunity to influence the opinion of the judges and sway the audience toward the cause they are defending.

Quintilian, regarding judicial speeches, stated that the peroration should "be like the ancient tragedies and comedies, where the spectator was never left without a resolution." more interested, more moved, than when the play was about to end." Before reaching the end, the orator must prepare the audience for the upcoming conclusion of the speech.

This can be done through specific words or expressions that signal the closing, or by adjusting the tone to indicate that the speech is nearing its end. In this sense, the peroration is much like a plane getting ready to land at an airport, gradually guiding the audience toward the final point.

[128],[129]In this final stage of the speech, the orator will recap the main points and make a final emotional appeal to the audience, if the circumstances are favorable. This is the moment to leave a lasting impression, ensuring the audience feels the weight of the message and is moved to action. The orator should not merely skim over or lightly touch upon the major arguments covered in both the argumentation and the refutation as a way of refreshing the memory. They will highlight the strongest points and create a magical summary, which may appear in the form of a metaphor or image, to make an even greater impact. By using vivid language and powerful imagery, the orator enhances the emotional resonance of their argument, making it unforgettable for the audience.

The orator should not, as Cicero states, repeat the entire speech. The peroration is a moment full of powerful words, images, rhetorical actions, and, above all, emotions projected onto the audience. For instance, the orator might present a rhetorical situation that makes it clear to the audience and the jury that, given the circumstances, the only reasonable decision is to rule in favor of their cause.

In the trial of Maurice Papon (1997-1998), accused of crimes against humanity during World War II, in his closing statement after a judicial marathon lasting about five months with lyrical speeches, lawyer Gérard Boulanger (representing the civil parties) first recaps the case, the lies of the accused, and the points on which the jury should focus. He deliberately chooses to cite the statements made by the victims and their families during the trial.

This approach provokes emotions and brings the human dimension of the case to the forefront, diminishing its primarily technical aspects. By focusing on the personal experiences and emotions of those involved, the orator shifts the narrative from abstract legal arguments to a story that the audience can connect with on a deeper level.

He also emphasizes the significant fact that the victims were individuals, not just a faceless group of people, making them more relatable and identifiable. This personal connection helps the audience see the case through a more empathetic lens, making it harder to ignore the impact of the actions being discussed. He highlights the human consequences of Maurice Papon's actions and moves the jury with his multiple oratorical flourishes before they hear the defense.[130] As we can see, the orator who wins the goodwill of the judges automatically ensures their emotional involvement. The techniques used to enhance the speech and focus on elements that trigger compassion—like illness, hardship, or personal tragedies in the life of the person being defended, or even facts that emphasize the vulnerability of the victims—help to stir emotions that can have a significant impact on the audience. This can be notably seen in Cicero's peroration during his speech to defend Marcus Caelius: "Look at his youth, but also take into account that you have before you this unfortunate man, who, in front of your humanity, humbly pleads and prostrates himself not only at your feet but especially before your minds and senses. You will feel relieved as you remember your parents, the smile of your children, by exalting, in the pain of others Your pity and your kindness. Do not hasten, my judges, the end of this man, now in decline, more than by the law of time, nor break this young life, already rooted in the first bloom of virtue, in an unforeseen whirlwind or storm. Keep this son for his father and this father for his son, so that it may not seem that you have despised an old age without hope, nor have you sought to keep alive, on the contrary, struck and severed a youth rich in hope. If you keep him with us, for his family, and for the republic, you will gain his loyalty, bind him to you and your children, and through all his strength and efforts, you – my judges, more than anyone else in the world – will reap the greatest and most lasting rewards.[131]"

As we can see, it is not enough to merely recap the main points of the speech, but one must also know how to solicit emotions, and know when to announce the imminence of the peroration, which, it must be acknowledged, happens like an aircraft preparing to land at an airport.

II - On the Order of Presentation and The Weight of Arguments

The sequence in which the arguments are presented is crucial to both the structure of the speech and the persuasive impact it will have on the audience. A carefully organized order helps guide the listener's understanding and strengthens the overall argument. C. Perelman, in *The Empire of Rhetoric: Rhetoric and Argumentation*, asserts that "the arrangement of arguments, notably their order, is crucial when it comes to arguing in order to gain the audience's agreement.", "the order of presentation of arguments changes the conditions of their acceptance.[132]"

There is no doubt that the order in which arguments are presented significantly influences their acceptability, their reception, and their acceptance by the audience or the jury tasked with judging the relevance of the arguments the orator has submitted through his speech. Several methods and strategies exist to allow the orator to arrange the arguments they have carefully gathered from their research.

They must make a strategic choice and then establish a corresponding order. In this context, we observe a confrontation of different trends and theories. Some argue that beginning with strong, convincing arguments ensures that the audience is immediately engaged and receptive, laying a solid foundation for the rest of the speech. For some, the orator must impress the audience from the outset by presenting the strongest, most compelling arguments first, in a descending order (A).

For others, the orator should create suspense by reserving the best arguments for the end, following an ascending structure (B), as suggested by the rhetoric of Herennius, an anonymous Roman treatise: "Since the last words spoken are what are most remembered, it is useful to leave a solid, fresh proof at the end of the speech, in the minds of the audience. This method allows the orator to end on a high note, leaving the audience with a powerful impression that lingers after the speech is over.

This arrangement of the arguments, just like the order of battle, leads to success and ensures victory." Cicero, in his famous treatise *De Oratore*, opens new horizons by recommending a third approach: placing the weakest arguments in the middle of the speech and framing them with more convincing reasons. This order, which seems to have been endorsed by the ancient masters of rhetoric, is commonly referred to as the "Nestorian order"[133] (C).

In order to fully understand this important aspect of oratory, it is essential to carefully analyze the decrescendo order, crescendo order, and Nestorian order of arguments. By doing so, one can determine the most effective strategy for a speech that aims to win a case based on the strength of its ideas, the order in which the arguments are presented, and most importantly, the power of those arguments.

A - The Crescendo Order of Strength

An orator who completes their research, as described earlier, may choose to use an ascending order for organizing their arguments. This approach begins with the less important points and gradually builds up to the strongest arguments, which are saved for the end of the speech. Here, the orator reserves their best ammunition—their "joker" argument—for the end of the speech to emphasize even more the importance of this final point they wish to engrave and crystallize in the minds of the audience.

Thus, at the beginning of the argumentative development, one might see expressions like "first," announcing the initial argument generally of lesser importance; "furthermore," which signals the imminence of a medium-strength argument; and finally, "above all," which could introduce, like a flashing beacon, the key argument of the speech.

Given that the audience always remembers the last words spoken, the crescendo order of strength aims to leave a solid, fresh piece of evidence in the audience's mind—a situation that easily leads to the victory of the defended or pleaded cause. Furthermore, because of the ascending structure of the speech, the orator raises the tension and emotions of the audience, and eventually the jury, like a pump that inflates with pressure.

However, it must be noted that in the delivery of a speech, the beginning is the time when the orator has the most attention from the audience, which tends to be the most reactive at this precise moment.

From the first to the last words, a speech is like a long thread that must be kept taut to prevent the audience from wandering off course. One might see some audience members yawning simply due to a loss of attention. A speech that uses the ascending order of arguments or simply highlights the crescendo of argument strength could risk making the audience uncomfortable or displeased, especially when they are impatient.

The audience could then make a general judgment about the curve the speech will take, not assuming that the best arguments will appear toward the end of the speech. This expectation could lead the audience to become less attentive as the speech progresses, since they might anticipate that the most compelling points will come later. This strategy could distract the audience, which might lose focus early on and follow the speech erratically, rather than staying engaged from beginning to end.

One might wonder if this approach would be more effective, or if it would actually be counterproductive to the cause the orator is defending. In fact, the orator risks losing the audience's full attention at the most critical moments of the speech.

The great masters of rhetoric have long recognized this difficulty, which is why, in practice, they generally agree that the ascending order of strength does not always work. It is not necessarily a good idea. Therefore, it becomes crucial to explore other strategies of arrangement.

B - The Descending Order of Strength

In contrast to the ascending gradation logic outlined above, the orator who chooses a descending order of argument strength aims to capture the full attention of the audience from the very beginning of the speech, impressing them at the dawn of the address, rather than waiting until the night is about to fall on the debates of the day.

This approach works by establishing credibility and authority right away, setting a strong tone that encourages the audience to remain focused throughout the speech. He will use the strongest arguments at the beginning of the speech; considering that by the end, the audience is somewhat fatigued, he will instead use the weaker arguments.

This tactic ensures that the audience is engaged while they are most receptive, leaving the speech with a sense of closure rather than a lingering feeling of unresolved tension. At least, the essence of the message will have been delivered at the start, and the audience will have grasped the core of his thoughts. In his argumentative structure, one could note expressions such as "Above all," "First of all,"... introducing the rock-solid argument of the speech, which should captivate the audience; then, one could observe expressions like "Next, then," marking the second argument, though not of lesser importance. This second argument stands out with a decrease in intensity, marked by the strength of the first argument.

As the speech nears its conclusion, the orator introduces his weakest argument with "Finally...". This argument is presented with much more calm, given the high pressure and emotion stirred by the first two key points of the speech. While this strategy helps the orator earn the audience's trust early on and address the most important and sensitive points right at the start, it's important to recognize that the audience typically remembers the final words spoken by the orator the most.

The great challenge here is to maintain the attention that has been skillfully captured at the beginning of the speech, at the point where the audience, still eager, wishes to drink in more of his words. To ensure the audience stays engaged, the orator must pace the speech carefully, balancing the delivery of strong arguments with moments of reflection to sustain interest. In this regard, Quintilian, one of the greatest specialists of Roman eloquence, stated: "One must have foresight, directing everything and guiding the last parts of the speech as we speak the first, so that everything we say is illuminated by this foresight."[134] This careful orchestration of the speech ensures the conclusion feels just as powerful and purposeful as the beginning, creating a lasting impact. The last words remain fresh in the memory of the listeners.

This situation may harm the orator who uses the strategy of presenting arguments in a descending order of strength. In fact, by doing so, the orator risks leaving the audience with a final impression that is far from favorable. The effectiveness of the strongest arguments may be diluted by the time they are presented, weakening the overall impact of the speech. Unfortunately, despite all the effort put into presenting strong arguments and high-caliber ideas, the orator might fall short in leaving a lasting positive impact.

The orator needs to be aware that the final moments of the speech are crucial in ensuring the audience retains the intended message, not just the facts but the emotional connection. Beyond being a skilled researcher, the orator must be an excellent strategist who knows how to deploy their arguments strategically and, more importantly, when to deploy their "joker" argument.

This is why many great masters of ancient rhetoric warned against using this tactic, as it doesn't always prove effective. By employing this strategy, the orator essentially overlooks the principle that while the beginning of a speech is important, it is the conclusion that truly matters.

The closing words are what leave a lasting impression and serve as the culmination of the argument. The orator risks undermining their cause, even when they have the necessary "ammunition" to convince an audience, jury, or adversary who is waiting for the right argument at the right moment to be swayed. Cicero, in his memorable and contemporary work, clearly recommended another approach inspired by the Greek general Nestor, who had a special method for organizing his troops during battles.

C - The Nestorian Order135 Of Arguments

The great masters strongly recommended following the Nestorian order, which consists of presenting a strong argument at the beginning of the speech, an even stronger or at least irresistible argument at the end, and placing the weakest argument in the middle. This approach ensures that the audience is engaged from the start, then captivated by the strongest points, leaving them with a final, powerful impression. In memory of the arrangement with which the Greek general Nestor arranged his troops.

This method was vigorously defended by Cicero in his work De Oratore. By strategically placing the weakest argument in the middle, the orator avoids diminishing the impact of their speech and maintains the audience's attention throughout. More recently, many orators have been successful with the Nestorian order of arguments. This is the case with Kennedy, who in his speech about the moon landing "skillfully inserted the cost of the American space program between two exalted evocations of the lunar adventure."[136]

The Nestorian order is widely regarded as highly effective and incorporates the strengths of the other strategies discussed earlier. Its structure ensures that the orator captures the audience's attention at the start, builds momentum, and leaves a lasting impression at the conclusion. Moreover, it avoids significant drawbacks, making it a reliable and compelling choice for orators looking to craft persuasive speeches. The orator can thus capture the audience's attention both at the beginning and at the end of the speech. Its weak points will not be noticed since the weakest argument is subtly inserted in the middle of the speech, following a very strong argument.

Even though this way of presenting[137] arguments may influence the logical order of thought, with the consequence of distributing ideas in a so-called "nomadic" structure, the argumentation is not weakened but rather strengthened and accepted as a whole, especially since, in the end, the various arguments converge toward a common goal. The Nestorian order thus allows each argument to play its role, however small, for the triumph of the cause.

Each argument, by itself, will be able to demonstrate an aspect of the evidence and withstand objections, even the sharpest ones. This method also allows the orator to present their arguments in a way that builds progressively, ensuring that each point reinforces the others, making the speech cohesive. As can be easily seen, the Nestorian order of arguments appears to be the most complete and strategic for any orator who wants to maximize their chances of being right and thus defeat an opponent or win their case. It offers a balanced approach, allowing the orator to emphasize key points without overwhelming the audience with too much information at once. With great simplicity, it allows the orator to begin the speech strongly, end in the same way, and make a good impression simultaneously.

It allows the orator to subtly pass off weak points without necessarily harming the outcome of the case, just as the chances of leaving the audience satisfied at the end of the speech are high.

Board 1: The Nestorien Order Of Arguments

Credit: Dede Fotsa

A representation of the Nestorien order of arguments, which, like a military troop, places a strong argument at the beginning, a medium argument in the middle, and the strongest or most irresistible argument at the end of the speech.

The Speaker Is an Architect of Words

The speaker is an architect of words, as Quintilian already recognized in his work *Institutio oratoria*. The construction of the speech is comparable to building a structure, where it's not enough to gather stones, materials, and everything necessary if one hasn't first applied a technique to arrange and order the materials needed for construction. Just as a builder relies on a clear blueprint to ensure the structure is stable and coherent, the orator must outline their speech meticulously to avoid inconsistencies or gaps that could weaken their position. In structuring the speech, the speaker must demonstrate skill and artistry, knowing in detail what might be useful for the speech, pleasant, or superfluous.

This planning phase also allows the orator to anticipate potential counterarguments, embedding subtle responses within their framework to preempt opposition. Like a poet or a flutist, the speaker will begin their speech with the exordium; then, they will proceed with the persuasive exposition of the facts they assume have occurred, through an oratorical maneuver we have called "narration." The speaker will then develop the arguments provided to support their thesis and will not forget to refute the opposing arguments if necessary.

They will "crown" their entire speech with the peroration, a maneuver that offers them the chance to persuade further and to involve the audience by appealing to emotions and feelings. Beyond their talent as an architect of words, the speaker is a strategist of argumentation and persuasive force, who, by arranging their arguments, ensures more opportunities to triumph over the audience and thus win their cause or defeat a contradicter. By carefully selecting their emotional appeals, the speaker can strengthen the audience's connection to the speech, transforming logical arguments into deeply resonant messages. In this regard, the great masters of ancient rhetoric, as well as those of contemporary rhetoric, recommend opting for the Nestorian order of arguments, considered the best because it allows the speaker to emerge victorious in every circumstance.

He balance of strong opening and closing arguments, with weaker points tucked strategically in the middle, ensures that the speech maintains its persuasive power throughout its delivery. We fully agree with this opinion.

However, is it intimidating to be overwhelmed by emotions at the very beginning of a speech? Some argue that this initial rush of emotion can actually humanize the speaker, helping them forge a bond with the audience as someone who cares deeply about the subject. When we know that power, tone of voice, and rhythm of speech are important elements to convince, should the speaker who experiences increased heartbeats, sweating, or chills at the beginning of the speech be intimidated by such a situation? On the contrary, such physiological responses, when harnessed properly, can serve to amplify the speaker's passion and sincerity, making their delivery even more compelling.

Cicero experienced this and believed that it was nothing serious: "At the beginning of a speech, I become pale, and all my mind and limbs tremble..."[138] Is the speaker's emotion at the beginning of a speech always negative for the case being defended? We might have reasons to doubt that.

SECOND PART:
ETHOS[139]

After demonstrating the truth of his assertions, the orator must win the goodwill of the listeners. To make his cause and ideas go down smoothly, like butter in a pan. Beyond his rational arguments, he is, above all, a charmer, or rather, a flirt who, like a courtier wooing a particular lady, uses various maneuvers to win the sympathy of an audience whose hopes, sometimes well-founded, are placed in a tribune who does not just state certain facts and arguments, but presents them in a certain way. The orator tickles the hearts and, at the same time, ensures an unparalleled credibility with the listeners. The ability of the good speaker to charm his audience and please them is a fundamental pillar of ancient rhetoric that still holds its strength today: ethos. This term refers to "the moral credibility of the orator and the trust he inspires, often based on the proximity he is able to create and maintain directly with his audience."

Through the image the tribune has of himself, his character, his personality, and his behavioral traits, he will inspire his audience more if, at least, they are captivated by these aspects of his person.[140] The orator who demonstrates prudence, kindness, and virtue generally earns the favor of those listening, as they feel more confident in the presence of a speaker who inspires trust. The way the orator presents themselves is very important during this part of the speech. If they come across as trustworthy and admirable, the audience is more likely to listen and take their words seriously.

The attitude and morality of the debater are sources of authority for the strength of the speech he is delivering or will deliver. Ethos is, therefore, an aspect of the speech in which the orator himself is questioned as an "argument of authority,"[141] with his ethics and morality as sources of authority. This is more connected to what the orator represents as a person than to the ideas he is trying to present to the jury or audience from his platform. Through the seductive power of his words, he tries to conquer his audience by eliminating the distance between himself and them, creating an atmosphere that better fosters the audience's alignment with his cause. Ethos is undoubtedly the presence, ethics, and reputation of the orator in order to favorably influence his audience.[142]

Therefore, how can the orator ensure that he makes a good impression on his audience, beyond the content of his speech? That is the question every orator should ask themselves when preparing to speak in defense of a cause. To try to answer this question, it becomes valuable to focus on delivery (Chapter IV) and oratory action (Chapter V), in the hope of better understanding this equally strategic aspect of the art of speech.

CHAPTER IV:
ON ELOQUENCE143

It is no longer a well-kept secret that the orator is a remarkable seducer. Through the pleasure and emotion he evokes, the orator charms as much with his ideas as with the enchantments orchestrated by his rhymes, verses, and phrasing. This ability to captivate relies not only on the orator's creativity but also on their deep understanding of how language evokes feelings and connects with human experience. It's this artistry that transforms a simple speech into a memorable performance. Eloquence, or elocutio, appears in this context as the act of giving linguistic form to ideas once the content and arrangement of the speech[144] have been found.

The pronunciation of the speech is by no means of lesser importance, especially since it is the act that brings the speech to life, while contributing significantly to the persuasion of the audience. Aristotle acknowledged this from the dawn of rhetoric when he stated, "There is a certain difference when speaking in one way or another.[145]"

The tone, pauses, and rhythm chosen by the orator act as tools to direct emotions and focus, ensuring the audience remains fully engaged and responsive. These nuances in delivery can make the difference between merely being heard and truly being felt. The orator, who is essentially defined by mastery of language, is fundamentally built upon language, which constitutes the greatness of an orator and the very framework of eloquence, the foundation of "the power of well-saying.[146]"

Eloquence itself, which comes from *eloqui,* means exactly: "to express everything conceived in the mind and convey it to the knowledge of the listeners." Without this, the art of oratory would be superfluous, like a sword hidden in its scabbard (similia gladio condito intra vaginam suam[147]).

Even though a certain tendency remained reluctant until very recently toward elocutio, the art of speaking well, which was wrongly accused of developing debates of pure form, sterile verbalism, and endless chatter turned into a system at the expense of substantive issues, elocutio in its variations—form and word—holds its full relevance in multidimensional persuasive strategies. However, it must be acknowledged that the art of words and form could never replace a lack of substance or a nearly chronic argumentative crisis.

The orator who holds the best arguments must therefore know how to express them adequately. Without this skill, their speech would feel dull and lifeless, like food without any flavor. It wouldn't convince an audience that cares not only about strong arguments but also about the beauty and impact of well-spoken words.

A situation Cicero reveals in a dialogue on eloquence in De Oratore, Brutus, Orator. Academics, Book 1.[148] It goes without saying that, in such circumstances, elocutio becomes one of the main elements of the art of persuasion, which every orator must master if they wish to adorn themselves with the vibrant colors of eloquence in order to persuade and convince.

The choice of words, phrasing, and rhythm can transform a simple argument into a captivating and memorable presentation, ensuring the audience remains engaged and attentive throughout. Therefore, how can the orator's elocutio influence the persuasion of the audience? And thus, make the cause they fight for triumph? It would certainly be fitting, before analyzing how the eloquence of the orator can influence the delivery of the speech (II), to first proceed with a catharsis of the value of elocutio and the persuasive power of the speech (I). Moreover, the way an idea is expressed can evoke emotions that resonate deeply with the listeners, creating a connection that logic alone cannot achieve.

I - The Power of Persuasion and The Virtues of Eloquence[149]

Eloquence is undoubtedly a key to unparalleled persuasion. It serves as a facilitator for the intelligibility of the speech, its adaptation to the historical circumstances of its delivery, particularly the atypical audience receiving it. The grammar and specific vocabulary that rise like smoke from the speech contribute significantly to giving color, style, but most importantly, clarity to the speaker's words, which appear in the minds and imagery of the audience as clear and pure as crystal water. By tailoring the language to suit the audience's cultural and intellectual background, the orator can create a stronger connection and make their message more relatable.

The question has often been raised as to whether rhetorical embellishments can be an indispensable condition for eloquence and, by extension, guarantee the persuasive power essential for the speaker embarking on his oratory flights. The prevailing tendency is to consider these embellishments as part of pathos. Additionally, the use of vivid metaphors and analogies can turn complex ideas into easily digestible concepts, ensuring the audience stays engaged and comprehends the message fully.

Therefore, we will emphasize, on one hand, the appropriateness of the speech (A), grammatical and lexical correctness (B), and clarity (C), while demonstrating how the speaker must attend to these aspects of eloquence that are essential to ensure the necessary persuasive power of the speech and, more than ever, provide the speaker with the confidence and credibility required to elevate the oration in the public arena. Eloquence, therefore, has merits, and there is always a difference when it comes to how one expresses oneself and the impact the speech can have on the audience.

A - Adapting the Speech to The Audience

The speaker needs to make sure their speech is suited to the audience they are speaking to. This means understanding who they are, what they care about, and presenting ideas in a way that connects with them effectively. A speech before a scientific committee must differ from one used in an electoral campaign or in a courtroom. Each context has its own rhetorical customs, and it is a strategic and tactical mistake not to account for this when preparing the speech. The speaker must choose the style of eloquence best suited to the particular circumstance they are facing.

From the "humble" style (humilis) to the "moderate" (mediocris) and "solemn," the speaker will select the most appropriate style based on the object, the circumstances, and the purpose they aim to achieve. The chosen style must also align with the audience's expectations and level of understanding, ensuring the message resonates without appearing overly simplistic or unnecessarily complex. The "humble" style appears to be the simplest and most modest. It is notably marked by the use of everyday language, which is generally precise and concise.[150] However, it must still be coherent and, as Cicero emphasized in Orator ad M. Brutum, "in good health."

This style does not lack appeal, nor does it fail to charm: "as some women, without adornment, are considered beautiful because of this lack.[151]" A speaker who chooses this style values demonstration over decoration. They might still use rhetorical figures, but "their presentation will neither be too passionate nor theatrical, but will be characterized by a moderate movement of themselves.[152]" One of the best examples of adapting a speech to the audience is provided by Lysias, who demonstrates a strong ability for clarity, brevity, and narration.

This approach allows Lysias to strategically achieve his goal while adapting to the circumstances and the purpose of his speech. In such a context, he demonstrates appropriateness by delivering the most suitable speech for the specific circumstances. However, when the orator must confront a specialized or highly specialized audience, he will resort to what Cicero referred to as the "middle style," which, according to Traversi, a criminal defense lawyer, is quite common in judicial oratory. By opting for this style, the orator better accommodates the circumstances, the subject, and the purpose of his speech, hoping to make it more persuasive.

The "middle style" is, by nature, "richer and a bit more robust than the humble style, but more modest than the highest style.[153] It strikes a balance between simplicity and grandeur, allowing the orator to present arguments with sophistication while maintaining accessibility to a diverse audience. This adaptability makes it particularly effective in situations requiring a persuasive yet relatable approach. It includes various embellishments like garland knots.[154] The orator using this style can argue more effectively, but also charm his audience, as Cicero illustrated in his speech to defend Morena, accused of electoral fraud. The "solemn style," for its part, consists of noble words and a structure that is both "elegant and adorned." It is rich in "varied, abundant, and austere[155]" concepts, aiming not only to charm but also to move the audience, to affect their hearts and minds, and to change their feelings. This style demands meticulous preparation, as the orator must carefully choose their words and structure to evoke a deep emotional response, ensuring that the message resonates long after the speech concludes. The exordium of Cicero's first action against Verres for extortion is one of the lasting examples of this.[156]

Therefore, depending on the specific characteristics of the circumstances, the rhetorical genre, the desired outcomes through the speech, and the goal, the orator will adapt his speech. Above all, he must be in harmony with his audience, adjusting not only his style but also the duration of his intervention.

Only under these conditions will he be able to influence the hearts and minds of the listeners, and only in this way will he be able to change their worldview and feelings, delicately, while demonstrating high levels of seduction and, by extension, credibility. An ill-suited speech risks losing its persuasive power, even if its substance is relevant. The orator would benefit from knowing his audience in advance, but also from being able to sense their moods during the delivery, so he can react accordingly.

Hence, the urgency of avoiding pre-written texts, the reading of which could strip the speech of its very existence, especially if unforeseen circumstances require its modification. Appropriateness is an important part of eloquence that helps persuade the audience, just like using correct grammar and words is essential for the speech to work well.

B - Grammatical and Lexical Requirements

The speaker, when delivering their speech, will refrain from using improperly formed words in relation to the morphological and phonological requirements of the language in which they are speaking. This careful attention to the form of words ensures that the speech remains clear and professional, maintaining the credibility of the speaker.

They will therefore avoid vocabulary errors that affect the form of the word they are using. Whether it is an existing word that is distorted or words that are almost non-existent in their language of expression, stylisticians and linguists refer to this distortion of vocabulary as "lexical barbarism" when it infects or alters an element of the lexicon. By avoiding these errors, the speaker strengthens their authority and prevents the audience from being distracted by language mistakes.

For example, if the speaker says "arborigène" instead of "aborigène," "aréopport" for "aéroport," or "ituliser" for "utiliser," they are committing a "lexical barbarism" that could be fatal to the effectiveness of their speech, regardless of the possibly impeccable argumentative support.

Similarly, a "grammatical barbarism" occurs when the grammatical part of the word suffers from morphological or phonological flaws; for instance, when the word "courrirait" is used instead of "courrait." The speaker must be careful and focused when giving their speech. They should avoid mixing up letters, adding extra ones, or using wrong word comparisons.[157]

Additionally, words and expressions from a certain past, from a bygone era, outdated terms that are no longer used in the speaker's time, known as "archaisms," should not be part of the speech. The speaker should resonate with the vocabulary of their time in order to better convey the ideas they defend and thus ensure the success of their cause. It would be difficult to argue a cause in the third millennium with a vocabulary inspired by the medieval period. It would be hard to digest, despite the weight of the arguments that could arise from the speech.

Similarly, the speech should be free from syntactical errors or constructions that do not conform to the rules of syntax in the language the speaker uses, that of their time, and constructions that are not accepted within a norm or an acceptable usage. These errors can confuse the audience, making the speech difficult to follow and diminishing its overall impact.

The solecism[158] that constitutes this syntactical error further discredits the speech and even the speaker, casting doubt in the minds of the audience, who may still be charmed by the speech, but not by doubt. The audience might begin to question the speaker's authority, which undermines their ability to persuade.

The use of pleonasm in a speech, meaning unnecessary and sometimes incorrect words, does not always help make the speech persuasive. This situation can become burdensome for the audience and sometimes counterproductive in terms of the objectives to be achieved through the speech. The speaker should therefore regulate or limit the presence of pleonasm.

The speaker must know when to leave the stage, as contemporaries say: "know when to leave the stage before it leaves you." Speaking longer than necessary is one of the ailments of many speakers who, through overly long, diffuse speeches full of unnecessary details, get lost in superfluous developments that distract the audience and naturally cause them to lose interest. An audience's attention is finite, and the longer the speech drags on, the more it risks disengaging them. Prolixity, which consists of speaking longer than necessary, is a flaw that obstructs the persuasive power of a speech. The more unnecessary content added, the less impact the core message of the speech will have. Does this mean that one must always be concise? We have reasons to doubt this, because an excessively concise speech does not allow the audience to appreciate its scope and details.

As Cicero stated, a speaker who quickly delivers their speech is "like someone entering a rich and well-furnished house, where the carpets are rolled up, the silverware is put aside, and the paintings and statues are pushed away, where all the magnificent things and utensils are stacked and hidden." An overly concise speaker does not always allow the audience to discover the argumentation and the words used to express it. Today, it is agreed that an excessively long speech is inconceivable, considering the demands of time management.

Therefore, the speaker should refrain from unnecessarily prolonging their speech and giving excessive attention to facts and arguments that are not strictly necessary. However, they must focus on the essential points, without being too brief or too verbose. Only in this way would he ensure the possibility of charming, captivating, flirting with, and winning over those who are listening, thus making the truth triumph with a speech that is clear in both the minds and hearts of the audience.

C - The Necessary Clarity

The speech, after all, must be understandable and intelligible. The clarity of the speech shows that the speaker, like a great master, has mastered the subject; indeed, what is generally well conceived is always expressed clearly, and the words to convey it come easily.[159] The clarity of the speech is the sine qua non condition for winning the case, charming the audience, presenting the essential arguments, and thus achieving the desired objective through the oration; as Aristotle said, "if it is not expressed clearly, it does not achieve its purpose.[160]" To do this, the speaker must deliver the speech as audibly as possible.

The volume of his voice must be sufficient, and the diction clear as crystal. This eliminates any potential obscurity that could have clouded the luminous momentum carried by the speaker. Clear pronunciation ensures that the audience can easily follow the message, which strengthens the persuasive effect of the speech. The speaker must therefore work daily to improve his pronunciation, diction, and overall elocution. It is said that Demosthenes, affected by stuttering and respiratory insufficiency, overcame these difficulties by reciting verses aloud and holding his breath while climbing a steep hill.[161] Through this consistent effort, Demosthenes not only overcame his physical limitations but also sharpened his ability to deliver speeches with power and clarity. The speaker will make sentences easy to understand, easy to hear, and even easy to memorize. Therefore, he will avoid complex sentences, slapdash sentence structures, and ambiguous grammatical, syntactical, and semantic constructions.

In his anthology *De Oratore*, Cicero, an esteemed lawyer, writer, and Roman politician, offers a secret that allowed him to deliver clearer speeches and improve his elocution. He strongly recommends the enjoyable activity of reading. As he writes: "When I have time, I make a habit of reading books... after having read these books diligently at Cape Misene, I feel that, in their presence, my way of speaking becomes, so to speak, higher in color.[162]" Reading, therefore, would help develop clarity in reasoning and elocution, and consequently, the persuasive devices that the orator should employ in any oratorical flight to ensure the persuasion he intends to achieve with his words, phrases, and circumlocutions.

However, clarity can depend partially or fully on the attitude of the audience. A distracted and detached audience requires the orator to make a greater effort to maintain clarity. It is therefore essential for the orator to remain aware of the audience's engagement and adjust the delivery accordingly to maintain focus.[163]

That is why Quintilian, a skilled lawyer, recommends that in an oration, especially a judicial one, "one should never say more or less than the arguments" and that "the arguments should be clear and easily understood, even for those who pay little attention... the judge's attention is not always strong enough to push away the obscurity on its own and to bring light from his intelligence to the darkness of the speech... while being distracted by several thoughts, our words must be clear to ensure that our oration touches his mind as the sun touches his eyes... we must make it so that he cannot not understand."

The orator must say what is necessary, the necessary, and nothing but the necessary. Regardless of the attitude of the audience or even the judges, the orator's words must be clear enough to "touch" the judge's and audience's minds, "just as the sun (touches)" their eyes. In this case, the speech would be very clear. The judges, impressed and persuaded by the orator's charm, would likely be influenced by the speech and agree with the orator.

II - The Art of Presentation and Oratorical Seduction

In his role as a seducer and charmer, beyond the clarity of the speech and the various decorative artifices it contains, the orator must know how to put his speech into motion. This involves a deep understanding of timing and emphasis, where the orator uses pauses and inflections to build anticipation and impact.

Hence, the urgency of mastering the art of presentation and exposition is truly essential to maximizing the persuasive power he seeks to achieve through his words. It is the art of presentation that gives value to the speech. It is the art of presentation that highlights the seductive devices skillfully crafted by the inventive genius of the orator.

Ultimately, it is the art of presentation that allows one to persuade and convince even the most skeptical and delicate audiences. A well-delivered speech can transform a dry argument into a compelling narrative, keeping the audience's attention and making them emotionally invested in the message. But one must know how to master this particular art of presenting a speech for seductive and persuasive purposes.

The art of presentation is similar to the acting of cinema, where the orator embodies the speech he is delivering like a Hollywood or Nollywood actor. In this process, the orator becomes a storyteller, shaping their words to create a vivid mental image for the audience. He will certainly highlight his skills in dramatic arts, musicology, and improvisation.

The presentation of the speech requires the orator to engage his diction and gestures, without which the speech would be but a shadow of itself, lacking the liveliness and sensuality so crucial for its methodical journey into the heart and mind of the audience.

The gestures aspect of non-verbal communication seems more related to oratory action (Chapter II) than to the art of presentation. This is why emphasis will be placed on diction. From start to finish, we will analyze, on the one hand, pronunciation (A), on the other hand, pauses (B), and finally rhythm (C). Further down in the reflections, we will challenge the place of the orator's memory in a seductive, artistic, and rhetorical logic.

A - Pronunciation

Pronunciation refers to diction, which, according to the Larousse dictionary, is the manner of speaking. It encompasses the rules that standardize the pronunciation of a language, viewed from an aesthetic or normative perspective. The best pronunciation systematically influences the seduction of an audience and the persuasive power of the speech. How can the pronunciation of the speech be approached while disregarding the voice that carries it? The orator's voice must suit the speech and the context in which it is spoken. Regarding this, Quintilian believes that diction is: "effective and elegant when supported by a voice that is not forced but is strong, rich in modulation, solid, soft, constant, sonorous, pure, that cuts through the air and penetrates the ears.[164]" The orator's state of mind and the nature of the issues discussed will determine the intonation used for the speech. Like the tuning of violins in music, the orator will adjust their voice to the emotions they wish to convey through their oration. Pronunciation will allow, beyond reason, to transmit passions that arise from various mechanisms of seduction and charm, capable of touching the sensitivity and hearts of the audience.

The tone changes based on the speech's key moments to highlight essential points or emphasise issues. Cicero mentions a trick in his work De Oratore when he suggests that "he must bring out a vibrant tone when he wants to be passionate, a muffled tone when he wants to be soft, a deep tone when he wants to appear serious, a plaintive

81

tone when he wants to evoke pity.[165]" The pronunciation of the speech should never evolve like a calm river but rather, as it seems to us, like a sinusoidal curve that clearly demonstrates variations in tone, feelings, moments of passion, gentleness, great gravity, complaint, or pity. The orator will strive to remain natural. A forced pronunciation could break the clarity necessary for the persuasive power of the speech. Finally, he should neither speak at the speed of a hare nor the speed of a tortoise, as such a situation could obscure the pauses and emotions on the one hand and, on the other hand, distract the audience's attention, which is essential to triumph in his cause.

B - Pauses

A speech without pauses would be classified as "verbal diarrhoea" and would, therefore, be devoid of seduction and persuasion. Traversi defines the pause as: "a brief suspension of the speech, intended to be inserted between one period and another[166]..."

The pause allows the orator, after expending energy in the delivery of the speech, to take a breath towards the end of a sentence or paragraph, ensuring that he concludes without major incident. Above all, the most interesting effect of the pause is that it gives an additional elegance to the speech, making it fluid, clear, easy to listen to, and even easier to memorise. In this context, the speech, the plea, or the argument: "flows continuously like a river[1676]" (ne infinite feature ut flumen ratio).

The pause helps establish various sequences in the speech, different moments, and strong ideas. The orator could also use the pause to highlight exceptional moments of attention, where the audience, captivated by the speaker's words, delicately drinks from the wisdom of the orator's perch.

It is, therefore, an opportunity for the speaker to seize the moment and engrave his plea into the audience's memory or simply to emphasize a particular point in the speech, offering the listeners a moment of reflection to grasp its contours and nuances[168]. Thus, the pause in the speech is a crucial moment of the delivery, a time when the speaker, through the suspension of the speech, conveys powerful moments, strong expressions, a moment of communion with the audience, better watered by the speech and able to grasp the ins and outs of the argument; a moment of rhetoric where the listener can better understand the arguments that naturally rise above the fray, appreciate them, and, without weakness or pity, but also without vengeance or anger, make use of his *spatuim congitandi* (grasp the depth of the speech). At this stage, the audience is naturally charmed, and the persuasive power of the speech is not only reinforced but further consolidated.

C - The Oratorical Rhythm

The orator, just like the musician, must follow a certain musical cadence in order to achieve their goal, which is not only to teach but, above all, to move and, even more importantly, to please. The speech should appear harmonious to the listener. In the opening, ancient rhetoric recommends that the orator appear calm and serene and avoid, as much as possible, showing aggression because, as we have seen, the orator's goal is to solicit the attention and goodwill of the judge or audience.

This first impression the orator gives should, it seems, be good and even respectful. The narration of the facts that follow the exordium should be succinct. Indeed, an overly long narration would be boring and sometimes airy, as it will never be the focal point of the speech, although it sets up the logical sequence of the arguments that will follow.

However, when addressing the refutation of the opposing thesis, the speech, the plea, or the oration must rise a notch. The tone will become a little higher, and the intensity of the speech will increase as well. In the argumentation phase, or the actual presentation of the orator's thesis, the tone and intensity of the speech will reach their peak. This is the climax of the oration, where the orator demonstrates the validity of their thesis while proving how their opponents have been mistaken.

The speech must naturally increase in intensity, as the outcome of these two stages will be crucial for the cause. At this level, the orator will appeal to various seductions to various passions in order to conquer the sensations beyond reason. Then comes the peroration with a tone that is equally vibrant but not as prominent as the one highlighted during the argumentation and refutation.

The rhythmic question has been the subject of many debates for over two thousand years. The Roman lawyer Cicero resolved it by observing that "the speech must be constructed with art so that the beginning is calm, the animated discussions have a quick pace, the narrations of facts are gentle, and in any case, it must flow according to a rhythm such that, when it reaches the end, the pause is natural.[169]"

Board 2: The Rhythm of Elocution[170]

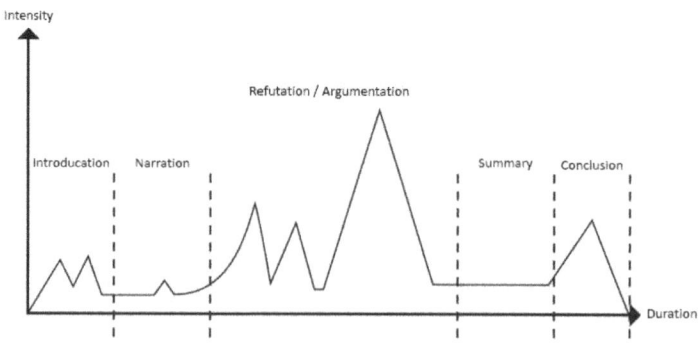

The delivery and the rhythm of the speech should vary depending on the parts of the discourse. By this method, the speaker allows their audience to distinguish what is more important and what is less so, what is useful and what is pleasant. The rhythm of the delivery has always been different depending on the parts of the discourse. Each part of the speech corresponds to a well-defined rhythm. It is a sacred principle of revolutionary rhetoric.

The Orator Is a Seducer

The orator is a charmer who, beyond presenting arguments, uses speech techniques to appeal not just to reason but also to emotions. He does not simply choose to state certain facts like an ordinary person, but to present them in a way that pleases and certainly triggers an emotional process, creating adherence to the thesis defended, the cause argued.

There is indeed a difference when one expresses oneself in one way or another, as Aristotle already acknowledged in Book III of his Rhetoric. In this vein, the orator will highlight the virtues of elocution by adapting his speech to the audience, taking into account the grammatical and lexical particularities related to the speech with a seductive approach, and ensuring the clarity of said speech. Like a film actor, he will master the art of presentation and oratorical seduction based particularly on the quality of pronunciation, moments of silence and pause, as well as the rhythm of his elocution, which will make the speech a harmonious whole, a real symphony similar to music, its cadence, and its various beats.

Similarly, the memory of the orator would be a significant asset for his elocution. Indeed, an orator who knows his case inside and out, the cause he defends, could make use of his memory, which would contribute significantly not only to reinforcing his credibility but also to seducing an audience amazed by this orator who delivers specific phrases constructed in order, as if they were disparate, and gives the impression of searching, in a meditative and hesitant manner, for the elements prepared for the oration.[171] To do this, the orator must have full mastery of their cause, much like an object held in hand.[172]

Using the ancient rhetorical technique of associating ideas, the orator memorizes key concepts by recalling their order. This method, called "artificial memory," allows, according to Quintilian, for the lasting engraving of images of chosen places, just as a wardrobe circus would.[173]

One is not born a great orator... one becomes one! Only daily practice allows for the improvement of the art of eloquence, much like Demosthenes, the Greek lawyer and great orator, who, suffering from stuttering and respiratory insufficiency, managed to overcome these handicaps by declaiming verses loudly and holding his breath while climbing a steep hill.[174]

CHAPTER V:
THE ORATORICAL ACTION

Board 3: The Action

Credit: Dede Fotsa

A real debate at the University of Paris-Sorbonne inspires this image. It brings to life a fundamental aspect of oratory: the oratorical action, one of the powerful tools of revolutionary orators that allows them to change the course of a debate.

An orator's words and gestures are potent tools for persuasion. Action is to the orator what fragrance is to the flower or what bright feathers are to a rare bird. Action is "the eloquence of the body,[175]" as it essentially derives from the voice and gestures.

Gestures may include hand movements that describe the flow of thought, facial expressions, or simply body postures that make the speech expressive, illustrative, and persuasive. The speech also has its tone, its music, and its rhythms, though this musical aspect is at least somewhat masked, not always rising above the fray as in traditional musical art.

With its emotions and inflexions, the voice awakens the audience. The voice helps maintain the tension, as the speech is like a long thread that must be kept taut in order to avoid losing the listeners along the way.[176] It is the ultimate vehicle for expressing feelings but, above all, for rhetorical seduction, which, due to its diverse tones, can produce in a speech a "song with accents of a delicious variety.[177]"

As Cicero acknowledged in an epistolary treatise written at the request of the famous Brutus in 46 BC, oratorical action would be the very cornerstone of eloquence. Eloquence cannot emerge without it. One can understand how crucial action is in the process of seduction and persuasion that constitutes the delicate mission of the orator at the heart of his oration.

Action alone, due to its beauty, can make men who cannot express themselves collect the fruits of eloquence, just as a smooth talker, lacking elegance in his actions, would be considered a speaker of bad taste, useless to society. Oratorical action is thus at the heart of the speech, and any orator wishing to adorn themselves with the luminous and brilliant colors of rhetoric should master its uses and mechanisms.

It thus becomes crucial to evaluate the contribution of oratorical action in the seduction of a jury or an audience; in other words, how the voice, gestures, and facial expressions of an orator, beyond charming and seducing, can strengthen or consolidate the persuasive power of the speech that the orator brings and submits to the sagacity of an audience.

In order to address the above problem, it would be appropriate first to conduct a thorough analysis of the power of gestures (II) and then consider a study of the orator's voice (I) in the process of charm and persuasion that the orator hopes to achieve through a flowery oration, adorned with sympathy.

I - The Voice and Oratorical Seduction[178]

The voice is undoubtedly one of the essential vehicles of expression at the disposal of the orator. It is one of their seductive tools, which, in the process of action, gives color to the oration. A judicious use of the voice would have a rather pleasant and positive effect on a speech. The audience, informed by a voice rising above the crowd due to its quality, its various tonalities, its softness, its consistency, or simply its elegance, will be more captivated by its power but, above all, seduced.

The orator's voice, more than ever, appears in this context as a seductive device capable of conquering, beyond rationality, the emotional fiber of the listener. The latter, veiled by the scent and fragrance of the voice highlighted, will be drawn even more, like a bee that seeks to consume, certainly with less moderation, the nectar of knowledge carried by a voice with angelic flavors, harmonious melodies, provoking, to the limit, shivers, and emotions.

The voice thus brings a certain musicality, sensitivity, and cadence to the oration, which, in this case, also serves as a work of art for the audience, who, in one way or another, will not be indifferent to the various modulations it carries. Well-modulated and adapted to the circumstances of the speech, the voice adds power to its content, allowing it to have a greater impact on the listener. Similarly, it grants much more credibility to the orator, posed here as the "actor-musician" of his own speech.

The speech, here staged like a movie, placing the orator as the main actor. Could it make him the hero of his own "film," the star of his own oratorical stage? Only his ability to use his vocal cords to maximize his persuasive power will help answer this question. The voice and the seduction of the speech require first knowing the quality of the voice (A) in order to understand better its tonality and modulations, as well as their impact on the persuasive power of the speech (B). The answer to these two questions will help better understand the "oratorical scene" that highlights the orator, his voice, and the persuasive power it can have on his audience.

A - On the Quality of The Voice

The orator should wish to have a good-quality voice, given that, in general, the quality of the voice does not depend on the orator. However, should the orator simply accept the voice that nature has given him? He must undoubtedly work daily to improve the quality of his voice, especially since it plays a major role in his oratorical seduction process and persuasion.

In this regard, Quintilian, in his book *Institution Oratoria* (Book XI), believes that the orator should have a natural voice, that is, not forced. A forced voice would fatally undermine the clarity of the speech. It could even be harmful to the audience, who would be disturbed by it and would thus lose the attention necessary for the orator to persuade.

According to Quintilian, the voice should be strong and rich, soft, consistent, and modulated. Such a voice would facilitate the clarity of the speech and seduction based on vocal codes and voice variations. The audience, carried away by the beauty of the voice, its natural colors and variations, would give more attention to the person of the orator and, most importantly, to the content of the speech, which would gently, delicately, and naturally enter the hearts and minds of the listeners.

How should the speaker strive to improve their voice and, consequently, their vocal seduction technique? It is clear that, lacking control over the intensity or timbre of their voice, the speaker can, through declamation practice, gradually acquire greater flexibility. This not only regenerates the audience's ear but also builds the speaker's self-confidence.

For his part, Demosthenes believed that the best quality of a speaker is far from the search for arguments or the art of arranging ideas effectively; it is "action," in other words, the way the speech is delivered. As a side note, Demosthenes himself was shy and unsettled in public early in his career as a speaker. He imposed strict and rigorous training on himself in order to face the Athenians without losing his composure. Among other things, to improve his articulation, he practiced speaking with pebbles in his mouth. In order to cover the noise of a murmuring assembly, he declaimed in front of a waterfall.

He practiced in front of a mirror, locking himself in an underground room for several weeks, shaving half of his head to be too ashamed to go out, and forcing himself to work even harder. Caius Gracchus, a Roman orator, would have a piper accompany him who played a note so that he could place his voice above each speech.

It is through constant practice that the orator improves their voice and delivery. Various breathing exercises and practice declaiming in front of the sea are necessary to improve the voice and guarantee the powerful effect it should have in captivating the audience and persuading the judges. Let's imagine, even for a moment, a speech with the best possible arguments, the most artistic arrangement that could exist, but a speech with faltering pronunciation, an unsuitable voice, forced, weak, inconsistent, and monotonous...

This speech would, in reality, have no flavor or scent, simply bland. This speech would be nothing but a shadow of itself, far from changing the present or the future. That is why, more than the Greeks, the Romans had already focused on the importance of the orator's physical presence, as the power of the intonation of the voice seemed essential to seduce, persuade, and convince a jury. Like an actor, the orator must interpret their speech and master their voice and their breath.[179]

B - The Tonalities of The Voice

The tonality of a speech holds unprecedented power for seductive devices and the force of persuasion. As discussed earlier, it is a crucial element of oratory that gives the speech a rhythm, a musicality, and an artistic aspect that is essentially close to the performing arts and cinema.

The orator, like an actor, must rely on variations in tone to maintain the audience's attention.[180] This variation will make the speech more interesting or prevent the audience from being bothered by the monotony of the speech. Such monotony could become boring and negatively impact the persuasive efforts that have been activated.[181]

Monotony in speech removes all its spices and artifices, and like a house of cards, the attention of the listeners collapses. Immediately, the oratorical seduction fades, and the persuasive power vanishes like smoke. Hence the urgency of giving prominent importance to the intonation of the voice, which seems to have more power than the argument itself or the art of arranging the arguments.

In practice, as stated since Antiquity, the speaker will move from calm tones, like the one used at the beginning of the speech (exordium), to higher tones that are generally suited for moments of argumentation or rebuttal. He will then lower his tone slightly when making proposals, stating hypotheses, asking questions, or evoking emotions. The modulation of his voice is based on the emotions he wants to convey at any given moment of the oration.

In this regard, Erasmus (1467-1536) in *The Praise of Folly* expresses concern about the orators of his time who try to impress the audience indiscriminately through varying tonalities: "They have taken, I don't know where that the exordium should be delivered slowly and without éclat. What do our people do? They begin in such a way that they cannot hear themselves, an excellent method for not being understood by anyone.

They have been told that, to stir passions, one must raise the tone; to obey the precepts, at the moment least expected, they suddenly burst into furious outbursts. It is still traditional for them that the orator must warm up gradually. Thus, after beginning haltingly, they suddenly start to shout, even in the coldest place, and then they end so low that one would think they were about to breathe their last."

This is fundamental in order to touch the hearts of his audience and secure the necessary sympathy to ensure the triumph of the cause he passionately defends. The tone gives rhythm to the oration; indeed, this musicality based on the modulation of the voice captivates the audience's attention, leaving them hanging on the speaker's every word, simultaneously demonstrating receptivity to the cause he is pleading for. The speaker would use tonal variation to express the delicate nuances of his speech, just as a painter would with his colors to create nuances in his artwork.

In his anthology work *Orator ad M. Brutum*, Cicero shows the importance for the orator to change his voice according to the emotion he wishes to express at a given time or moment of his oration, in order to seduce and persuade further:

"Nature has assigned each emotion a specific expression, a tone of voice, and a gesture... the tones of the voice are tuned like the strings of an instrument, and yet each stroke produces high and low sounds, fast and slow, loud and soft... They are at the disposal of the orator to express the different nuances of speech, just as a painter does with his colors... Anger will have a particular tone, high-pitched, excited, with frequent interruptions... Compassion and pain will have another tone: flexible, full, broken, and plaintive... Fear's tone will be low, hesitant, discouraged... Pleasure will require a different tone, clear and tender, joyful but subdued... The tone of discouragement will be low, but without compassion, uniform in the articulation of the voice[182]... ".

The tone of the voice is of great importance to the art of oratory in general. The tonality makes the orator a singer, a seducer, a storyteller, and even a griot, who, through their speech, convey emotions to instill the change they wish to see through the outcome of the cause they defend.

Like a sine wave, the listener can better understand when the orator refers to an important point that demands their full attention or when they wish to convey a particular emotion that would help the listener grasp the ins and outs of the cause they are fighting for. The seductive and persuasive value of tonal variations is, therefore, undeniable.

A well-modulated voice gives real chances for the triumph of the cause being defended. However, the mastery of one's body and gestures by the orator would give even more power to the speech.

II - The Power of Body[183] Movements and Oratory Seduction

As we have mentioned, gestures are the eloquence carried by the orator's body. The body embodies a form of rhetoric that can either serve or harm the orator, depending on its use. Gestures are at the heart of oratory. It is the gesture that carries the speech, it is the gesture that brings the speech to life. Indeed, since Antiquity, gestures have always been regarded as an indispensable complement to verbal communication. Cicero notes in a very famous work: "Words only move those who are connected by a common language and deep thoughts, often incomprehensible to the minds of superficial men, whereas gestures, on the other hand, which express the feelings of the mind, touch everyone because the minds of men are moved by the same feelings they recognize in others through the same signs with which they show them in themselves.[184]"

The gestures, therefore, have a broader impact than language alone. Through gestures, the orator communicates the emotions embedded in their speech. This would allow the orator to "quickly reap the benefits of eloquence with their audience, whereas the ugliness of gestures has made many a smooth talker appear as a poor orator.[185]" Cicero adds: "Often, incapable orators have gained praise for their dexterity in gesturing, while many capable orators have been considered inept due to their false gestures.[186]" It is not by chance that Demosthenes attributed the first, second, and third places to gesture.[187]

The great masters of rhetoric agree that gestures are undeniably one of the cornerstones of the art of seduction, supported by the orator and, by extension, of persuasion of the audience. From ancient times to today, this truth has lost none of its relevance. Beyond the oratorical posture and the associated hand movements, particular attention is given to facial expressions and eye movements, which Cicero defines as the "interpreters of the soul." Gestures undoubtedly have a significant impact on the process of oratory seduction and, especially, on the power of persuasion that determines the outcome of the cause presented by the orator.

In this context, it becomes wise to analyze this crucial rhetorical process. Such an analysis requires emphasizing the posture of the orator and the movements of their hands (A) in terms of seduction and persuasion before focusing on the facial expressions that many orators consider essential and even indispensable in the context of seduction and persuasion (B).

A - Posture and Hand Movement

From ancient times to the present, an orator wishing to adorn themselves with the artifices of seduction and thereby hoping to persuade, must take care of their posture. The orator, as an educator, must choose a position, a manner of standing, and an attitude that, beyond aggression, should at least be inspired by the classical model of restrained eloquence—calm but firm.

While certain aspects of this oratorical tradition may be almost obsolete in light of contemporary realities, others have not lost their persuasive power. In any case, an upright posture and relative stability are now indispensable for any orator who wishes to make their posture a valuable addition to the speech they deliver. Cicero, in a treatise written at the request of the famous Brutus, absolutely acknowledges this when he states: "...he should stand upright, head held high, avoid pacing constantly, rarely advance toward the audience, and always in a moderate manner, never tilting his head weakly[188]..." Such an attitude, far from discrediting the orator, makes them a charmer who knows how to contain themselves while respecting the rules of decorum, which help guide their speech to the hearts of the listeners.

Like an artist of the stage or a movie actor, the orator must interpret their own speech, which implies that in order to be more expressive, they must methodically use their hands, which, like the voice, must carry and express their emotions. Indeed, hands, like tone, convey the rhythm of the speech, the intensity of the discourse, moments of great excitement, and moments of calm.

The orator will extend their arms during moments of high rhetorical excitement and "bring them back to themselves during calmer passages.[189] "In a contentious debate, they will gain strength or power by raising their index finger, even though Quintilian believes that only the right hand should move, "with the middle finger against the thumb, the three other fingers extended, a slight movement to the right and left, without ever rising above the eyes or lowering below the chest.[190]"

In a rhetorical speech, they will either face the palm upward or forward to explain their metaphors or charm the audience. The orator will, in any case, regulate their own movements to make them more natural "so that nothing appears exaggerated.[191]" Hand movements add a bit more spice to the elocution, making the speech more digestible, more attractive, and more persuasive.

The opposite would make the speech dull and hinder its impact. Quintilian observes in this regard that the movement of the hands: "speaks for itself"; indeed, "isn't it true that with them we ask, promise, call, bring out, threaten, beg, express hatred, fear, question, deny, and manifest joy, sadness, uncertainty, and other emotions, regret, modesty, a quantity, a number of times? And aren't our hands always the ones that reveal excitement, embarrassment, approval, astonishment, and modesty? In the enumeration of places and people, don't they take the place of adverbs and pronouns? So, despite the linguistic differences between all peoples, the language of the hands truly seems to be a universal language.[192]"

The movement of the hands transcends languages and cultures. Through this technique, the orator could even reach those who cannot hear or speak. It is the language of universality essential in a speech, just like the expressions on the orator's face.

Board 4: The Power Grab

Credit: Dede Fotsa

The raised index and the open fingers are power indicators.

Board 5: Determination

Credit: Dede Fotsa

The clenched fist symbolizes a strong expression of conviction and determination. A powerful moment of oratorical passion, a communion between the orator and their audience.

Board 6: Oratorical Precision

Credit: Dede Fotsa

The hand movements here indicate a moment of precision expressed by both orators. Precision in a statement made, precision on a particular point of the speech.

Board 7: Calmness

Credit: Dede Fotsa

A highly passionate female speaker, evident in her face and gestures, which show a rise in oratorical passions. However, in contrast, a male speaker with his outstretched hands tries to calm these passions, certainly to return to reason.

B - Facial Expressions

Because facial expressions are sometimes more eloquent than any other words[193], Roman rhetoricians paid special attention to them. It is the first impression left on the audience.[194] Facial expressions must harmonize with the content of the speech; otherwise, the speech risks losing credibility and effectiveness.

The gaze, for its part, must follow the direction of the gesture. The eyes are of great importance for seduction, so it is important to know how to control one's gaze. Cicero in De Oratore demonstrates how facial expressions can be decisive in oratorical seduction and the persuasive power of the speech.

As he writes in The Orator: "The face, which after the voice is the most powerful, brings either dignity or grace! When one ensures that nothing improper or affected appears on it, it is the eyes that need to be monitored. Since the face is the mirror of the soul, the eyes are its interpreters[195]; they will be joyful or serious in turn, depending on the things discussed."

The orator, in this perspective, will be mindful of the movement of his eyes, for as Cicero asserts: "If the face is the mirror of the soul, the eyes are its interpreters." The eyes reflect either joy or sadness, depending on the subject discussed by the orator. This allows the orator to convey messages of joy, sadness, pity, or melancholy through their facial expressions in connection with the cause they defend.

The audience, moved by these actions, will be more flattered and will better understand the fundamentals of the thesis presented for their consideration by the orator – the actor of the moment.

The orator must finally harmonize their physiognomy with the speech being delivered, as well as the tone of their discourse. Specifically, as Quintilian states in *Institution Oratoria*: "... either the gesture precedes the voice, or begins after the voice.[196]" The opposite effect would be particularly unpleasant for the audience, who may become uncomfortable with an orator appearing out of sync with the circumstances.

The Orator Is An Actor

Photo credit: Batoul Ajrouche

At the Cyber-justice Lab of the University of Montreal, we were tasked with acting as defense lawyers in a simulated trial. We realized just how crucial the eloquence of the body is in a rhetorical contest with revolutionary fervor.

As we have seen, oratory action is nothing more than "the eloquence of the body, since it relies on both the voice and the gesture.[197]" It is a process that allows the orator to bring attention to their body, gestures, and vocal cords with the goal of captivating the audience and persuading them of the validity of the cause they present through their oration for their supreme consideration.

Oratory action is undoubtedly the backbone of oratory art. Action complements elocution; oratory action allows one to reap the fruits of eloquence even with a flawed diction. Speaking well is not always enough and can even prove to be very insufficient if the orator disregards oratory action, which undeniably occupies the first, second, and third places in the art of oratory.

Therefore, the greatest quality of the orator is not the invention of arguments or the art of organizing and arranging their ideas[198]; rather, it is the way they deliver their speech, the art of interpreting it, the mastery of their voice, body, gestures, and even facial expressions. "The face is the mirror of the soul, and the eyes are its interpreters.[199]"

The orator is ultimately like an actor who, through oratorical maneuvers such as voice, gaze, and gestures, positions themselves as a seducer of an audience whose favor they wish to win, hoping to see their plea triumph and, if necessary, overthrow the established order. These maneuvers, deployed methodically and artistically, aim to conquer the hearts and minds of the judges and the hearts of the listeners. Certainly, the rules of ancient rhetoric do not always apply mutatis mutandis, like those derived from the Haranguer of Lake Trasimene.

However, it must be acknowledged that most of these ancient rules have not aged a bit, hence the urgency to draw inspiration from them and imbibe them. Ultimately, what would a speech be without gesture? What would a speech devoid of body movements be? What would a speech that disregards facial expressions, appropriate tonalities, or musicality be? Such a speech would be the shadow of itself! It would be "bland and incomplete,[200]" lacking flavour, because devoid of its essential artifices and spices. Such a speech would simply fail to capture the hearts of the listeners, who would remain mere spectators.

THIRD PART:
PATHOS

The orator must not only be able to prove the legitimacy of a cause and please those who listen to them. Above all, they must move their audience to hope for victory. Whether it is a plea or a political speech, proving has always been a necessity, a delight, and moving, a moving victory.

When the orator moves the audience, their cause is won.[201] The orator will rely on various genres in this perspective: the simple to prove, the tempered to please, and the vehement in which they concentrate all their power to move the audience. The ability of the orator to stir emotions and passions during their speech has been recognized in ancient rhetoric as *Pathos*. "This part of rhetoric deals with means aimed at moving, as opposed to ethos, which deals with morals.[202]"

It is almost the same reasoning we find in Michel Meyer's work *La rhétorique*, which notes that pathos is: "the set of implicit values of responses outside questions that nourish the questions an individual considers pertinent.[203]" Through pathos, the orator provokes emotion in the audience by playing on the values that are sacred to them: what can anger them, calm them, what they despise, or what they indignantly oppose.

Through their speech, the orator stirs emotions and passions in the audience, which can stem from hope, fear, love, despair, pleasure, displeasure, and many others. The emotions provoked by the speech, the passions thus stirred[204], contribute to touching the heart of the audience, which, beyond reason, is carried away by a speech that speaks more to their feelings than to their reasoning.

The listener in this context is not much different from someone passionately in love, who no longer sees much difference between the qualities of the loved one and all the good they could think of them. Like a magic spell, the listener finds in the orator marvelous, exceptional qualities, thus elevating these passions to the value of the speech and the one who embodies it. This is the effect we can observe after the famous "I have understood you" by General De Gaulle, the *"Ich bin ein Berliner"* from Kennedy, the *"I have a dream"* from Martin Luther King, the *"Yes, we can"* from Barack Obama, or the very memorable "Congolais, Congolaises" from Patrice Lumumba, at the Independence ceremony of the Congo... Through this art of emotion, the orator will make the audience vibrate, make them dream, make them anxious, reassure them, and make them laugh or cry. There is no doubt that well-executed pathos undoubtedly strengthens the power of persuasion and ensures victory for the cause being defended, just as the stories told, the arrangement of words and thoughts, the images, parables, and techniques used all contribute to stirring the rhetorical passions and leading the orator to victory.

Rhetorical figures are essential for raising passions and emotions during a speech, and those with decorative qualities are even more crucial. The distinguished orator, in addition to mastering dialectics and semantics, must adorn himself with high-level stylistic artifices to ensure, beyond seduction, the stirring of passions and the ability to move from the courtroom, carried away by the lyricism of his impassioned speech.

Thus, it becomes crucial to analyze the rhetorical maneuvers capable of evoking emotions and leading to victory. In this effort, it is important to recognize that ornamental rhetorical figures and speech amplification techniques are indispensable. Therefore, we will systematically analyze the decorative style figures (Chapter VI) and various amplification techniques of the speech (Chapter VII). In doing so, we will gain a precise understanding of the place of pathos in rhetorical passions, emotion, and persuasion of the orator.

CHAPTER VI:
DECORATIVE STYLE FIGURES

The sublime orator will express himself with distinction. He will use a brilliant, floral, colorful, and polished style in which the listener can easily uncover various seductions of speech, various seductions of thought. It is the brilliant style carried by rhetorical figures that seizes souls and hearts. It is this flamboyant style that subtly slips into the hearts and sows new ideas, uproots old ones, and changes the world[205]. The orator, in addition to impeccable argumentative support, a solid argumentative structure like reinforced concrete, diction, and gestures worthy of great speeches, must master the figures of style. These rhetorical figures have shaped the greatness of eloquence in antiquity and in the city.

Decorative style figures, that is, this particular way of expressing things to modify ordinary language while making it more expressive, give the speech all its weight in gold. This expressive value, worthy of great intellectual nobility, influences the emotions and persuasive power of the speech, which, by this fact, is above the fray.

Ancient rhetoric, in its various aspects, made a general classification distinguishing tropes from "figures of thought" and "figures of words," also called *Lumina, flores, and colores*[206]. The most relevant division seems to come from Fontanier, who organizes figures of speech into seven classes, divided into figures of meaning and figures of expression[207]. This classification fits with the traditional one that already distinguished between "figures of thought[208]," which express ideas, and "figures of words[209]," whose main function is purely to embellish the speech. For a long time, clouds obscured these classifications, preventing objective clarifications of the different classifications mentioned above.

In an effort to settle the debate, Cicero does not seem to convince further when, in the wake of making this differentiation, he states that: "the figure of words disappears if we change the words, but the figure of thought remains, regardless of the kind of words we use[210]. "Thus, in order to methodically balance both sides, we will focus in this reflection on figures of speech with essentially decorative functions for the oration. These could be "figures of words" as well as "figures of thought." Therefore, we will especially focus on what ancient rhetoric called "tropes[211]," although other techniques should not be neglected in the emotional and persuasive processes of speech.

It thus becomes logical to question our rhetorical heritage in order to see which figures can be decorative and thus contribute to moving the audience, who in one way or another will be convinced of the validity of the cause pleaded by the orator from the height of his perch. In the perspective of analysis, the spotlight will be placed on the main ornamental rhetorical figures (I) before we lift a veil on various other stylistic techniques that also decorate the speech (II). But above all, we will see at each stage of the process how these figures add value to the speech, particularly how they allow emotions to rise and strengthen the persuasive power essential to the triumph of the cause to which the orator has dedicated himself.

I - Major Rhetorical Figures with Decorative Flavors

The orator will methodically use figures of speech, particularly those that add more decoration and ornamentation to the speech. The more decorated and adorned the speech, the better it will evoke emotions while strengthening its persuasive power. The orator will prioritize noble and elegant words and expressions. Figures of speech, like the decorations that adorn the theater and halls during grand celebrations, add more color and aesthetic value to the speech, as evidenced by various wordplays and identical endings that excite the mind, inflame the emotions, and help win the victory.

The orator will use these figures that give a brilliant turn to thoughts, simultaneously creating a bright ray in the listener's mind, like a firefly illuminating the heart of a dark night. Decorative figures replace literal words or expressions with figurative ones to enhance aesthetics. They give the speech a very particular flavor based on a certain emotional fiber, thereby improving the persuasive power[212] of the speech and the triumph of the cause that is dear to the orator's heart, who does not hesitate to unfold in a nearly torrential lyrical outpouring. Masters of both ancient and contemporary rhetoric identify many rhetorical figures that can lend height, elegance, and nobility to the speech[213]: from onomatopoeia to oxymoron, passing through catachresis, litotes, allegory... There are many rhetorical figures capable of making a speech flourish[214]. We must focus more on the most essential, common, and prominent decorative rhetorical figures. Although other rhetorical techniques still abound with vigor, we will now proceed to analyze: metaphor, and a few figures of comparison (A), synecdoche, and substitution figures (B), in order to discover the rhetorical process related to their construction, their use, but most importantly, how they allow for the raising of passions, emotions, and ensure the victory of the orator, who, with exceptional mastery, highlights them in a persuasive context.

A - The Metaphor and Figures of Comparison

The metaphor[215] is undoubtedly the most important decorative figure. It has held a central and almost generic place since Aristotle, as if all other figures stemmed from it.[216] According to Aristotle, the metaphor aims "to give something a name that belongs to something else.[217]" The orator constructing their metaphor will substitute one concept or word with another concept or word used figuratively, establishing a plausible relationship between the two terms. It is a veiled and, to some extent, implicit comparison. This situation leads Quintilian to state that a metaphor is "a shorter similarity" *(in totum autem metaphora brevior est similitudo)*. With comparison or similarity, the orator makes a direct comparison with the thing they wish to express, for example: "Cellini is as courageous as a lion." However, with a metaphor, the orator says what they mean by substituting the thing itself. In this perspective, saying that Boniface is a lion is metaphorically saying that Boniface is courageous. In other words, Boniface, in the circumstances, is to humans what the lion is to animals[218]. When an orator develops a metaphor by completing the comparison with several related elements without directly expressing the thing being compared, we are presented with a sustained metaphor[219].

The metaphor is thus an elegant figure that creates a sense of presence in the speech and involves speaking about something using an image. If the image is accurate and well-chosen, it enriches the speech and facilitates attention. It adds brilliance to the speech and can even, to some extent, have an argumentative effect. By using the right image, the orator can condense an argument or even construct a solid counterargument.

To the question of why speakers prefer figurative terms over those used literally, the great master Cicero provides a highly relevant answer: 'I think this happens... either because the listener's first thought goes elsewhere, which gives great pleasure... or because, when used at the right moment, the figurative meaning awakens the senses, particularly sight, which, among all the senses, is the most useful.[220'] Through well-placed metaphors, the speaker captivates the attention of the audience and awakens their senses. It is the ultimate tool of seduction and rhetorical passions. One can understand why it is the mode of expression par excellence in poetry, especially lyrical poetry, whose one of its features is to stir emotions. This is easily observed in *The Song of Songs*:

"How beautiful you are, my friend
How beautiful you are
Your eyes are dove's eyes
Your lips are a thread of purple
And your mouth is charming,
Your two breasts, two fawns,
Twins of a gazelle,
Who pass among the lilies.[221']"

How could one not be carried away after such a speech, such lyrical poetry with honeyed verses? It is in this way that the speaker can move their audience, and through this emotional thread, achieve victory. According to Cicero, the metaphor should be natural; it must be subtle to increase its effectiveness. The metaphor, when well used, adds color and ornament to the speech, captivating more, seducing more, enchanting more. It alone: 'like the stars, it gives the speech a particular charm and splendor[222]. 'No longer is it surprising that the metaphor has been the hallmark of great orators, in particular times. From Aristotle to Obama, Cicero, Mélenchon, Victor Hugo, Jean Jaurès, Mandela, Lumumba, Martin Luther King, to Fidel Castro... the metaphor has always been the rhetorical device par excellence in every great speech or plea, systematically changing the world[223].

In addition to the metaphor, the orator may invoke other figures of comparison, namely similitude and allegory, which, like the metaphor, can prove decisive in moving and, thus, winning the victory. In a comparison, the orator links two ideas or objects—or an object and an idea—to show their similarity. The orator will always distinguish the compared (what is being compared) and the comparator (what is used to compare). One of the best examples comes from La Rochefoucauld, who says: 'Absence diminishes mediocre passions and increases great ones, just as the wind extinguishes candles and lights the fire[224].'

Similitude, for its part, allows for comparisons of greater scope than the comparison itself. It brings to the speech rays of light, illuminating like the morning sunrise, the spirit of the listeners, who are carried away by its considerable power of suggestion. Similitude is very present in preachers or in literature of religious inspiration. Thus, one can read in the Bible:"

"The man! His days are like grass, he blooms like the flower of the fields. When a breath passes over him, he is no more, and the place he occupied no longer knows him.[225]"

As we can see, comparisons and similarities contribute to giving more vigor, color, and strength to the speech. These realities can only move the listeners and lead the orator to hope to win the cause. This can be observed in a very famous defense speech for an accused electoral fraud case:

"There is nothing more changeable than the people, nothing more enigmatic than the will of men, nothing more illusory than the general conduct of the elections... indeed, as sometimes storms break out due to a certain premonitory sign from the heavens, they often explode suddenly for no precise reason and for unknown causes, just as in the democratic storm of the elections, you may often understand by which sign they were determined, but frequently it is so obscure that it seems like it was born by the effect of chance.[226]"

Allegory is the representation of an abstraction, an idea, either through images or living beings. Quintilian believes that it consists of: "indicating with words something different from what is implied" or "sometimes even conveying the opposite of what is said.[227]" Allegory brings a certain mysticism to the speech that the listener will seek to decode in order to better perceive its essence, consistency, and quintessence. Baudelaire, in one of his poems, offers an example of allegory:

"---And long hearses, without drums or music, / Slowly pass through my soul, Hope, / Defeated, cries, and the atrocious, despotic Anguish, / Plants its black flag on my bowed head.[228]"

The orator must ultimately deliver his speech in such a way that it rises above the crowd. Such a speech will be like the owl of Minerva with its beautiful plumage and lyrical song, which comes to enlighten through its chant and various artifices, healing social ills with words and rhetorical turns that soar from his speech, sounding like a soft music, equally in the delicate ears and hearts of his listeners.

B - The Synecdoche and Various Figures of Word Substitution

In his project of seduction and incitement to emotions for persuasion, the orator would do well to list and praise his audience with words as sweet as honey during his oration. By doing so, he ensures his chances of stirring the passions, increasing his chances of succeeding. Whether it is a periphrasis[229], pleonasm[230], or anastrophe, the orator will highlight figures that add more decoration and rhetorical passion to his speech.

In this case, the speaker could strategically use synecdoche,[231] Catachresis, or metonymy, tropes that particularly ennoble the oratory moment, giving it a bit more solemnity and even an extra touch of majesty.

The orator wishing to move the audience could strategically use synecdoche, a rhetorical figure that consists of "using a word by attributing it a broader or narrower meaning than its usual meaning."

The word thus used "maintains a special inclusion relationship with what it designates[232]" (Office québécois de la langue française). Thus, the speaker could, in a speech, name the part for the whole (for example, having a roof over one's head to say one owns a house, or traveling by sail to say one is traveling by boat). Similarly, but inversely, the speaker could start from the whole to designate the part[233] (for example, going to Africa instead of going to South Africa, going to America instead of traveling to the United States). In the same logic, they could also go from singular to plural and vice versa (the Cameroonian instead of the Cameroonians, the Canadian to say the Canadians...); finally, they could designate the species by the genus and vice versa (bread for food, "mortals" for "humans"). As we can easily see, synecdoche adds color and breadth to the speech, better yet, it gives the liveliness it needs to assert itself objectively among the listeners, evoke emotions, and lead to victory.

In their lyrical ascent, the speaker may also invoke catachresis or "abuse," in Latin, or "abuse" in French. In the circumstances, the orator will resort to a neologism[234] or existing terms to fill gaps in vocabulary. He would thus use a figurative word in the absence of the specific, proper word. For instance, one might hear expressions like: "the neck of the bottle," "the bed of the river," "the head of government," "the teeth of a saw," "the feather of a pen," "the sun sets"… In general, to achieve this, the speaker will employ a detour or an abuse of language, justified in this context by the urgency of using the most appropriate vocabulary for the speech.

Thus, far from providing clarity and a little more light to the speech, the speaker, through the use of catachresis, brings powerful images that easily imprint themselves on the audience's memory, while stirring the impulses they carry with them. In such circumstances, the speaker's speech, like a tranquil river, can only proceed smoothly toward victory.

Finally, "metonymy," with its strong ornamental capacity, helps to evoke emotions and add even more color to the speech. From the Latin "Denominatio," metonymy is "a change of name." The speaker designates a reality by a name that refers to another reality. The name thus used "metonymically belongs to the same semantic field as the usual name of the thing designated. The two are linked by a relationship of contiguity, meaning proximity.[235]" The examples of metonymy are numerous and varied.

The speaker, in their oration, could name an author instead of speaking of their work, for example, listening to Beethoven. They might instead refer to a producer or the place of production in place of the product itself (e.g., drinking a Martini, drinking Bordeaux...). The orator may refer to the leader or head of a religious institution, for example: "Saint Peter," "Notre-Dame"; or to a seat to indicate an institution, such as "The White House" for the President of the United States, "The Élysée" for the presidential power in France, "The Palace by the Sea" for the presidential power in Gabon, and "Étoudi" for the executive power in Cameroon... The orator might refer to the color of a team jersey to designate the team wearing it: "the Blues" for the French team, "the Indomitable Lions" for the Cameroon national team, "the Red Devils" for the Belgian team...

The examples of metonymic uses are numerous, and the orator's imagination could flourish if he masters the modus operandi of this figure. A beautiful use of metonymy allows for avoiding unnecessary repetitions. But above all, this figure of style colors the speech, giving it strong images that could not only provide pleasure but also stir the passions that, as we have seen, lead to victory.

II - Various Other Decorative Stylistic Devices

Does not the accessory always follow the principal[236]? Beyond the major rhetorical figures with a decorative flavor, the orator, in the process of building his speech, might equally call upon various other devices that, like the ones we have called major, provide the speech with more decoration, color, and weight. These figures can be words, expressions, or thoughts. Through their use, the orator hopes to stir passions and move his audience in order to achieve victory.

Alliteration, assonance, the insertion of a letter or syllable within a word – commonly known as epenthesis – homoioteleuton, and paronomasia are all sound-based devices that cajole the ears, hearts, and beyond, appeal to the emotional fiber of the listeners while soliciting their goodwill.

This particular category of words, characterized by the assembly of phonetically identical terms but with different meanings, gives the speech a certain cadence, a musicality that is certainly emotional. To possess verbal magic is also, in one way or another, to be the memory and the soul of the society in which one lives. In this regard, the orator, like the griot[237] in the distant and ancient African lands, the ethnophilosopher[238], or the philosopher in the Greco-Latin sense of the term, should, in certain circumstances, not ignore the ancestral wisdoms that, from generation to generation, have garnered unanimity and pride in society.

He could mention social maxims that have been established over time as norms of socially acceptable life, universally accepted by all. These maxims and wisdoms embody, far from aesthetics, a clear idea of ethics and morality, likely to restore the orator's honor. It is certainly pleasing and moving for an audience to hear an orator say out loud what he thinks privately, although sometimes in a different context. Therefore, before analyzing this section dedicated to wisdoms and maxims in an emotional tone [B], it would be appropriate first to consider an analysis highlighting the impact of sound or homophonic figures on the emotional fiber necessary for persuasion [A].

A -Figures of Sound

Figures of sound play a key role in the orator's approach to move, inciting the passions of his audience.

They concern a special category of words that are deceptively similar in their phonetics but have different meanings; for example, the words: ver, vers, vert, verre, and vair. This is the quintessential style of poetic language which, through its very rhythmic musicality, caresses the audience, who is swept away by the lyrical orator. In order to better understand the contribution of these figures to rhetorical passions and the victory of the cause being defended, it would still be necessary to review alliteration, assonance, homoioteleute, and paronomasia, which form the backbone of figures that charm and stir passions leading to victory.

Alliteration consists of the orator repeating the same syllable or consonant in a series of closely related words. This repetition produces a harmonious effect. One of the best examples comes from a collection of poems by Victor Hugo, *La Légende des Siècles*, particularly the poem "Booz Endormi":

"A fresh scent rose from the clusters

of asphodel;

The breaths of the night floated over Galgala.[239]"

One can note similar examples in Jean Racine's *Andromaque*, where he makes this statement worthy of the most brilliant alliterations in literary history:

"For whom are these snakes hissing above your heads![240]"

The orator may, therefore, in his speech, allow himself to make constructions of phrases inspired by classical rhetoric,[241] as well as from its authors, who never run out of inspiration. Expressions like "the objective <u>objection</u>," "the in<u>conceivable incongruity</u>,[242]" and "<u>tendentious tendency</u>" come from this emotional approach to

117

discourse. Without a doubt, alliteration is a high-level seduction tool that calls out the passions of the audience, making them feel more sympathy for the cause the orator defends with all his might from his perch. However, some masters of contemporary rhetoric believe that alliteration should be used sparingly, or else it may seem more like a flaw than a positive aspect of the speech. This opinion has certainly not lost its relevance.

One of the key maneuvers at the orator's disposal is indeed assonance, which consists of repeating the same vowel within the same sentence or verse.[243] Like alliteration, assonance produces an effect of harmony, giving the speech rhythm, musicality, and cadence, all necessary to seduce and make the speech more accessible to the listeners. One of the best examples of assonance comes from Verlaine, who in *Mon rêve familier* states:

"I often have this strange and penetrating dream

Of an unknown woman whom I love and who loves me

And who is not quite the same every time,

Nor quite another, and loves me and understands me (...)[244]"

We can clearly observe the assonance in (E) and (A) in this stanza. Another example comes from Verlaine, who in one of his most famous poems, makes brilliant use of assonance with the vowel (O):

"The long sobs

Of the violins

Of Autumn

Wound my heart

With a monotonous

languor."

Assonance, like alliteration, has seductive virtues capable of influencing the passions. It allows the orator to more easily reach the heart and emotions of the audience, thus increasing the chances of seeing their cause triumph.

Certainly, the orator is not a poet, but they can use their poetic talent to add value to their speech. This mechanism occurs when they invoke "homoetoteleute," a figure that happens when the orator uses words with identical, similar, or nearly identical endings, so that, as in a poem, a rhyme with particular sonic effects can be recognized. Therefore, it would not be an exaggeration to say that it is poetry introduced into prose that creates an emotional, charming, and enchanting effect.

Paronomasia involves bringing together phonetically similar words with different meanings. This figure appears in various proverbs and in popular wisdom. For example: "Those who resemble each other, unite," "errors... and judicial horrors," "He who sleeps, dines," "a good cat, a good rat," "urbi et orbi," "He who steals an egg, steals an ox..."

Paronomasia helps reinforce the memory of the audience, who will always remember the magical points of the speech. Such a situation adds color to the speech, making it more digestible while enhancing the persuasion it has on the listeners. In preparation, the orator must keep in mind that the listener has both reason and passions. They must not forget that the speech also has a cadence, a music, a rhythm, a culture that should resonate in phase with the values of their audience. Moved by various rhetorical techniques, the audience will not hesitate to give credit to the speaker who has charmed them throughout their address.

B - Maxims and Wisdom

If it is true that a fish cannot live once it is out of water, the same applies to humans outside of their cultural environment. Culture is the soul of the people; it is what remains when everything else is forgotten.[245] The orator must adapt to the culture of their audience in order to make a significant impact, an even greater impact. There is no better way than to make strategic use of maxims and wisdom that have been established as universal norms and thus hold authority.

A maxim refers to a formula that summarizes a moral principle, a rule of conduct, or a general judgment.[246] It is a community rule formulated in a sentence, claiming to be recognized as a barometer of life in society. The orator will mention it in their speech to involve the audience's values in the cause being defended. It is always a real pleasure for a listener to recognize themselves in the principles presented during a speech. This situation, which gently strokes their ego, also awakens the emotions that were still dormant within them.

In a famous work of ancient rhetoric, Aristotle, the master of rhetoric, acknowledges this fact when he states: "Listeners take pleasure when one says, in universal terms, what they may have previously conceived in a particular case.[247]" (Aristotle, *Rhetoric*). Proverbs or popular sayings are part of this category; for example: "The sweetness of honey does not console the bee's sting[248]," "A good reputation is better than a golden belt[249]," "When it rains on St. Aubin's day, water is more expensive than wine[250]"... Like legal maxims. For example: *"ubi societas ibi jus[251]"* ("Where there is society, there is law"), *"Si vis pacem, para bellum[252]"* ("If you want peace, prepare for war"), *"Cujus regio, ejus religio[253]"* ("Whose realm, his religion"), *"Fraus omnia corrumpit[254]"* ("Fraud corrupts everything")...

It is also the case with literary quotes known to all nations. Maxims are, to a certain extent, important for the orator. Indeed, when they embody morality, the orator appears as an individual who represents virtue, as Aristotle says in *Rhetoric*. It is, therefore, wise to know which maxim to put forward in a very particular time or moment. This, it seems to us, should be inspired by the current values in society at the time when the orator delivers his speech. It is well known that a truth within the Pyrenees may be an error beyond; thus, the context and the pretext of the speech should influence its text. What would a speech be that does not take into account the culture or context of its time? The emotions thus aroused could diametrically oppose the orator's objective, who wishes to accumulate the maximum amount of sympathy capital necessary for the triumph of the cause he cares about. In Africa, it is recognized that when an elder dies, it is a library that burns, and that what an elder can see while sitting, a young person will only see when perched on a tree. This situation highlights the fundamental place of wisdom and orality in African culture.

An orator wishing to speak before an audience that values African culture should, it seems, draw from the elders to understand the context of the issue and how it has evolved over time. But above all, they should draw from the nectar of the wisdom that flourishes in all regions and nations, and from the precedents that have been consolidated and crystallized, guiding the destinies of nations.

Regardless of the orator's culture of origin, the multicultural world we live in suggests that the orator must make a back-and-forth journey between their own culture and other cultures to maximize their persuasive power. African culture is a rich source of wisdom that, within a speech, has the ability to evoke emotions, in addition to the seductive tools it possesses, potentially leading the orator to the expected victorious glory. For example: "When you don't know where you are going, look at where you came from[255]," "When a tree falls, it is heard; when the forest grows, not a sound[256]," "A woman is the belt that holds a man's pants[257]," "Lies give flowers, but no fruits,[258]" "The one who wakes up late never sees the turtle brushing its teeth in the morning[259]"...

Maxims and wisdom undoubtedly bring more seduction, more emotions, and, of course, the persuasive strength needed to achieve the sacred objective of the speech: victory! Provided the orator uses them methodically and strategically.

The Orator Is an Artist of Speech

Photo credit: FFD[260]

Speaking in an amphitheater at the Sorbonne, adorned with symbols of the French Revolution and the Age of Enlightenment, one can easily understand that an orator is someone who expresses things in a particular way, that speech is an art, and this is not a recent development.

It is clear that relevant arguments, a masterful argumentative structure, and a voice worthy of opera are not enough to persuade. Beyond these basic techniques, emotion and passion can change the course of history. The orator must master the most pertinent rhetorical figures capable of adding color to their speech. Certainly, decorative figures are essential, but other rhetorical and stylistic devices such as hypotyposis, irony, character painting, allusion, insinuation, apostrophe, prosopopoeia, permission, surprise effect, frankness, antistrophe, and synonymy... are equally important in this process of evoking passions. It will not be enough to merely list them in order to praise them in the speech; their use must be highly appropriate, methodical, and strategic, depending on the context and the purpose of the oration.

Decorative rhetorical figures add depth to the speech, bringing emotion, which is the essential tool for addressing the hearts of the audience by stirring their dormant emotional fiber. In this movement, the speaker will not ignore the culture of the audience, which could be useful, particularly in the choice of maxims or wisdom to be used in the speech, in order to achieve a higher quality persuasive impact. In this regard, proverbs, legal or literary maxims, as well as sayings and wisdom, represent the best source of emotional incitement in the context of oration. However, the speaker must show discernment, but must not lose sight of the fact that a truth on this side of the Pyrenees could be an error on the other side. Hence, the urgency of calibrating the maxims put forward and the wisdom used, which must reasonably align with the culture of the audience or the location where the speech is delivered. Otherwise, the speaker risks witnessing an opposite effect, as if by a wave of the hand or a flick of a magic wand, where a well-prepared, well-pronounced, well-interpreted, and well-paced speech is rejected.

Decorative rhetorical figures are undoubtedly like a ray of light that adds more brightness to the oration. They are like those spring flowers that give the garden more attraction and evoke positive feelings in listeners. One should not be surprised by the speaker's ability to arrange the crowds, much like bees are attracted to flowers and their nectar. Through these stylistic techniques, the speaker manages to move their audience, which certainly confirms their victory. However, it would still be necessary to master the mechanisms of rhetorical amplification.

CHAPTER VII:
THE AMPLIFICATION OF THE SPEECH

As we have seen, the orator is above all a strategist who, through a speech, aims to convince the audience to adopt a particular stance or approach towards a specific situation. To achieve this, he highlights both major and minor arguments, as well as various rhetorical, semantic, stylistic, and morphosyntactic devices. Like music, a speech also has its moments of calm, moments of pressure, times of emotion, and great passions. Like a river that flows, the speech is also dotted with quieter periods, but also various noisy moments marked by falls and rises, floods and recedes.

Thus, in every communication, there would be points that form the keystone of the oration, points that are essential and capable of allowing the orator to achieve his ultimate goal, which is to lead him towards victory and convince the audience. The urgency of these points requires not only that the orator uses a much more expressive tone, but also that emotions are heightened, and an appropriate style for the occasion is employed—one that is sought after and that rises above the fray: this is the amplification of the speech.

Amplification is a method that involves highlighting a subject or specific aspects of the speech, bringing its importance into focus through various rhetorical maneuvers to touch the emotional fiber of the audience truly. This is the opportunity for the orator to strike and make the greatest impact on his audience. It is the moment more than ever to imprint, engrave, and crystallize an idea in the minds and hearts of the listeners. In this context, one might be tempted to conclude that the very essence of a speech lies in the amplification of the moment when the orator highlights a central idea through various means, various rhetorical maneuvers.[261]

An ancient rhetorical tendency suggests that amplification only includes rhetorical maneuvers that give "grandeur to the argument.[262]" This tendency seems rather restrictive to us. Quintilian, for his part, believes that the amplification of a speech relies on four methods: amplification, comparison, reasoning, and accumulation.[263] However, as criminal lawyer Florence Traversi acknowledges, the forms of amplification are varied, and the definition is broader, considering the means of expression that "with persistent intensification, strengthen the exposition.[264]"

Therefore, how could the orator insert words or expressions into his speech that could provide more persuasive strength to the facts or arguments presented in his plea? This is the question that will guide our reflections throughout this discussion on oratorical amplification.

This question forces us to review our rhetorical heritage in order to determine the most pertinent figures of speech, both of thought and of words, and to figure out how they help stir oratory passions, how they foster the expression of feelings necessary for the triumph of the cause for which the orator speaks. Thus, it becomes essential, before analyzing various amplification techniques (II), to first analyze the most common amplification techniques (I).

I - Amplification Figures

Great orators, both ancient and contemporary, specifically use particular rhetorical figures to give more punch to certain aspects of their speeches. In a situation where the orator highlights blame or praise, they will call upon the rhetorical figures that express horror or beauty, aiming to elevate, like the white papal smoke, the emotions necessary to make their speech historic, an iconic speech that will be engraved in gold letters in the annals of history for having marked and changed the world. The figures requested come from various models of basic construction. One of the most common amplification techniques draws its foundation from the repetition of words within sentences (in this case, we are dealing with "epanalepsis")[265]. This repetition found here and there grants the speech a certain solemnity and definite intensity.

Perelman and Tyteca, in their treatise on argumentation, *The New Rhetoric*, believe that "this type of repetition in speech, through these figures, doubles what would be called the 'effect of presence,' making not only the theme of the speech even more present to the audience's consciousness but also bringing a higher value to the second utterance.[266]" By extension, it would be difficult for listeners to remain indifferent to the amplification tactics that significantly enhance the speech, while adding weight to aspects of the discourse deemed critical by the orator for the cause's outcome.

Anadiplosis involves repeating the last part of each sentence at the beginning of the next. This scene, taken from a famous play by Paul Claudel, serves as a living example: "The void produced the emptiness, the emptiness produced the hollow, the hollow produced the breath, the breath produced the bellows, and the bellows produced the soufflé.[267]"

The repetition of the same word, according to Cicero, is a method that "strikes the listener violently," inflicting on the opponent a "serious wound, as if a weapon were hitting the same part of the body multiple times.[268]" This can be seen in this excerpt from his *Catilinarian Orations*[269]: "According to this decree, Catalina, you should already have been executed without delay. And on the contrary, you live! And you live not to renounce your mad intentions, but by persisting in them.[270]"

In order to better understand how the most commonly used rhetorical figures by speakers can have a significant impact on listeners, thereby provoking passions and emotions that lead to victory, we will analyze one by one and thoroughly: anaphora and its variants (A), antithesis and emphasis (B). The focus on these particular figures is justified by their recurrent use by both ancient orators and modern-day speakers. This in no way diminishes the amplifying value that other rhetorical constructions embody, which, it must be acknowledged, also have considerable worth.

A - Anaphora and Its Variants

From the Greek *anaphora*, meaning "the action of carrying up," anaphora is one of the oldest rhetorical figures. It is an excellent method that allows the orator's style to shine,[271] as Cicero notes in one of his iconic works, *Rhetoric to Herennius*. In practice, anaphora is a figure of repetition, consisting of the repetition of the same word or group of words at the beginning of each sentence or several lines. The repeated words are highlighted, drawing the listener's attention, who should regard them as essential in the final interpretation of the speech or plea; a fact that would be decisive for the outcome of the cause presented by the orator. In a specific context, the speaker may use anaphora to emphasize certain sounds, creating through the speech a certain musicality, a cadence, or an atypical rhythm in order to seduce more effectively. In most cases, it is highlighted to convince the audience or to convey the urgency of a situation.

This is the case of many political speeches that have marked history, as well as various famous pleadings and orations that have left a lasting impact on judicial history, including trials classified as historic cases.

In a famous oration delivered by Cicero to defend Marcus Caelius, the anaphora demonstrates its irrefutable ability to elevate the oration and evoke the necessary emotions to bring forth the cause at hand.

"This is the defense of the innocent, this is the language of the cause, this is the singular path of truth. The accusation cannot invoke, not a suspicion, not a fact of the conspiracy they want to concoct, not a trace of word, place, time, not a witness, not an accomplice whose name we could mention."

After World War II, following the liberation of Paris, General de Gaulle, with genuine emotion, delivered an iconic speech marked by anaphora to show the French people the scale of this liberation and the national pride restored. He was widely acclaimed by his people, who immediately understood the full significance of the moment and the oration: "Paris! Paris outraged! Paris broken! Paris martyred! But Paris liberated![272]"

During the 2012 French presidential election debate between François Hollande and Nicolas Sarkozy, When asked what kind of president of the Republic he wanted to be, François Hollande raised the emotions and feelings of thousands of listeners with a methodical and strategic use of anaphora in a sentence that became historic: "Me, President of the Republic." This ability to move his entire audience through speech amplification led him directly to victory in the elections, against a talented orator, Nicolas Sarkozy de Nagy-Bosca. This statement by François Hollande seems to us to be a living example of speech amplification and the incitement of the emotional fiber of the listeners, who were glued to the TV screen:

"Me, President of the Republic, I will not be the head of the majority... Me, President of the Republic, I will not treat my Prime Minister as a collaborator. Me, President of the Republic, I will not participate in fundraising for my own party in a Parisian hotel. Me, President of the Republic, I will ensure that justice functions independently... Me, President of the Republic, I will not claim the right to appoint public television channel directors. Me, President of the Republic, I will make sure that my behavior is exemplary every time. Me, President of the Republic, I will also ensure that the criminal status of the head of state does not apply to me... Me, President of the Republic, I will create a gender-equal government. Me, President of the Republic, there will be an ethical code for ministers. Me, President of the Republic, I will take action on decentralization..."[273]

Nicolas Sarkozy seems to be one of the contemporary speakers who uses anaphora effectively and tactfully. His speeches are generally built around successive anaphora, one after the other, giving a more intelligible effect to his orations.

This could explain why, during his campaign speeches, the crowd is almost beside itself with emotion. This situation may be explained by the rhetorical and amplification techniques used by the speaker, who makes elegant and perfect use of various anaphoric constructions: "I loved, I loved the sky under which I lived, and yet it was not, Mr. Mayor, the sky of Marseille. I loved the sound of words. I loved songs. I loved music. I loved books. I loved cities, a way of aligning houses, of planting trees along roads, so typically French. I loved the seashores. I loved a way of laughing. I loved a way of being free. I loved a French way of savoring life. I loved a way of loving. In the end, I loved France without knowing it.[274]"

As a figure of repetition, anaphora ultimately allows the speaker to highlight aspects of the plea or speech. It allows the speech to rise in intensity, to the point of evoking a sense of ecstasy or exaltation in audience.[275] This can be seen in the speech of Nicolas Sarkozy and many other orators: "We have two months. Two months to build the greatest adventure. Two months to shake up uncertainty. Two months to overturn everything. Two months to make them lie. Two months to make the truth triumph. Two months for the France that you represent (...) This France is the France of Joan of Arc, it is the France of Victor Hugo, it is the France of De Gaulle, it is the France of Schuman, it is the France of Monet, it is the France of humanists. Help me (...)[276]"

This is the same cadence we observe in a speech by Emmanuel Macron, which has remained historic since it was delivered: "Being patriotic is not the left that has shrunk to its utopias. Being patriotic is not the right that loses itself in its disgraces.

Being patriotic is not the National Front, withdrawal, and hatred. Being patriotic is wanting a strong France, looking at the world.[277]"

Sometimes, the speaker finds it wise to repeat words or groups of words at the end of their sentence, paragraph, verse, or stanza. In this case, the speaker uses a rhetorical device called epiphora, which is slightly different from anaphora. Epiphora means "to bring more" and involves repeating one or more words at the end of a statement. One of the best examples of epiphora comes from *La rhétorique à Herennuis*: "Since the time when good harmony in the city was abolished, freedom was abolished, friendship was abolished, the state was abolished.[278]"

One of the key uses of epiphora comes from Canadian writer and poet Anne Hébert, who, in a very popular poem, makes brilliant use of this construction, which we find ideal and represents this nuance of anaphora called epiphora:

"Music of the water,

Attraction of the water,

Betrayal of the water,

Enchantment of the water."

Epiphora, like anaphora, aims to amplify the speech by raising passions to the exaltation of the audience.

There are situations in which the speaker sprinkles the sequences of the speech with anaphora and epiphoras in sentences that begin and end with the same words. This symbiosis gives rise to a very particular rhetorical device, bringing more brightness to the oration: the symploque. In a memorable speech delivered in Évry, Manuel Valls uses it masterfully:

"We are told that the left has no chance, but nothing is written. We are told that it will never unite, that it is incapable, nothing is written. We are told that the far-right is automatically qualified for the second round, nothing is written.[279]"

The orator could finally use a figure of repetition that, by its structure, resembles the anaphora, without actually being one. It is called *polysyndeton*, which, like anaphora, participates in rhetorical amplification. Meaning "tied together" from its Greek origins, polysyndeton consists of the orator repeating a recurrent conjunction before each term in a list.

It contrasts with *asyndeton*, which occurs when a coordinating conjunction is omitted. Like anaphora and epiphora, polysyndeton aims to give the speech greater amplification and more rhetorical passion—essential elements for the impact the speech is meant to have. One of the best uses of this rhetorical construction is provided by Jean Racine in his tragedy *Iphigénie*: "Have you heard any sounds in the air?

Would the winds have answered our prayers this night?

But all is silent, the army, the winds, and Neptune.[280]"

B - The Antithesis and Emphasis

In the search for relevant rhetorical techniques for amplifying the speech, the orator may very well turn to *antithesis*, whose amplifying powers are widely recognized in the community of stylistics and rhetorical art specialists. Antithesis (*contrarum*) in itself is a rhetorical device by which two opposing terms or sets of terms are strongly contrasted. Although it is a means of expressing contradictory ideas, antithesis is also, and above all, a maneuver in which the orator highlights a key idea of the speech while reviewing the opposing idea, which they systematically dismiss by demonstrating how it is flawed and always in need of support to stand.

As can be observed, antithesis thus has a persuasive power that is not only related to its expressive form but also to its dialectical strength, which is its foundation. From two opposing ideas, the orator will use one to prove the other more easily and concisely. As in this passage from Cicero's *Rhetoric to Herennius*: "How can you hope that someone who has always been harmful to his own interests can be useful to the affairs of others?[281]"

In this example, Cicero clearly highlights the inability of someone who harms their own interests to manage the affairs of others. This rhetorical maneuver, through its stylistic construction, directly strikes the mind and even the heart of the audience, who are now better equipped to consider this parameter when evaluating the relevance of the speaker. Another living example comes from Jean-Jacques Rousseau, who in *The Social Contract* states: "Man is born free, and everywhere he is in chains.[282]"

Sometimes, the antithesis can take the form of a chiasmus, another rhetorical device. This device consists of reversing the order of words to create a certain discordant parallelism between the words and expressions used. The orator will achieve rhetorical constructions inspired by this famous maxim:

"One must eat to live, and not live to eat."

In addition to antithesis, the orator may resort to insistence, which consists of "insisting" repetitively on a particular theme or idea in the speech to highlight it and draw the audience's attention to this specific point of the oration. By linking one statement to another to clarify and enrich the thought just expressed, the orator can emphasize this rhetorical device, just as by retouching, meaning revisiting the same theme multiple times with varied experiences and vocabulary, in an effort to add details and reaffirm concepts already stated.

However, before triggering this rhetorical maneuver, the orator must ensure that the argument being emphasized is exceptionally pertinent and essential for the decision that will follow from the matter at hand. Beyond the emphasis and amplification it brings to the speech, insistence, it seems to us, should be recurrent throughout the speech in order to maintain the audience's attention on the cornerstone of the speech, or simply its pivotal point, which would prove more than useful for the resolution of the case.[283]

Ancient masters of rhetoric had long acknowledged this technique, which seems to have lost none of its relevance today.

One of the best examples of insistence is highlighted in a speech by Cicero, which has become iconic. It is the speech delivered against Catiline in the Senate: "How long, Catiline, will you abuse our patience? For how much longer will your madness mock us? How far will your unrestrained audacity go... do you not see that your plans here are uncovered? That your conspiracy is surrounded here by witnesses, chained from all sides? Do you not think that none of us is unaware of what you did last night? And the night before that?[284]"

As we have seen, insistence and antithesis are figures of repetition that, within the framework of an oration, provide additional ammunition to the orator. Through these figures, the orator has the opportunity to focus the audience's attention on key points of the speech, which are crucial to the decision that will be made. Just as they prevent the audience from scattering their attention, they help them concentrate on what matters and will be decisive for the triumph of the cause the orator is dedicated to during this sacred moment of oratorical elevation. Their amplifying effect is undeniable when brought forth with tact and mastery.

II - Various Processes of Amplification in Speech

A speech's effectiveness is determined by its capacity to hold the audience's tension and focus. It resembles a long thread that the speaker must keep tight, requiring ongoing engagement from the initial spark of interest oration. How can such tension and attention be maintained without referring to the various processes of amplification in the speech, which, with their seductive artifices and ability to stir emotions, raise the passions necessary to ensure the emergence of thoughts, arguments, and streams of consciousness that rise like papal smoke?

Both contemporary and ancient masters of rhetoric invoke various amplification processes. Some are common and recurrent in various speeches, pleas, and orations, while others, although possessing their amplifying skill, are less frequent. Depending on the orator's rhetorical background, certain techniques will be emphasized to the detriment of others, while some will be put aside, much to the disappointment of others. Whether it's the anastrophe[285], hyperbatons,[286] oxymoron,[287] interrogation[288], or prosopopoeia, the speech can be amplified by multiple tricks, techniques, and methods that, far from just adding the necessary color to seduce an audience drinking in the words of the enchanting orator, elevate emotions and passions without which the brilliantly argued and battled cause would not triumph.

In this context, examining specific rhetorical amplification techniques is crucial, as ignoring them would strip our analysis of a vital aspect. Cicero's first speech against Catiline in the Senate, famous enough not to need full elaboration here, exemplifies the emotional and persuasive power of interrogation.

Its importance is evident; these techniques are strategic and nearly decisive, contributing to the speech's brilliance and the orator's success. Consequently, it is essential to delve deeper into how hyperbole, gradation (A), and suspension (B) can evoke emotions and passions that favor the cause's success. Moreover, the amplification techniques discussed only scratch the surface of a broader range of rhetorical figures, all capable of enhancing oratory effectiveness.

A - Hyperbole and Gradation

Originating from the Latin term superlatio, hyperbole is a rhetorical device that relies on exaggeration or caricature to accentuate a particular aspect the orator wishes to underscore.[289] Ultimately, it presents a somewhat paradoxical interpretation of reality—a grandiloquent discourse where the orator emphasizes certain elements through hyperbole.[290]

By employing hyperbole, the orator intends to provide greater weight and clarity to their ideas, directing the audience's attention to a specific point while helping them understand the scale of the issue. The intent is not to deceive the audience with exaggeration, but rather to effectively magnify the truth[291] to enhance the speech and elicit the passion and focus necessary for the success of the cause.

The audience will therefore exercise discernment to determine the meaning and applicable deductions. The orator, to ensure effectiveness, must avoid excessive zeal in using hyperbolic images that may render their assertion ridiculous rather than giving it the necessary strength it requires. As Longinus notes in *On the Sublime*[292]: the best hyperboles are those that do not reveal themselves as hyperboles. The orator can construct hyperbole through figurative language, comparison, or paradox. Victor Hugo, in this description, meticulously uses this technique to inspire any orator: "They were giant men on colossal horses.[293]"

Alfred de Musset, in his poem *La nuit de mai*, does not shy away from using hyperbolic expressions, as seen in this excerpt: "Console me tonight, I am dying of hope.[294]"

François Fillon, the former Prime Minister of France, uses hyperbole to express his distress regarding his summons by investigating judges in the inquiry into the fictitious employment of his wife while he was campaigning for the presidency. The statesman, in a style adorned with metaphors and hyperboles, denounces a "political assassination": "It is not only me they are assassinating, but the presidential election.[295]"

The hyperbole, as we have just seen, would give more value to the speech, more flavor and height, a height high enough to have the necessary influence on the emotions stirred in the audience. It may occasionally happen that the orator contradicts this by saying less to suggest more, attenuating a concept in order to strengthen it in the hearts of the listeners. This exceptional turn is the litotes[296], a rhetorical figure also imbued with revolutionary grandeur.

Gradation is one of the figures par excellence for amplifying speech, as it brings tension and rhythm. From the Latin *gradatio*, meaning "staircase," gradation is a rhetorical device where the orator organizes the terms of a sentence referring to a similar idea, following a progression logic that can be either ascending or descending, depending on the circumstances.[297] Gradation in a speech allows for a certain progression of ideas that leads to the strong impact the orator wishes to engrave in the audience's memory. The orator, like a bird carefully building its nest, constructs a speech resembling a staircase, with each step being crucial before moving on to the next, following a crescendo or decrescendo approach. Thus, when the approach is ascending, there is a progressive increase in the power of the speech, and conversely, when descending, there is a decrease. Undoubtedly, gradation adds more intensity to the speech and the necessary rhythm to raise passions and grab attention while maintaining the tension of the speech.

Due to its ordered structure, the persuasive power of gradation also comes from the rigorous arrangement that characterizes it. One of the best examples is taken from Cicero's second speech against Catiline: "... we expelled him from the City, or if you prefer, we let him leave, or better yet, when he left, we saw him off with a nice farewell. He left, he fled, he threw himself out of here[298]..."

Lamartine, in a memorable poem, offers another example of gradation:

"The river is born, rumbles, and flows.

The tower rises, ages, and crumbles.[299]"

Similarly, we can highlight this living example from Baudelaire, in a poem with undeniable rhetorical momentum and certain amplifying virtues:

"When they have thrown me, old sorrowful bottle,

Decrepit, dusty, filthy, abject, slimy, cracked.[300]"

B - The Suspension

One of the rhetorical tricks that proves effective in giving the speech more weight is indeed the suspension, which, when used well by the speaker, maintains the audience's attention by building up emotions that are favorable to the cause being defended, tooth and nail. In itself, the suspension is a rhetorical figure that involves the speaker making the audience impatient for what has been previously announced but not yet stated. Through this device, the speaker highlights a particular aspect of their speech to persuade the audience further, keeping them glued to their lips, waiting for the resolution of the figure. By talking about something for a long time without clearly stating it, the speaker creates a surprise at the moment of resolution when they finally specify what they were talking about.

The suspension, like other figures, adds musicality to the speech. This situation makes it easier to maintain attention, and in a sense, sweeps the audience along. They won't notice when the speech gets long, because it is easy to listen to and even to memorize. They won't notice at all. The suspension creates suspense. This is evident in this excerpt from François Hollande during a speech on the margins of the 2012 French presidential election:

"I'm going to tell you something. In this battle that is starting, I will tell you who my opponent is. My true opponent. He has no name. No face. No party. He will never run for office. He will therefore not be elected. And yet, he governs. This opponent. It is the world of finance.[301]"

This second passage from François Hollande further demonstrates the suspense and tension that the suspension can create in the audience: "The French must know that if they elect me, I will ask myself as president, just one question. Before any further effort. Before any reform. Before any decision. Before any law. Before any decree. I will ask myself only one question. Is what is being proposed just? If it is just, I will accept it; if it is not just, I will reject it. Only justice must guide our actions.[302]"

As we can see, the suspension helps to elevate the discourse by making certain aspects of the speech memorable and striking. The suspense created by this figure can, in some cases, evoke humor and even laughter from the audience, who are usually excited by this particular rhetorical device.

Once again, François Hollande demonstrates mastery of this technique when he uses humor to ridicule his opponent in the presidential election:

"The outgoing candidate will promise us something new. He will try to turn his weaknesses into strengths. The president has made mistakes for 5 years, and that will be his experience. They will tell us, but he has governed for 5 years, so he knows what not to do! He knows the mistakes to avoid! The proof is that he made them all... You know today's news... the president candidate is now a candidate president[303]..."

In this rhetorical technique, the concept of time is important. This fact creates tension and captures the audience's attention. The suspense and surprise generated and then revealed create emotional sensations that give the orator the goodwill he or she will necessarily need to move towards or simply win the victory.[304] Finally, we note inspiring examples of suspension from many classical authors and orators, such as Victor Hugo[305] and Madame de Sévigné, just to name a few.

The Orator Is a Lyrical Poet

What would a speech be, truly, if it disregarded oratorical amplification? Certainly without height, value, or flavor, simply monotonous. The amplification of speech is therefore one of the cornerstones of the triumph of the cause for which the orator speaks. To demonstrate the prominence and sequences of his oration, he will undoubtedly resort to a certain height of tone, an elevation of feelings, but also and most importantly a special style rising above the crowd. In this analysis, we have reviewed various rhetorical techniques that, with persistent intensification, make the exposition stronger.[306] It will be up to the orator to practice the techniques of speech amplification, each of which works according to its own logic. He must know how to introduce them into his oration, and he must know when to introduce them, depending on the objectives. There is no better way to highlight them than through regular practice. It cannot be said enough: "Nascuntur poeta, fuint oratores." (Poets are born, orators are made.[307]) While it is true that anaphora, gradation, insistence, antithesis, hyperbole, suspension, anastrophe, and oxymoron are major techniques that help amplify sequences of the oration, it is equally true that these rhetorical techniques are like the tree hiding the forest, as the rhetorical heritage is full of many other techniques we have not explored, which are just as relevant.

It is not always necessary to be right in order to win a case. Sometimes, even the most compelling arguments fail to convince the audience. The favorable outcome of a case can, to some extent, be influenced by the jury's level of goodwill toward the orator. The orator will do everything possible to win the jury's favor, acting in a way that makes them: "so moved by judging, not through a thoughtful judgment of the mind, but under the push of an impetuous movement of the heart.[308] "Furthermore, it seems wise that the orator does not limit himself to the amplification of the speech to evoke emotions that lead to the expected victory. He would act in such a way that the audience naturally perceives that the facts mentioned in the speech come to life: such a technique evokes even more emotions, with the audience feeling directly involved in the issue highlighted by the orator. How can such a result be achieved if the orator does not use methods of participation? How can this be accomplished without focusing on specific rhetorical techniques such as apostrophe[309], interrogation, and prosopopoeia[310]? These techniques seem relevant in a logic of emotional[311] participation and inciting oratory passions.

FOURTH PART:
THE STRUCTURED PARLIAMENTARY DEBATE

Photo credit: FFD[312]

The speaker Eugène Afarin is an expert in parliamentary debate. He has debated in Canadian, French, and Chinese debate formats. As the World Champion of French-speaking Debate as a Second Language, he contributes to training the orators of tomorrow in Shanghai.

The birth and essence of parliamentary debate are closely linked to the rise of democracy in the Western world. In other regions, it is an integral part of ancestral and cultural heritage. Oratory, parliamentary debate, and democracy are like twins born from the division of a single cell.

Every time a dominant model of thought disappears and its successor is awaited, parliamentary debate resurfaces as a mode of expression for political plurality, allowing the expression of democracy that addresses the affairs of the city.[313] Recognized as "The set of deliberations carried out by the parliament in the exercise of its legislative power and in overseeing government actions,[314]" parliamentary debate has its origins in ancient Greece, notably in its mythical city, Athens, the birthplace of democracy. It was the only means by which Athenians could directly participate in the governance of the city. All classes, without exception, could participate actively in the management of the city through parliamentary debate. It was the golden age of Greek oratory, embodied by sophists like Gorgias, Isocrates, and other famous orators like Demosthenes, Aristotle, Plato, and many others.

In 509 BC, the abolition of the monarchy in Rome gave birth to a unique political regime: the Republic. From the Latin *Res publica*, meaning "public thing," it allowed certain groups of citizens to participate in the management of the city's affairs. Although limited to a specific social elite, the advent of the Roman Republic and its political institutions allowed its citizens to have a say in public affairs, whether through popular assemblies, magistracies, or the Roman Senate. The very aristocratic nature of the Roman Republic did not prevent the parliamentary debate and oratory art in general from experiencing a certain rise.

During this time, an orator of high stature and superior resonance embodied and carried this parliamentary debate in his ardent desire for justice, as seen in his numerous orations in the Senate, such as the speech against Catiline in the Roman Senate or his speech *Pro Roscio Amerino* delivered in 80 BC. Cicero certainly made a significant mark on parliamentary debate in Rome.

With the rise of the Middle Ages, the monarchy and serfdom, centralization, the personification, heroization, and sanctification of political power in the hands of the king, the funeral oration of democracy was pronounced, along with the demise of parliamentary debate, relegated to the Greek calendar, and the accessories store, in various Western regions, particularly in France, where Louis XIV reigned like a god, and in England, where King John Without Land established a divine right absolutism, capable of doing anything except, of course, turning a man into a woman. This royal absolutism, however, could not prevent an irresistible and irreversible movement leading to the signing of the Magna Carta, which limited the future financial powers of the king of England by institutionalizing checks and balances. Later, the Habeas Corpus was introduced, which imposed a judgment before any condemnation. This "Glorious Revolution" also laid the foundations for the British parliamentary system, materialized by the establishment of the House of Lords and the House of Commons, which the kings did not appreciate, as they reduced their political and economic maneuvering power. Later, with colonization and the expansion of the British Empire worldwide, the parliamentary system spread to several Commonwealth countries, including Canada. Canada thus, *mutatis mutandis*, adopted the British parliamentary system with a few exceptions. This political regime also gave rise to a particular oratorical tradition that we had the opportunity to experience as a debater for the University of Montreal's debate team and within the Canadian inter-university and inter-collegiate debating society.

With the Enlightenment and its ideals of justice, we witnessed the emergence of men of law, letters, and sciences such as Locke, who, in 1690, already recognized the necessity of separating the legislative, executive, and judicial powers to prevent them from resting in the hands of a single individual.[315] It was in this same perspective that, a few years later, Montesquieu began conceptualizing the need for the separation of powers. As he wrote in *The Spirit of the Laws*: "It is an eternal experience that every man who has power is always inclined to abuse it... In order that power may not be abused, it is necessary that, by the disposition of things, power should stop power.[316]" These ideals of freedom spread like wildfire across the world and directly or indirectly led to the

American Revolution in 1776 and the French Revolution in 1789. In France, this revolution fueled the creation of a constituent national assembly, which led to the adoption of the Declaration of the Rights of Man and Citizen. This declaration marked the end of monarchy and absolutism. It was also the beginning of French democracy and parliamentary debate as an embodiment of political plurality, a model of oratory that continues to inspire young speakers committed to making history for tomorrow.

As an orator and debater, we were fortunate to experience French-style parliamentary debate at institutions like the Sorbonne, Assas, Sciences Po in Paris, and Quai d'Orsay[317] during various international debate competitions or cultural events aimed at celebrating the beauty of words under the guise of parliamentary debate and historical trials.

While Africa has long been considered the cradle of world civilizations, some thinkers mistakenly believed that because it had a predominantly oral culture, it lacked philosophy or a traceable institutional system based on tangible evidence. The primarily oral nature of its culture was cited as the reason for this. In this part of the world, wisdom is not always passed down through manuals, as is common elsewhere, but typically through evening discussions around the fire, accompanied by palm wine and a hearty meal.

The elders seize the opportunity to impart to the younger generations tales, fables, and wisdom that have shaped history. It was this reality that led Amadou Hampâté Ba to say, during an oration that remains engraved in golden letters in history: "In Africa, when an elder dies, a library is burned.[318]" Oratory, therefore, undoubtedly forms the foundation of African societies, where, through the heroism of its griots, through its stories, proverbs, and legends, and through its glorious empires, oral traditions have always been a means of managing the city based on its customs. Like other countries in the Americas, Africa has also experienced imperialism.

It has also been influenced by foreign institutions, sometimes British, French, Spanish, or Portuguese. This openness to the world has profoundly influenced its political system at the dawn of decolonization. Notably, we find both British and French oratory styles coexisting with traditional African rhetoric; the latter predates various kingdoms, chiefdoms, and even the institutional management of young states emerging from the "sun of independence.[319]"

As a litigator at the prestigious African Moot Court competition at the University of Pretoria's Faculty of Law in South Africa, I had the opportunity to witness, beyond legal techniques, the African rhetoric in action, moving and emoting across various aspects, faces, and images. Parliamentary debate in Africa, therefore, seems atypical while still sparking curiosity, demonstrating hybridity adorned with specificities. To better understand the structured parliamentary debate and how it can help train quality orators, enlightened citizens, and those better equipped to inspire democratic ideals and revolutionary winds needed to change the world, it would be useful to analyze, on the one hand, the Canadian-style structured parliamentary debate (Chapter VIII), and, on the other hand, the French-style structured parliamentary debate (Chapter IX), in order to more easily approach the issue of African-style rhetoric or parliamentary debate (Chapter X). Beyond the theory linked to various oratory systems, we will base other analyses on the particular experiences and interactions acquired through exposure to these different debate systems.

CHAPTER VIII:
THE CANADIAN STYLE
PARLIAMENTARY DEBATE

Here, the very first Canadian delegation at the Paris-Panthéon-Assas University during the opening ceremony of the 2014 World Debating Championship. From left to right: Adam Samson, René Le Bertre, Marianne Amar, Cédrick Cormier, Isabelle JV (standing), Gabriel Meunier, Gabrielle St-Onge, Élisabeth Arsenault, and André Blondel Tonleu Mendou (seated).

The Canadian parliamentary debate, like Canadian law, is a child of English law. As a former English colony, Canada adopted the same parliamentary system as Great Britain.[320] The Canadian style of parliamentary debate originates from the British House of Lords and the House of Commons.

Each parliament has its own oral tradition, a code of conduct for debates, and a rhetorical procedure. It is through this procedure that major debates concerning the city and the future of communities take place. Inspired by Canadian parliamentary debate, contemporary speakers have imagined a unique concept used in the training of speakers, in debate competitions, and in the development of individuals who are meant to influence the world of tomorrow: the structured Canadian-style parliamentary debate. The structured Canadian style parliamentary debate is an argumentation based on a structure derived from the debates in the Canadian parliament. It follows an ancient tradition and has specific rules.

It consists of two debate teams representing the government and official opposition, presenting opposing speeches to defeat each other and convince the audience of their position, following an established structure and conduct code. Although the roles assigned in the debate are purely fictional parliamentary roles, Canadian parliamentary debate seems to be one of the best laboratories where the most brilliant, prestigious orators are molded, capable of discovering the missions assigned to them by their generation in order to accomplish them,[321] because they are surrounded by verbal magic that rises above the fray like a Hegelian bird migrating from the intelligible world to the sensible world.

This is truly the place for experimenting with techniques of argumentation and oratory that provide the necessary tools to carry out the revolutions needed, while bringing about systemic changes through small actions made in small settings. All of this is aimed at ensuring a better future for both present and future generations. As debaters, we have faced many high-level speakers in this debate format. We have personally felt the impact of engaging in this debate style, appreciating its grandeur while also recognizing its possible shortcomings. So, what are the mysteries of Canadian parliamentary rhetoric? In other words, what are the secrets of this style of debate that has brought glory to many orators and charismatic leaders in Canada and around the world? What is its contribution to the formation of the orator of tomorrow?

An effort to answer these questions would recommend that before addressing the criteria of persuasion (III) of the judges in this oratorical style, we first consider on one hand, an analysis of the actors involved, as well as the structure of the debate (I); and on the other hand, we will shed more light on the proceedings of the Canadian parliamentary debate (II). Only then can we assess with greater discernment the stakes of such a debate system for an orator who aspires to be distinguished, because living in a global village where the criteria for evaluating a brilliant orator may be a truth on this side of the Pyrenees, but an error beyond.

I - The Actors of Canadian Parliamentary Debate.

One of the keys to Canadian parliamentary debate is indeed the respect for a certain structure, a certain logic, a clear architecture of the discourse that allows any listener to easily follow the logical progression of the speech. It is the structure that will enable the judge to know whether the debater is in a preliminary phase, at the heart of an argument, or gradually moving from one argument to another.

The materialization of this structure is embodied by the debaters, each of whom must follow the nomenclature imposed by the role assigned to them by the rules of the debate. Respect for the debate structure is especially important, as it largely determines which of the two opponents will win the clash of ideas at hand. The actors in the parliamentary debate here refer to any speaker who, according to the debate grid, has a specific role to play, both for the affirmative and the negative.

It goes without saying that the panel of judges forms, undoubtedly, a group of strategic actors, because they must judge without weakness or pity, but also without vengeance or anger, which of the two teams has managed to prevail, according to specific criteria, in terms of the weight of ideas, the strength of arguments, ethos[322], and pathos[323] necessary to win the victory. We will detail the judges' role in part three of our demonstration, focusing on evaluating the debaters. One of the key actors is the timekeeper, the master of time. They are responsible for keeping track of speaking time and, if necessary, interrupting the speaker who exceeds the required time. The audience is also an actor in the debate, though passive, as the power of decision lies exclusively with the panel of judges, who are supposed, through their wisdom and oratory genius, to evaluate the debate.

However, their presence adds a theatrical effect to the debate, providing animation, especially since they can react depending on the emotions that the speaker provokes deep within them through their speech. A behavior that, it seems to us, can, to some extent, influence judges who are sometimes doubtful about the judgment they should give priority to. Sometimes, judges seek to enhance their credibility, to deliver a judgment that aligns with the various sensitivities present, a judgment that would find unanimity here and there, in order to impose themselves more easily with enforceable force. One of the specificities of Canadian parliamentary debate is the place given to fairness during oratory duels.

The fairness officer is one of the key actors who develops fairness principles for the competitions while reserving the discretionary power to sanction any debater or judge who violates these principles.[324] Can we truly invoke the actors of Canadian parliamentary debate while overlooking the prime minister, the cabinet minister, the opposition member, and the leader of the opposition?

That would deprive the analysis of a very important dimension of its relevance. It is crucial to focus on the government and opposition teams, as they are key actors in the structured Canadian parliamentary debate by debating both affirmatively and negatively on the motion of the day. Because it is a contradictory debate where one speaker from the government faces one from the opposition, and then two contradictory crystallizations, it becomes essential to analyze the actors of the debate according to the debate structure and their speaking order. This involves the prime minister (A), the opposition member (B), the cabinet minister (C), and the leader of the opposition (D).

A - The Prime Minister

The prime minister is the first speaker in the debate, having ten minutes divided into two interventions: one of six minutes and the second of four minutes. He defends the affirmative. After both teams have completed their research related to the motion being debated, it is the Prime Minister's responsibility to present the government's proposal. The statement must be clear, concise, and precise. For example, to introduce the proposal, he might say: "The motion presented for the chamber's consideration is as follows[325]..." In his introductory remarks, the Prime Minister will define any terms that are still unclear, provide a brief historical context, and, by doing so, aim to garner the goodwill of the judges and the audience.

Once this step is complete, the Prime Minister will announce, in the simplest and clearest manner, the government's position that he intends to defend in the debate: "We, the government, firmly believe that..." These first two steps of the debate allow the Prime Minister not only to adhere to the structure of the debate but also to establish a rapport with the audience so that both the judges and the public, knowingly or unknowingly, are encouraged to identify with him[326], as mentioned in the ancient rhetorical treaties. The third part of the demonstration requires the Prime Minister to give a brief overview of the arguments that will be developed by the government to prove the validity of the thesis it defends. He might say, for example: "To convince you of the merits of this motion, we will develop the following arguments... I will address points A and B, and my very excellent colleague will present, with a certain mastery, arguments C, D, and E."

Once this step is complete, the Prime Minister will need to elaborate on the first two arguments of the government as announced in the previous step. He will name the arguments, explain how these arguments support the government's thesis, and may invoke facts, authorities, or testimonies that support the argument and the thesis presented. He will conclude each argument following a syllogistic, inductive, or other logical approach. For example: "Therefore, hence, in conclusion, finally." To ensure that his speech has the effect of music in the ears of the judges, it is highly recommended to use linking words and logical connectors that allow the progression of the ministerial speech to be better appreciated.

It is important to note that this process must take place within a duration of six or seven minutes, as it is traditional in this debate format for the Prime Minister to introduce and deliver the closing argument of the debate. In his closing speech, which comes after the interventions of the other debate participants, the Prime Minister is expected to refute[327] the arguments of the member of the opposition before crystallizing[328] the debate for three to four minutes. During the Laurier Cup at McGill University,[329] I had the opportunity to work alongside my colleague Arnera Nathanaël in the role of Prime Minister. As if it were yesterday, I remember those pivotal moments in my career as a speaker. I recall how, through this first experience, we turned a trial run into a masterstroke. The position of Prime Minister, in addition to helping me structure myself more effectively, it also awakened the leader that was dormant within me. In reality, the Canadian parliamentary debate invites quick thinking, as we only knew the topics about ten minutes before the debate when we were in government: we didn't have enough time for in-depth research.

But this reality developed in me a certain spontaneity to take the bull by the horns in any circumstance, and no matter the topic, to remain logical, structured, and elegant in the face of the opponent. It seems to me that this is an ideal exercise that prepares us to face any situation, to cultivate memory as was practiced in ancient times, but above all, the sense of listening to others and the intellectual curiosity that encourages us to become more involved in the affairs of the city and the problems that shake humanity. I cannot ignore the exceptional improvisation skills, the sense of phrasing, and imagination that such time constraints can cultivate in an orator engaging in such an exercise.

B - The Member of The Opposition

After the first speech by the Prime Minister outlining a set of assertions, it is the opposition's turn to take the stage and provide the contradiction. Depending on internal arrangements within the opposition, a member of the opposition could speak first, or the leader might choose to do so as well. But traditionally, the member of the opposition speaks before the leader, for seven minutes. What exactly should they do during this sacred time? First, the member of the opposition must naturally present the opposition's thesis in general terms, showing how it stands in contrast to the one defended by the Prime Minister.

In General, before any substantive debate, a member of the opposition will typically introduce their position with a phrase such as: "We, on the side of the opposition, are against the motion as proposed by the government. However, we believe that..." The members of the opposition must either accept or reject the definitions put forward by the government. In the case of rejecting a definition, they must provide the definitions that, according to their understanding, seem appropriate in the circumstances. Then, the member of the opposition is expected to summarize the opposition's arguments and indicate those they will present. They will develop the most compelling arguments of the opposition, providing solid evidence, citing relevant authorities, referring to testimonies, and mentioning other facts that support these arguments and the opposition's thesis, which they will connect through clear logical links. This is how they will conclude each argument after presenting it. However, the members of the opposition must distinguish between an example and an argument. Confusing the two could work against their side. Once the argumentation is completed, they will proceed to a critical part of the debate: the refutation.

The refutation is the essence of the oratory duel, as it embodies the contradiction. The member of the opposition will uncover the flaws in the arguments put forward by the Prime Minister. They will particularly focus on the arguments that, according to their firm belief, are incorrect or simply weak. If possible, it is crucial to say exactly what was stated by the Prime Minister, hence the importance of taking notes to remember precisely what was said. It will not be enough to simply say that one is against such or such an argument; it is vital to demonstrate how and why those arguments are wrong. In this logic, the salient and vivid facts, evidence of all kinds, could help enlighten the judges. The opposition member will not forget to conclude each rebuttal: "This is why, honorable judges, this argument is erroneous... Therefore, Mr. President, this argument collapses like a house of cards..." The conclusion of each rebuttal helps the judge gain more clarity on the progression of the debate, allowing them to know that the debater is moving from one rebuttal to another, from one stage to the next. Finally, it is almost a categorical imperative for the opposition member to summarize the opposition's position and the arguments presented, revisit the motion as presented by the government, while highlighting the rebuttals made, as well as the arguments that would lend credibility to their side.

In the Canadian parliamentary style, it was a real challenge for me to debate in the position of the opposition. As a member of the opposition, the motion was often revealed during the Prime Minister's speech. On the spot, it was about listening, thinking quickly, and organizing to provide both a solid argument and a strong rebuttal within the time limits. I must admit that during my early practices with the University of Montreal's debate team, this was not an easy exercise for me; but with the help of my peers, I was able to overcome this difficulty, and like a rooster learning to crow, I was able to sing the debate's song. At the Canadian National Championship in 2013, I also discovered the strong capacity of this position to structure my thinking further, force myself to reflect quickly, and convey the essential in an extreme time constraint situation. It was a privilege for me to be supported by brilliant orators, sharp falcons[330], whose rhetorical abilities left me deeply impressed and only enhanced my learning efforts in a wonderful environment. As a member of the opposition, I gained more self-confidence. I was able to realize that the first inspiration is often the right one, and that with a touch of magic, one can present arguments capable of overturning a well-established order.

C - The Minister of The Crown

The Minister of the Crown is the second speaker of the government, that is, the team that affirms the validity of the proposal or motion. At the start of their speech, it is customary for them to repeat the motion word for word, just as the Prime Minister did in their opening speech. If the opposition member has contested the definitions presented by the Prime Minister, it is crucial for the Minister to clarify to what extent these definitions remain relevant for the debate. After addressing these general considerations, the Minister of the Crown must first develop new arguments in a way that complements those introduced by the Prime Minister. During these arguments, it is expected that they demonstrate, explain, and prove by various dialectical and rhetorical methods why these arguments are valid for the proposed motion. As with the other debaters, it would be in their best interest to avoid fallacious reasoning, disjointed arguments, and other maneuvers that fail to substantiate the assertion made in the premise. Then, like the opposition member, but conversely, the Minister of the Crown must contest the arguments of the opposition member. The rebuttal at this stage of the speech is essential. Arguments that are not refuted would remain valid and can give material for the prime minister, who, in their final speech, revisits the themes of the debate, but not necessarily the arguments. And, under the pressure of the moment, there are good reasons why such a refutation might be omitted, to the detriment of the opposition.

Finally, in this five-minute speech following the refutation of the opposition member's arguments, the minister should revisit those of the prime minister that were attacked before the judges: this is the reconstruction of the prime minister's arguments. The reconstruction involves either demonstrating that the opposition's refutation is not enough to undermine the weight of the prime minister's argument or simply allowing the minister of the crown to strengthen a weak argument previously defended by the prime minister. At no point should the reconstruction of the prime minister's arguments simply consist of a repetition of the argumentation presented by them. Such an approach would be purely counterproductive and would represent a serious failure on the part of the Minister of the Crown.[331] To conclude their speech, it is advisable for the minister of the crown to summarize their intervention, notably the strategic points addressed, to reaffirm their position and that of the government in the final sentence spoken. The role of the Minister of the Crown seems interesting; it allows one to understand what it means to work as part of a team. The mechanism of reconstruction is a valuable exercise that enables the speaker to evaluate, before their intervention, the impact of an argument, how the argument has been attacked, and to imagine what countermeasure to apply in order to tone and solidify it further, in a way that responds to the deepest wishes expressed by the opposition.

This is one of the best exercises in logic that structures the speaker's thinking while preparing them to face any eventualities once they are before the judges, who, in the context of the debate, are considered "gods" because they decide who wins and who loses, with their opponents not existing, as they are just a stuttering voice contesting the truth.[332]

D - The Leader of The Opposition

The leader of the opposition holds one of the most decisive interventions for the outcome of the debate. In a seven- or ten-minute speech, depending on the chosen format, they must contribute to the debate that has remained in suspense. They are expected to revisit the motion based on the opposition's argument. If they believe that the definitions presented by the government are lacking in relevance, now is the time to highlight the reasons why the definitions put forward by the opposition should be considered. From the outset, the leader of the opposition should present new arguments in addition to those of the opposition member and demonstrate how reason is on the side of the opposition. Then, the structure of the debate requires that they refute the arguments of the minister of the crown by proving how they lack logic, a reliable mechanism, and credibility. In the same perspective, the leader of the opposition will reconstruct the arguments of the opposition member to show the judges that despite the refutation by the minister of the crown, their arguments still hold significant weight. They will address the inefficacy of the refutation on one hand, and on the other hand, the argumentation itself, to either address their potential weaknesses or deepen the reasoning of the opposition member.

The leader of the opposition must also review the arguments of the Prime Minister to give them a final blow, one that will weaken them permanently. Finally, similar to the Prime Minister, they will move forward with clarifying the debate. It is important to note that the crystallization of the debate by the opposition occurs before that of the Prime Minister, who, according to tradition, must introduce and conclude the debate. In this final stage, the leader of the opposition will not introduce new arguments; this is the last opportunity to address the judges by highlighting the issues and themes that emerged during the debate, drawing attention to what their team has accomplished brilliantly, at the expense of the government, which has merely been scrambling to make sense of the situation. Crystallization is ultimately a moment of high tension, action, seduction, and passion that, if well-orchestrated, undeniably leads to victory.[333]

The French debate society at the University of Ottawa,[334] in its introductory guide to parliamentary debate, illustrates in the best possible way the actors in the parliamentary debate and their roles within the structure of the debate. This guide clearly summarizes the questions related to the actors, as well as those regarding the structure of the debate. We will be largely inspired by this for the development of the schematic demonstration that follows. In the same vein, we cannot overlook the guide from the Canadian University Debate Society and finally the guide created by Judith Wyatt in 1980, revised by Jocelyne Tessier for the Canadian Federation of Student Debates. Considering these interpretations of Canadian parliamentary debate, we will establish this brief schematic diagram concerning the actors and structure of Canadian debate.

Prime Minister (6 + 4 minutes)

Role: Introduce the motion and establish the debate's dynamics

Opening speech (6 minutes)

1- Announce and clearly explain the motion

(1 minute)

Motion

Context of the motion

2- Present the arguments

(5 minutes)

Argument 1

Argument 2

Argument 3

3- Debate summary: Reminder of the motion and synthesis of the argumentation.

Closing speech (4 minutes)
1- Recenter the debate and remind of the motion according to its context (30 seconds)
2- Brief rebuttal of the opposition's arguments (2 minutes)

Opposition argument 1......................rebuttal
Opposition argument 2......................rebuttal
Opposition argument 3......................rebuttal
Opposition argument 4......................rebuttal
Opposition argument 5......................rebuttal

3- Conclusion

(30 seconds)
Brief reminder of the government's arguments/our arguments were:

Argument 1

Argument 2

Argument 3

Argument 4

Argument 5

3- Crystallization

(1 minute)

Balance the themes and arguments of the debate, demonstrate why the opposition is wrong and how the motion is necessary and of public utility.

The Member of the Opposition (7 minutes)

Role: Create doubt about the validity of the motion by highlighting the main weaknesses of the government.

1- Context setting (30 seconds)

2- Present two arguments (3 minutes)

Argument 1

Argument 2

3- Rebuttal of the Prime Minister's arguments

Government argument
1......................rebuttal

Government argument
2.........................rebuttal

Government argument
3.........................rebuttal

4- Summary: Return to the opposition's position, summarize the arguments presented, and summarize the government's arguments (30 seconds).

The Minister of the Crown (7 minutes)

Role: Bring new elements into the debate while restoring the government's position.

1- Refocus the debate and remind the audience of the government's position (30 seconds)

2- Present two new arguments (2.5 minutes)

Argument 1

Argument 2

3- Rebuttal of the opposition member's arguments
(2 minutes)

Opposition member argument
1...................................rebuttal

Opposition member argument
2...................................rebuttal

Opposition member argument
3...................................rebuttal

4- Reconstruction of the Prime Minister's
arguments (1.5 minutes)

Argument 1

Argument 2

Argument 3

1- Summary: Brief reminder of the government's
arguments (30 seconds)

Le chef de l'opposition (10 minutes)

Rôle : Annoncer de nouveaux éléments dans le but d'apporter
plus de profondeur au débat et d'en faire une synthèse.

1- Recentrer le débat et mise au point (30 secondes)

2- Annoncer 3 nouveaux arguments (2,5 minutes)

Argument 3

Argument 4

Argument 5

3- Réfuter les arguments du ministre de la
Couronne (1,5 minute)

Argument du ministre de la Couronne
4...............réfutation 4

Argument du ministre de la Couronne
5...............réfutation 5

Argument du ministre de la Couronne
6...............réfutation 6

4- Reconstruction des arguments du membre de
l'opposition (1 minute)

Argument 1

Argument 2

5- Réfutation des arguments du premier minister

Argument du premier ministre
1.......................réfutation 1

Argument du premier ministre
2.......................réfutation 2

Argument du premier ministre
3.......................réfutation 3

6- Cristallisation

Summary of the argumentation, reviewing the key points of the opposition, highlighting the weaknesses of the government, and establishing the balance in favor of the opposition.

Board 8: Actors Of the Canadian Debate

Credit: Dede Fotsa

On the left, the government, formed by the Prime Minister and the Minister of the

Crown.

On the right, the opposition, formed by the Leader of the Opposition and the Member of the Opposition.

In the center, the timekeeper; in front of the speakers, the judges, and behind the judges, the attentive audience.

II - The Proceedings of Canadian Parliamentary Debate

Canadian parliamentary debate has particular rites, traditions, and customs—rituals that have crystallized over time into norms, imposing themselves on both passive and active participants in the debate. The proceedings highlight a series of situations that can arise during various interventions, speeches, or even in the middle of a speech. When an opponent violates the sacred rules of debate during their speech or simply, consistently disregards both the written and unwritten rules of the debate, specific mechanisms should apply to them in order to ensure the highest level of objectivity and absolute fairness that should prevail at all times in the arena. It is common for an opponent to distort the arguments made, not only for the sake of their own cause but also to ridicule the author of those arguments. It is clear that this maneuver is carried out with disregard for the ethical rules, which are fundamental in Canadian parliamentary style. This situation, unfolding under the heat of the action, may seem difficult to regulate. Fortunately, the principles of debate provide remedies designed to alleviate this situation, which could otherwise seem grim and somewhat pathetic in the presence of a jovial atmosphere during oratorical flights.

Debate also has a dramaturgical aspect. It has a theatrical dimension that adds value to the course of the competitions. This theatrical element fits into what is known as oratory action, taking place according to precise parameters, a well-defined nomenclature that establishes its scope and, to some extent, its limits.

The disruption (chahut) is the materialization of this theatrical side. It highlights the humor and weaknesses noted in the opponents' arguments.[335] During a debate, certain questions can sometimes be more important than the answers or lessons learned. In Canadian debate, questions have a history, and they respond to a tradition that dates back to the House of Lords. In the end, questions can influence the outcome of a debate, destabilize, or completely paralyze an opponent. However, the structure frames the questions to bring the speakers back to what remains essential: the contradictory debate, with a relative elegance in the interactions. To better understand the proceedings of Canadian parliamentary debate, it is essential to consider a comprehensive analysis that highlights the point of order (A), the ordinary question (B), and the privilege question (C). Only then can we know how to react as a debater to these key aspects of Canadian debate proceedings.

A - The Point of Order[336337]

As mentioned earlier, parliamentary debate has a structure, codes, and customs that impose themselves on all speakers who engage in the clash of ideas and the power of words. It would be natural under these circumstances for any violation of these oratory customs to be noted and taken into consideration both in the conduct of the debate and in its judgment, in both the first and final instance.

Debaters should therefore exercise extreme vigilance during the contest, so they can identify any irregularities that might compromise the elegance that is supposed to prevail at all times during the debates. It is the responsibility of each team to make such remarks, as the judge, having a passive role, may not necessarily do so. A speaker who does not respect decorum, making anti-parliamentary statements, particularly those with a certain vulgarity, should be called out. Similarly, a speaker who does not follow the protocol established by the structure of the debate should also be called out. A debater who demands to address the chair at the beginning of their speech and in key parts, and who refers to their opponent by their first name or nickname when they are supposed to use their title as per the debate structure, should be called out. Any debater who believes an infraction has occurred should simply rise during the debate: "*Point of order*, Mr. President / Madam President. The chair will ask the speaker who is engaged in their speech to sit down and request an explanation.[338]"

The accuser should state, in the most concise and precise manner, what infraction has occurred. For example: "The honorable member did not address the chair.[339]" The accusing speaker will return to their seat immediately after making the denunciation. The chair will judge whether the *point of order* is valid: if the point of order is valid, the speaker will be required to apologize before continuing their speech; if, however, the *point of order* is deemed invalid at the discretion of the chair, the speaker will be allowed to continue without further explanation, as the objection is rejected. The *point of order* is certainly a mechanism available to debaters to denounce any breach of the rules and traditions of parliamentary debate. It can be raised at any time a debater believes there has been a violation of the fundamental rules of debate.

B - The Ordinary Question

During a debate, it is strongly recommended that each team ask at least one question. Once the question is posed, the opposing team is required to provide appropriate clarifications when the time comes. The question cannot be asked during the protected moments of the speech, notably the first and last thirty seconds, during which a large margin of maneuver is granted to the speaker for the introduction and conclusion of their speech. Contrary to the norm that requires addressing the opposing team through the president of the chamber, the question can be asked directly to the debater who made the assertion that forms the basis of the question. Like the point of order, the question must be precise and concise. It must be a clear question that requires a precise answer. Hence, it is essential to clearly distinguish between a question, an assertion, a simple comment, or an opinion.

The debater asking the question thus seeks clarification or aims to establish a contradictory fact based on statements made by the opponent. However, there have been speakers who, when allowed to ask a question, were hesitant, recounting everything without actually posing a question. We have seen speakers, when asked a question, meander and play the lyre while Rome was burning. This is why it is imperative to think carefully about your question before posing it. A question that is irrelevant or without foundation will only serve to benefit the opponent, although they might, as an exception, fail to rise to the level of the debate. During various competitions, I have seen and even admired speakers who had the skill to use questions to destabilize their opponents. It's a maneuver I've often relied on in extreme circumstances that require high strategic rhetoric.

However, the danger of inflating the questioning or using it excessively can leave a bad impression with the judges, creating a sense of bad faith that could ultimately lead to our downfall during their deliberations. The custom of Canadian debate recommends that any team receiving one or more questions must answer at least one of them. However, the team receiving the question is not obliged to answer immediately; they may address it later in another part of the speech. In situations where time management is complex, the speaker engaged in their speech might choose not to respond to a question. If the question is based on a topic that will be addressed later in the debate by the speaker or their teammate, it would be wise to mention that. In any case, the debater answering the question should remain courteous in their response.

While it is essential to maintain courtesy in responding, one must also recognize a question that is purely off-topic, designed more for diversion than for reflecting on an essential issue being discussed in the debate. The methodical and strategic use of questions naturally improves with practice. In our early days, it was often difficult to find our footing through ordinary questions. But through continuous use, an expertise and strategy developed. Questions posed after some time felt like a real stir in the anthill. In short, the methodical use of questions, beyond just convincing, makes the debater first and foremost a strategist with words who, through a series of questions, can elicit from their opponent words and ideas they never would have imagined saying aloud.

Board 9: The Ordinary Question

Credit: Dede Fotsa

The raised hands here represent a tradition from the British House of Lords, which signifies: "I have no weapon, only words. I come in peace."

C - The Question of Privilege

During a debate, each speaker makes claims and presents arguments. The opponent, in their efforts to establish a contradiction and gain credibility with the judges or the audience, may claim to quote a statement made by their adversary, even if this is not the case. They may also gain the floor to make malicious and occasionally defamatory comments intended to win favor with the jury. Such a situation would be inequitable if the parliamentary debate tradition hadn't conceived and instituted a custom called the "question of privilege," which, in exceptional cases, allows a speaker who feels they have been wronged to correct the record.

As soon as the incident occurs, the affected speaker must rise like a soldier and declare: "Question of privilege, Mr. President / Madam President.[340]" Upon hearing this declaration, the president will ask the speaker to explain and will order the interrupted speaker to sit down. The complaining speaker presents their complaint in the most concise way: "Mr. President / Madam President, I did not say... but I actually stated that[341]..." The opponent cannot respond, and the complaining speaker returns to their seat. The president will use their discretion to determine the validity of the complaint. If it is found to be valid, the offending speaker will be required to apologize to the chamber before continuing their speech. It should be noted, however, that if the opponent merely summarizes the speaker's words without claiming to quote them, this does not lead to a question of privilege.

It is a normal part of the debate. Finally, the question of privilege is strictly personal, meaning it is limited to the allegations of the speaker who claims to have been misquoted or defamed. It is therefore prohibited to raise a point of privilege for one's teammate. Although the point of privilege allows for the necessary restoration of fairness for the smooth running of the debate, it must be used sparingly. An abusive interruption of the debate, sometimes for trivial reasons, can have a boomerang effect that risks being fatal for the interrupter, much like the tale of the "hoisted by one's own petard."

III - The Evaluation of Debaters

In a debate, the judges are like little gods. Indeed, they decide who they will bless and who, perhaps, they will condemn at the close of the speech. They decide who will receive the magistral grace and who will be left in disgrace. They decide which team will be awarded the victory over the heated debate that has unfolded under their wise gazes. In reality, the two teams that clashed in the exchange of ideas were but discordant and stammering voices contesting the truth. The

169

truth, only the judges can claim to possess it; only the judges, from their position of authority and intelligence, can hold the truth, which they do not hesitate to let triumph when the time comes by pronouncing the winner[342], rising above the fray. Once the spotlights are turned off on the debate, another particular debate begins, away from prying eyes: the "invisible debate[343]" a subtle stage of the debate during which the judges decide the winning team based on an objective basis, in the secrecy of their conscience, their discretionary power, without weakness or pity, but also without vengeance or anger. The sentencing process is initiated in a splendor that is uniquely objective and beyond comparison.

The Canadian parliamentary debate provides judges with guidelines that facilitate more rational decisions, decisions that are much clearer. The goal of any debate here is to convince, and the decision should be based on the exchanges that naturally emerged from the debates submitted for the judges' magisterial evaluation. It is customary for the decision first to be individual before a comparative study of the verdicts in the court of reason and oratorical passions is made, in order to render a collective decision that is intelligible and grants the glory of oratory to the team that deserves it. The evaluation of a debate, beyond the verdict, takes on a pedagogical importance of exceptional scope. It is, more than ever, the moment for the wise and intelligent judges to tell the debaters how to improve various oratorical performances that could make them distinguished debaters. In the Canadian style, the evaluation focuses more on the argumentation presented by the speakers, as well as the logical connections between their argument and the motion debated, rather than on other rhetorical artifices. This situation, it seems to us, extracts a certain flavor from the debate as we will see.

Because judges are wise, and because what they can see while seated, a debater can only see while perched on a tree, debaters are not required to discuss or contest the judges' comments, which are generally aimed at building the temple, not the gods to be worshiped.

Similarly, judges limit themselves to assisting, motivating, and supporting the debaters without showing excessive zeal.[344]

Panoramic analysis of the judge aims to verify how the speaker has used logos, ethos, pathos, and oratorical action during their speech, even though, concretely, logos seems to be prioritized over other factors. In any case, judges are required to base their evaluation of the debate on three inseparable criteria: respect for the structure of the debate as prescribed on the grid (A), the quality of argumentation and refutation (B), and the quality of style (C). Once these evaluations are completed and the decision is made, judges customarily invite the debaters to shake hands. This symbolic gesture of democracy clearly communicates that debate is a combat sport where the weapons are words, and these words serve to heal social ills. This is not the place to oppose one another because of a friend or comrade who opposes the ideas and convictions that are fundamental to us. The Canadian debate promotes freedom of expression, which, far from emphasizing the different accents embodied by the speakers, celebrates their various accents in a harmonious conviviality.

A - Respect for The Debate Structure

Respect for the structure is the foundation of any debate. It is the minimum that a speaker should respect in order to aspire toward the glory reserved for the winner of the debate. It is a form of container without which arguments and rhetorical techniques would have no solid support to ensure all the required effectiveness. Did the debater fulfill the functions imposed by their role in the debate? This is the first question that the judges will ask themselves. Depending on whether they were the prime minister, the minister of the crown, a member of the opposition, or the leader of the opposition, the judges will carefully examine their intervention to verify whether they respected the steps required by their role in the debate (for example:

refocusing the debate, argumentation, refutation, reconstruction, and crystallization for the leader of the opposition).

Is the debater's speech easy to follow, understand, and even memorize, based on a clear and precise plan? The judges will check whether the speaker followed a structure that made it easy to follow their process and the stages of their intervention. It goes without saying that a speaker who does not take care to announce their approach, highlight the importance with logical connectors that demonstrate they are moving from one stage to another of the argumentation, would have difficulty winning the jury's favor for this particular aspect of the evaluation.

Does the speaker succeed in making their ideas clear? In other words, is there clarity that leaves no room for doubt? Then the judges will assess the introduction and conclusion of the speech. This involves seeing whether the speaker introduces their speech according to the rules of the art demonstrated above and whether they provide the required conclusion at the end of each argument, signaling the end of the reasoning for that part of the speech. If so, the speaker will be rewarded; otherwise, they risk falling into disfavor.

Finally, and importantly, did the speaker use the required time, all the time, and only the time allocated to their speech? Respect for time is a cardinal value in Canadian parliamentary debate. This is evidence that the debater has not only conducted the necessary research but also knows what is necessary to advance their cause. Furthermore, they do not wish to abuse the audience's patience, which hopes to listen within a predefined time frame. However, they must strictly adhere to this time. A speaker who does not use the entire allotted time for their speech leaves a bad impression on the audience, which might begin to doubt their credibility regarding the cause being defended. Similarly, exceeding the time limit is not well appreciated by the very honorable judges, who, in accordance with the evaluation criteria, will not hesitate to enforce the necessary rigor. In any case, the ideal would be to use the time, and only the time, allotted to the speech. It is only within this framework that the debater can present convincing arguments that will be more highly considered in the overall evaluation process of the debate.

B - The Quality of The Argumentation

Debaters are required to present high-quality arguments that support the cause they are defending in the speech. A quality argument, it seems, should have an attention-grabbing title that serves as a signal for the jury and the audience, providing clear or unclear ideas about the content of the argument. The title of the argument should obviously align with the specifics related to the motion. This is why it is crucial to avoid overly abstract titles or metaphorical ones that are sometimes too distant from the essence of the motion.[345] Judges are quite rigorous about this important aspect of evaluating the debater. The argument itself must be highly convincing and constructive. It should be directly related to the position defended by the speaker. Regardless of the circumstances, the argument should answer the *why* and even the *how* of the position the speaker intends to defend. It should demonstrate why the judges should rule in favor of the speaker when the decision is made at the end of the debate.

As we have shown, the speaker can make use of relevant argumentative techniques such as reasoning by hypothesis, induction, abduction, and syllogism, which are highly valued by many speakers for their exceptional persuasive virtues. It is clear, therefore, that an argument is not simply an explanation of an action plan, a scientific phenomenon, or a statement of historical facts, which in a speech may serve as parts of the body, but not the core — which in this case is the argument itself. The argument draws upon facts, examples, quotations, articles, and jurisprudence, which, we believe, can support an argument without constituting its essence.

The argument here is summarized in a statement that logically connects with the motion or position defended by the speaker, explaining why the motion is acceptable, why the position defended is true, and thus why it should prevail.[346]

As we noted earlier, the argument is the cornerstone of Canadian parliamentary debate, and any speaker who fails to construct a high-quality argument is systematically reducing their chances of winning their cause. The evaluation of the quality of the argument extends to the refutations presented by the debater to demonstrate that their opponent is mistaken and that, ultimately, their own argument remains relevant. Like the argumentation, the refutation is based on a logical statement that demonstrates how an argument advanced by the opponent is more than ever in need of support to stand firm. The judges will assess the objectivity of the rebuttal to see if it truly destroys the opponent's argument. If so, it is an advantage; otherwise, the speaker will certainly lose favor. The same applies to reconstruction, where the judge evaluates to what extent the speaker adds value to their teammate's arguments to prove they are still valid. The judges pay particular attention to crystallization[347], which is a key phase of the debate for both the opposition and the government. The judges will check if the speaker has synthesized the debate in an organized and persuasive manner, identified the main issues, and demonstrated skillfully how, based on these issues, they should naturally prevail over their opponent, who presents a model that is useless to society.[348] This final step of the speech also provides the judges with the perspective they need to assess whether the speaker has a deep mastery of the debate topic.

As we have recognized, some questions are sometimes more important than the answers or lessons. Judges will give particular attention to the questions posed by the debaters to their opponents. Questions that create panic in the opposing camp would likely bring more glory to the team that initiates those questions. In the same vein, the debaters' ability to respond to questions with tact and strategy is highly considered in the evaluation process of the debate.[349]

C - The Quality of Style

Since antiquity, a successful debate should be formed around logos, ethos, and pathos. Recognizing in this evaluation grid for debaters the urgency of maintaining a clear structure, the necessity of developing quality arguments, the Canadian debate also acknowledges the values of logos, as desired by the founders of Greek and Roman rhetoric. The evaluation grid for speakers has also provided favors to speakers when techniques related to ethos and pathos are emphasized in the debate. These include the confident and credible personality of the speaker, the ease and fluidity of expression, the primacy of a solemn style free of anglicisms and swear words, the ability to evoke emotional reactions favorable to persuasion, the use of striking figures of speech, and respect for decorum.[350] However, from my experience as a speaker, I have reasons to believe that these valuable mentions regarding style, particularly ethos and pathos, are more a matter of principle than empirical observation.

The structured debate in the Canadian parliamentary style still seems to have a long way to go in a world where the value of a debater can be assessed beyond logos. From my memory as a speaker, I've seen debaters win debates without any reference to rhetorical devices, without resorting to persuasive techniques. I've seen speakers win competitions without highlighting their oratorical memory, let alone the oratorical action that leads to victory.[351] I've seen speakers win debates with sentences sometimes littered with swear words and a semantically and morphosyntactically questionable structure. I have seen with my own eyes, yes with my own eyes, speeches that stirred no emotion, no passion, no sensitivity in the audience, yet were written in golden letters in the history of parliamentary debate. Lovers of rhetoric and beautiful phrases, we have often dealt with judges who gave us the impression of not understanding the meaning, the consistency, or even the essence of our interventions. I remember, during the national championship with my friend and teammate Yrech, we faced off in the opening round against speakers from the University of British Columbia (UBC). In the comments, the judges mentioned that our level of rhetoric was very advanced compared to our opponents, and that this situation was unfair, and for this reason, we should lose the debate. This was to the great dismay of the UBC debaters who, even surprised to have won, still showed humility by coming to admit their surprise at having won the round. Troubled by the situation and concerned about the fairness of our rhetorical practices, Yrech and I, after much reflection, came to the conclusion that there can indeed be judgments with a double standard. Because we wanted to improve more than necessarily win, we did not create any controversy. It was a great learning experience...

Beyond this isolated case, we have seen several debates in which, although the evaluation criterion of style is mentioned in black and white in the evaluation grid, the judges make no mention of it in the evaluation of the debater, and even less in the comments... Well, even when the speaker uses rhetorical techniques necessary for persuasion, such as metaphors or other techniques, both their opponent and the judges quickly label such a maneuver as sophistry. Yet, the sophistry we discussed earlier corresponds to other criteria. In this context, one is tempted to conclude that the Canadian parliamentary style debate boils down to a single articulation: logos, and specifically, the argument, contrary to the wishes of the great masters of oratory and rhetoric who, from 46 BC to the present day, have built it brick by brick, granting as much nobility to ethos and pathos as to logos. The style! Where does it stand in the concrete evaluation of the debater in Canadian parliamentary structured debate? It simply does not exist! Although its shadow may appear on the result sheet of the Canadian Debating Society, intended to apply it for the comprehensive evaluation of debaters.

The Greatness and Challenges of The Canadian Structured Debate

Canadian parliamentary debate, in the background, is a mode of rhetorical expression, an oratorical culture with its own history, a well-defined custom, a structure, actors, but also a game and stakes. It is undoubtedly one of the best systems for training in the art of argumentation, dialectics, and even rhetoric. From our interactions with Canadian parliamentary debate, we can confidently assert that beyond training the orator, it shapes the debater, but also, and most importantly, the engaged citizen of tomorrow, concerned about the well-being of their community and the world in which they practice their art: debate. Canadian parliamentary debate has the merit of initiating the orator into quick and effective reflection.

It is a system in which the substance of the speech is prioritized. What would a speech devoid of substance really be? Pure sterile verbiage, an intellectual masturbation with no foundation or conclusion. The orator trains to recognize, through daily practices, the qualities of a better argument, without which their speech would be superfluous and, at best, airy. At the same time, they acquire excellent research skills that help find the best arguments for a given cause. The structure of Canadian debate seems to us to be the best modern tool for organizing arguments that exists. Finding arguments is one thing; organizing and arranging them to get the best for the cause we care about is another. The debater here is a thinker who skillfully employs reasoning through hypothesis, induction, abduction, and syllogism. The debater here is a researcher who masters the techniques of specific and common places developed by Cicero in *De inventione*[352].

The Canadian orator is also a fine strategist who masters the arrangement of arguments, knowing how to ask the questions that upset without getting angry, but also knowing how to provide answers in a jovial, relaxed, and cool manner when circumstances require it. Canadian-style debate presents itself as a laboratory for democracy, coexistence, and civic engagement. Orators feel invested with a social mission aimed at promoting freedom of expression, unity in difference, and the values of multiculturalism that characterize any distinguished society, leading towards an ideal of justice. As mentioned earlier, the challenges of Canadian style debate are many: giving more consideration to ethos and pathos as full-fledged criteria and not entirely separate from the art of oratory—the tendency for judges here being to consider these aspects as accessories to the art of oratory; yet they pursue the same goal as logos: persuading and convincing.

Through their bilingualism in French and English, we find French-speaking debaters who, in reality, have an anglophone culture, and English-speaking debaters with a francophone culture. The tendency for an anglophone judge is to apply an evaluation method that does not take into account the specificities of the French language when judging a very francophone debater, and vice versa. Thus, a real problem of training for judges arises. Some even work in the field of speech, but in reality, they don't seem to be sufficiently aware of the subject of rhetorical literature and its applications.

The issue of impartiality among judges has often been raised by debaters who feel they are "facing a group of friends all debating the same subjects on which they all agree." This is why the professionalization of debate seems to us to be a viable path, allowing rhetoric to be integrated into traditional education and thus become a discipline recognized by both the academic and professional worlds. Only then could we have debaters who are a little more offensive during major global gatherings of oratory and debate. It is only in this way that leaders embodying the positive revolution of societies will slowly but surely emerge in a sustainable way, to the great benefit of humanity. Only then could we have debaters skilled at persuading any type of audience and any category of jury, whether Asian, European, or French.

CHAPTER IX:
THE FRENCH PARLIAMENTARY
DEBATE STYLE

Photo credit: FFD[353]

In the solemnity of the ceremony of this final joust, the debate took on a new direction. The prepared arguments needed support. Thus, one orator found it useful to face their opponents without notes. A technique that is certainly demanding in terms of memory and action, but was useful in front of this passionate audience and attentive, prestigious jury. The Sorbonne is undoubtedly the sanctuary of revolutionary orators. Under the monarchical regime, the King of France was all-powerful. Omnipresent and omnipotent, power was concentrated in his person at a time when the heroization, sanctification, and even the divinization of royal power was the principle. Because after the night comes the day, the Enlightenment and its democratic ideals did not hesitate to criticize royal absolutism at a time when the king had created an island of happiness reserved

179

for the clergy and nobility, opposed to the ocean of misery in which the people of France slept. In this revolutionary momentum, Diderot boldly stated that "no man has received from nature the right to command others. Liberty is a gift from heaven, and every individual of the same species has the right to enjoy it as soon as he possesses reason.[354]"

The Enlightenment sounded the death knell of divine-right absolutism, leading to the French Revolution of July 1789 and the establishment of a national assembly that would shape the political regime for the future, but especially the parliamentary debate that would found democracy. French rhetoric also rose from its ashes after several centuries of absolutism. It experienced a golden age during this period. Illustrious orators embodied it, and parliamentarians did not hesitate to make rhetoric and parliamentary debate a tool for revolution. Since that time, the French-style parliamentary debate has been one of the best exercises contributing to the formation of orators. Oratorical societies such as Lysias, the Francophone Debate Federation, the French Debate and Eloquence Federation, and Debating at the Sorbonne continue to perpetuate this oratorical culture through various debates, speech competitions, and pleadings, aiming to transmit this revolutionary momentum of the Enlightenment, this love of speech to rising generations eager to make an impact in various aspects of daily life through the strategic and methodical use of verbal magic. It is this structured French parliamentary style that we encountered when we debated at Sciences Po in Paris, in the context of the World Debate Championship. It is the same style that we also discovered in the amphitheaters of Assas University, Sorbonne, and even on the gilded halls of the Quai d'Orsay.

Like the Canadian parliamentary debate, the French parliamentary debate has a history, customs, rites, and traditions that give it its specificity and uniqueness. Like the Canadian debate, it is punctuated by various questions during its course.[355] However, unlike Canadian debate, there are particularities that make this model atypical, and its exploration becomes necessary to understand various other secrets of rhetoric that the Canadian style does not necessarily explain.

Therefore, what are the actors in French parliamentary debate? What are its challenges? We will strive to answer these questions based on our experiential knowledge and available documents on the subject. Only then can we better evaluate its strengths, but also the challenges that an orator in such a system might face in a world increasingly marked by globalization and the realities of multiculturalism, which call for orators capable of handling the changes being imposed. It would therefore be wise to analyze, on the one hand, the actors of such an oratorical model (I) and on the other hand, its challenges (II), in order to better determine its greatnesses and shortcomings compared to other highlighted systems.

I - The Actors of The French Parliamentary Debate

Parliamentary debate in France seems to merge with the great revolutionary and rebellious trends of the 18th century. While we were at the Sorbonne, we noticed that several societies of speakers had names that evoked the ideals of justice, equity, and democracy driven by the French Revolution, such as "Révoltetoi![356]" (Revolt yourself!). A deep analysis allowed us to understand that the parliamentary debate in France is rooted in a highly revolutionary tradition inspired by the Age of Enlightenment. It is a debate that, like other systems, has its own history, customs, context, pretexts, texts, structure, and, most importantly, the actors who embody it.

The French debate is atypical because it is embedded in both the distant and recent history of the country. This is the debate that sparked the major legal, institutional, and social changes seen not only in France but also in many Western, African, South American, and even Asian nations.[357]

For this reason, debate here is a cultural aspect, and the orators are celebrities who make oratory not only an art of words or speech but a vehicle and instigator of social change. A visit to the Louis Liard[358] amphitheater at the Sorbonne or the Palais de Justice in Paris—where the annual competition for the "conference du stage" has been held for three hundred years—helps us understand without much difficulty how, in France, eloquence is sacred, the art of speech is valued, and the technique of debate is revered. This is probably what justifies the growing and almost galloping interest of the Parisian and French public in debate and eloquence. The lecture halls are generally packed with people. It is a passionate audience, much like a sports fan who comes to an arena to support their team, here for the love of words, addicted to debates and eloquence, ready to give the debate its spectacular flair. The audience here is a real participant, either through applause to approve the substantive arguments or rhetorical constructions used by the orator, or through laughter or murmurs that express their deepest feelings regarding a particular situation that arises in the debate. The agoras are as crowded as bird nests full of eggs, with spectators hanging on the words of the master of ceremonies presiding over the debates. In the context of French-style debate, the master of ceremonies is an orator with exceptional charisma who acts as the impresario during the verbal joust. They are also in charge of the time, granting and retracting the speaking rights of the orators, and timing each one. But before all of this, they are responsible for gaining the audience's trust and animating them with various rhetorical devices; they are tasked with introducing the jury members in the room. Once the jury is introduced, the master of ceremonies proceeds to present the debaters who will engage in the clash of ideas. In addition to maintaining order during the debate, they must distribute the speaking time to the debaters when their time arrives. They are a key figure who adds a ceremonial, harmonious, and highly formal element to the debate.

Once introduced by the master of ceremonies, the jury comes into play. Typically consisting of six to seven prominent figures from the world of oratory (lawyers, law professors, judges, journalists, politicians, ministers, highly renowned orators), the jury is an essential actor in parliamentary debate and French rhetoric. They determine, with their discretionary power and impeccable wisdom, which orator or team has made the most effective use of logos, ethos, pathos, oratory action, and even memory in order to convince better and persuade the audience.

After the debate, at the invitation of the master of ceremonies, the jury will retire to deliberate. When the jury returns to the stage, its members will provide comments, and the president or chairperson will deliver the final verdict. In this atmosphere, the journalists and photographers, in their effort to immortalize the event, temporarily illuminate the scene with flashes from their cameras and the zooms of their lenses. With the scene set, the crowd, jury, and media await the signal from the master of ceremonies, who will initiate the proceedings by inviting the prime minister to the podium for their introductory speech. At this moment, we are at the heart of parliamentary debate, manifested by the orator-actors mounting the podium to defend their opinions and convictions with perseverance, in a style adorned with eloquence and sometimes resplendent grandiosity. This is done to the great pleasure of the enchanted audience, but above all, under the calm and watchful observation of the jury. The debaters are, it seems, the actors who give the debate all its meaning, its substance, its full value, and, of course, its most delicate flavors. Therefore, we will focus particularly on these specific actors, grouped into government (A) and opposition (B), to ultimately establish the structure of French-style parliamentary debate and see how they could contribute to the formation of a new type of orator, destined to play leading roles in the battles that will shape the world of tomorrow.

A - The Government

The government is a key actor in French-style structured debate. The motion here is, in principle, announced to the debaters at a specific time during the debate, in contrast to the Canadian style, where, in the distant past, the government would prepare the motion, and the opposition would have the obligation to attack it with vigor. Once the motion is announced, a drawing is held to determine which team will form the opposition and which will form the government.

In French parliamentary debate, the government plays a crucial role, which goes beyond explaining and demonstrating why and for what reasons the motion is preferable to the status quo. The government must prove that the opposition is wrong. In other words, the government needs to show that failing to adopt the motion would be a mistake that would harm society, or even humanity, in the long run.

The government exhibits a robust sense of unity among its speakers, who, despite offering slightly varying yet complementary arguments, defend the same choice and stance. In their opening speech, the prime minister establishes the context by presenting the overarching thesis of the government, emphasizing one specific argument for further development. The first deputy will refute the opposition leader's speech while proposing and developing a new argument. The second deputy of the government will criticize the first deputy of the opposition before presenting their own alternative. Finally, the secretary-general, in addition to refuting the argument presented by the second deputy of the opposition, will focus on the themes that have emerged during the debate, demonstrating how the government has positively distinguished itself during the rhetorical exercise. It thus becomes necessary to analyze the government in its composition, particularly its debaters, their roles, and their challenges as defined in the structure of the debate. From start to finish, we will review: the prime minister (a), the first deputy (b), the second deputy (c), and the secretary-general of the government (d).

A - The Prime Minister

The Prime Minister is an essential figure in parliamentary debate. As the leader of the government, he is the first speaker of the debate and carries with him the motion being debated. He is granted four precious minutes to introduce the motion and capture the audience's attention while gaining their favor. The early moments of his speech are "like the prologue in poetry and the prelude for the flutist.[359]" Before the debate begins, the Prime Minister must break the silence, create a rapport with the audience that encourages them to feel identified, sometimes unknowingly, with the Prime Minister. If the motion allows for a brief narration of the facts, the Prime Minister must proceed in a clear and believable manner.[360] Once the formalities are completed, the Prime Minister will present the government's general thesis, name the arguments that will support this thesis, their order of presentation, and the deputies responsible for presenting them at various points in the debate. After unveiling this plan, the Prime Minister will take up one of the government's arguments and develop it in-depth. Argumentation is one of the key points of the speech, in which the Prime Minister explains the reasoning behind the argument, using syllogism, induction, hypothesis, or abduction, and then relies on authorities and examples to illustrate his thoughts, ultimately concluding the argument in connection with the motion. The role of questions in this phase of the debate should not be overlooked, whether they are questions of principle, definitions, or substantive questions addressed by the Prime Minister.

In the French style, the argument alone does not seem sufficient; the audience, hanging on the speaker's every word, expects beautiful semantic and stylistic constructions, but also the intonations of the voice, the exercise of memory, and oratorical action, which give the debate its splendor and style. The Prime Minister must also manage and handle the reactions of the often fiery public, especially when the speaker adopts a seductive tone that stirs passions in the audience! In this format, the Prime Minister only has one intervention, unlike in Canadian parliamentary style, where he is the alpha and omega of the debate. The role of the Prime Minister in this format can sometimes be delicate, as he holds significant responsibility: the outcome of the debate will depend largely on his performance. Therefore, the orator embodying this role must inspire confidence and demonstrate charisma.

B - The First Deputy of The Government

After the Prime Minister's speech and the opposition leader's rebuttal, the government's first deputy steps in with a specific purpose: to refocus the debate that the opposition leader has disrupted, arguing that the current situation is much better than the motion put forth by the Prime Minister.

In the same spirit, before advancing the government's thesis, the first deputy will proceed to refute the argument presented by the leader of the opposition, demonstrating its lack of foundation. He may draw inspiration from the Aristotelian method, which in a "refutory impulse" seeks to demonstrate "either that the fact does not exist or that the extent of the damage is not as claimed[361]..." The refutation must be clear; the deputy must precisely identify the inconsistencies and weaknesses in the refuted argument. In refuting the opposition leader's argument, the first deputy simultaneously prepares the jury and the audience for the unfolding of his argument, which, like a lighthouse in the dark, will provide the much-needed clarity for the debate. The first deputy will methodically demonstrate how his argument fits within the scope of the motion, showing how it adds value to the debate by employing the logical and rhetorical techniques previously analyzed. It is important to note that this government member has five minutes to conclude his intervention.

The master of ceremonies grants him protected[362] time at the beginning and end of the speech, respectively, for introduction and conclusion.

The deputy will undoubtedly face fierce questions from his opponents, sometimes raising objections or simply trying to take a few minutes of his precious time. It will be up to him to manage his time effectively, knowing when to take a question and how to handle any disruptive or destabilizing elements from his adversaries. Unlike his Canadian counterpart, the first deputy has less time, but this seems justified by his less heavy responsibility: refocus the debate, refute the opposition leader, present his argument, and conclude the debate. This time seems sufficient for the speaker to employ various rhetorical maneuvers, which are as valued and appreciated as the argument or even the action.

C - The Second Deputy of The Government

Credit: Dede Fotsa

It is customary to formulate questions to try to distract or destabilize a compelling debater. Like in this real scene where the second deputy from the opposition creates panic within the government, which in turn tries to overwhelm them with questions. (This image reflects a real scene.)

After the prime minister introduces the debate, the opposition leader contradicts them while presenting a different option, the first deputy of the government refocuses the debate, refutes the opposition leader, and presents the second argument of the government. The first deputy of the opposition refutes the first deputy of the government while presenting an argument supporting the opposition's thesis. Now it's time for the government to introduce new elements into the debate. The second deputy comes on stage to restore order and tip the balance in favor of the government. Like the first deputy, if necessary, they will refocus the debate, refute the arguments presented by the first deputy of the opposition, and introduce a new argument that further justifies why the government is right in the debate.

In the five minutes they have, the second deputy will also participate in any potential questions from the opposing team. They will need to manage the reactions and moods of the public that might influence the course of the debate. Playing the role of second deputy in a debate can be delicate. In reality, they often arrive late, like the owl of Minerva only taking flight at dusk. They often come when the strategic points of the debate have already been addressed. That's why it seems crucial that beyond the argument, they should be an excellent rhetorician who will impress the audience with their figures of speech, proverbial and vivid vocabulary. They should also be a good actor who can embody, like in theater or cinema, the role entrusted to them by the structure of the debate.

D - The Secretary General of The Government

The Secretary General of the Government is an indispensable figure for the outcome of the debate. They intervene only after the debate and primarily aim to dismantle the arguments of the second deputy of the opposition in order to give value to the government's thesis with their final speech, which constitutes the last impression the government will leave with the judges and the audience.

However, before crystallizing the debate, the Secretary General must conclude the government's thesis by revisiting the various arguments that remain relevant because the opposition has not been able to dismantle them. They should not introduce new arguments, but may revisit the arguments of their team in order to proceed, as much as possible, with a clear and brief reconstruction.

Once the conclusion is made, the Secretary General will perform a thematic study of the debate, in other words, a debate on the debate itself, in which they objectively show, through rhetorical maneuvers, how the opposition has not been able to create doubt in the minds of the audience. They will demonstrate how, despite everything, the position held by the government remains the best and must be adopted for the greater good. Finally, they will show how maintaining the status quo would be highly dangerous for the future and that, under these circumstances, there is no other choice but to support the government's proposal for a public utility motion. During the four minutes of their speech, the Secretary General will certainly have to answer one or more questions. However, they must be vigilant, as their speech is the last card of their team, their joker, and they must achieve their goals: refute, conclude, crystallize, and, if necessary, respond to questions.

Compared to the Canadian style, the speech of the Secretary General resembles the final speech of the Prime Minister, in which they crystallize the debate. The only difference is that here, the government does not bear the historical responsibility of closing the debate, and the Prime Minister only has one speech: the introductory speech, not the final one. We might be tempted to conclude that the Secretary General is the second most important figure in the government, as they often enjoy privileges and honors that other deputies may not have. Ultimately, they are an essential link in the cause championed by the government, and their role will certainly, like the Prime Minister's, set the tone and outcome of the oration, before the opposition can respond.

B- The Opposition

As its name suggests, the opposition, or the opposition team, positions itself against the government. It acts as the counterargument in the parliamentary debate. The opposition, therefore, fosters contradiction, giving meaning to the term "debate." Like the government, the opposition receives the motion an hour before the debate and is tasked with preparing arguments against it, as well as the refutations that will break the government's argument structure, thus sowing reasonable doubt in the minds of the jury, which could tip the balance in favor of the opposition. Like the government, the opposition is composed of four speakers who take turns at the podium to support the opposition's thesis: the leader of the opposition (a), the first deputy of the opposition (b), the second deputy of the opposition (c), and finally, the secretary general (d). It is important to examine in detail the roles of each speaker in both the defensive and offensive strategies of the opposition against the government.

A - The Leader of The Opposition

Once the Prime Minister has finished their speech, the Leader of the Opposition is the person authorized to speak. After the master of ceremonies formally hands them the floor, the Leader of the Opposition, who embodies the contradiction, must begin with the *exordium*. The *exordium*, as Cicero conceived it, is about capturing the audience's attention and winning their goodwill, so that they can identify with the speaker, even if they are unaware of it at times. The Leader of the Opposition will present the general thesis of the opposition, then provide the necessary critique of the argument made by the Prime Minister, drawing the audience's attention to the fact that this argument lacks logical foundation. The argument of the Prime Minister, having lost its capacity to harm due to the refutation, the Leader of the Opposition returns to what they believe to be true in the debate, presenting their argument. Furthermore, they will outline the following arguments by naming the opposition deputies responsible for them, aiming to make the truth prevail—a truth overshadowed by the Prime Minister's lack of insight. It is in this revolutionary momentum that the Leader will conclude their intervention. Like any speaker in this style, the Leader of the Opposition will have to withstand pressure from the audience, sometimes enchanted, sometimes disenchanted. The Leader of the Opposition will also need to respond to questions from their adversaries, which can sometimes be virulent and destabilizing. Acting as the Leader of the Opposition requires the speaker to assert their charisma and leadership qualities, without which they could be subjected to intimidation. Finally, the Leader of the Opposition is expected to display presence, style, and rhetoric worthy of distinguished orators during the four minutes allocated to them in the structure of the debate.

B - The First Deputy of The Opposition

The Prime Minister has delivered their speech, and the Leader of the Opposition has contradicted them. The first deputy of the government has just left the podium after a demonstration that revitalizes the government's position, which seemingly rises from the ashes with a wave of a magic wand. The first deputy of the opposition, after capturing the attention of their audience, will, in highly contested rhetoric, refute the argument of the first deputy of the government.

They will coldly demonstrate how this argument has limited or absolutely no objective support or logical backing. After having dismissed an argument that would overshadow the rays of light projected by the opposition in the debate, the first deputy will proceed to present their argument, as outlined and announced by the Leader of the Opposition in their introductory remarks. The presentation of such an argument could rely on logical methods like syllogism, induction, abduction, hypothesis, and various rhetorical devices that, beyond charming the jury, will stir the emotional fiber that might lie dormant within them. During the five minutes allocated for their speech, the first deputy of the opposition, like any speaker, is required to respond to the questions from their opponents.

However, they must know how to manage the response to the questions within the time available. In fact, paying too much attention to a question might give the impression that the question has embarrassed the speaker, that it is relevant, and has the potential to determine the outcome of the debate. That is why it is suggested to respond as briefly yet effectively as possible. The first deputy of the opposition must finally conclude by reaffirming the central position of the opposition.

C - The Second Deputy of The Opposition

The second deputy of the opposition speaks after the second deputy of the government. In practice, their task will be to refocus the debate towards the wishes of the opposition. This operation allows the second deputy to challenge the argument presented by the second deputy of the government and, subsequently, to introduce a new argument to once again conclude by reaffirming the position embodied by the Leader of the Opposition since the beginning of the debate. Like the second deputy of the government, the second deputy of the opposition often arrives late in the debate, either when the fundamental issues have already been addressed, or when the debate takes a different turn that requires insisting on refutation, or on rhetorical actions that stir passions in favor of the speaker and their team.

This role can be quite delicate in that it requires exceptional improvisation skills, but more importantly, imagination. I had the opportunity to embody the role of the second deputy during the final of the World Debate Championship at the Sorbonne's management amphitheater, which, for the occasion, was packed with participants in a debate that required us to defend the importance of the French language in France. As the second deputy, I found it wise, due to the direction the debate was taking, to focus on refuting the second deputy of the government.

Ultimately, given the turn of events, it became necessary for me to debate without notes so that I could have more moments of grace, allowing me to stir emotions through pathos in a debate that seemed to be moving away from this dimension, which was also highly relevant. As we can see, it is highly recommended that the second deputy of the opposition, like that of the government, be able to read the debate, identify its trends, and recognize the direction it is taking in order to know how to position themselves. The risk for the second deputy is sometimes to intervene with a tone, argument, or refutation that no longer fits the trajectory of the debate. Like a strategist, they will act. Like an actor, they will behave. Like a poet, they will craft their speech. Like a researcher, they will bring forward the most suitable refutation and argument for the circumstances of the debate. Hence, the urgency to continue dialoguing during the debate, even if through signs, with the leader of the opposition and other deputies. During the five minutes available to them, the second deputy will respond to one or two questions from the opposition but will not forget to conclude by reaffirming the opposition's position.

D - The Secretary of The Opposition

The secretary of the opposition has the privilege of being the final speaker in the debate. They have the opportunity to revisit the opposition's thesis, review the arguments presented by their colleagues, and methodically show the jury how, despite the government's refutations, those arguments have lost none of their weight. They will go over the government's arguments and demonstrate how these arguments now need more than ever to be supported to survive, highlighting how, during the debate, the government has treated the motion in a partial, biased, and even fragmented way. This initial step, which primarily aims to dismantle the government's stance while rehabilitating the opposition's, leads to the second and final part of the opposition secretary's role: crystallization. Like the secretary of the government, the secretary of the opposition must, during their four minutes, list the themes that have emerged during the debate. They will demonstrate how it would be a mistake for the chamber to side with the government by adopting its motion, which would strike a fatal blow to development. In contrast, through various rhetorical devices, they will show how the truth lies with the opposition. And it will be up to the judges, with their intelligence and wisdom, to make it triumph for the greater good of society as a whole.

Summary: Structure of the French-style Parliamentary Debate

Prime Minister (4 minutes)

Role:

1- Introduce the motion, define it, and set the tone for the debate.

2- Announce the government's arguments and team members.

3- Develop the first argument of the government.

   Argument 1 of the government

4- Conclude the speech.

Leader of the Opposition (4 minutes)

Role:

1- Introduce the opposition's stance, challenge the motion's definitions, and refocus the debate.

2- Refute the Prime Minister's argument.

3- Develop the first argument of the opposition.

4- Announce the upcoming arguments of the opposition and assign team responsibilities.

5- Conclude the speech.

The First Deputy of the Government (5 minutes)

Role:

1- Refocus the debate.

2- Refute the argument of the Leader of the Opposition.

3- Develop the second argument of the government.

4- Rebuild and reaffirm the Prime Minister's argument.

5- Conclude the speech.

The First Deputy of the Opposition (5 minutes)

Role:

1- Refocus the debate.

2- Refute the argument of the First Deputy of the Government.

3- Develop the second argument of the opposition.

4- Reaffirm and rebuild the argument of the Leader of the Opposition.

5- Conclude the speech.

The Second Deputy of the Government (5 minutes)

Role:

1- Refocus the debate.

2- Refute the argument of the First Deputy of the Opposition.

3- Develop the third argument of the government.

4- Rebuild and reaffirm the argument of the First Deputy of the Government.

5- Conclude the speech.

The Second Deputy of the Opposition (5 minutes)

Role:

1- Refocus the debate.

2- Refute the argument of the Second Deputy of the Government.

3- Develop the third argument of the opposition.

4- Reaffirm and rebuild the argument of the First Deputy of the Opposition.

5- Conclude the speech.

The Secretary of the Government (4 minutes)

Role:

1- Recap the government's arguments and rebuild them:

Argument 1...........................reconstruction 1

Argument 2...........................reconstruction 2

Argument 3...........................reconstruction 3

2- Recap the opposition's arguments and refute them:

Opposition argument 1.....................refutation 1

Opposition argument 2......................refutation 2

Opposition argument 3......................refutation 3

3- Crystallize the debate:

Weigh the themes that emerged from the debate, demonstrate why the opposition is wrong, and explain why the motion is preferable to the status quo and should result in the government's victory.

The Secretary of the Opposition (4 minutes)

Role:

1- Recap the government's arguments and challenge them:

Government argument 1........................refutation 1

Government argument 2........................refutation 2

Government argument 3....................refutation 3

2- Recap the opposition's arguments and rebuild them:

Opposition argument 1..........................reconstruction 1

Opposition argument 2..........................reconstruction 2

Opposition argument 3..........................reconstruction 3

3- Crystallize the debate:

Weigh the themes that emerged from the debate, then demonstrate why the government is making a mistake in proposing this motion, emphasizing, if necessary, the weakness of its arguments in order to sow doubt. Finally, demonstrate why the status quo is preferable to the motion, which would not be of public utility. This situation is likely to lead to the opposition's victory.

Credit: FFD[363]

The actors in the French parliamentary debate. The government and opposition are respectively composed of the prime minister, the first deputy, the second deputy, and the secretary of the government on one side, and the leader of the opposition, the first deputy of the opposition, the second deputy, and the secretary of the opposition on the other side. The two teams face off at the Constitutional Council during the final of the World Debate Championship.

II - The Stakes of The French Parliamentary Debate

The French parliamentary debate is truly a magical and unique moment that allows the audience, the jury, and the speakers to savor together the essence of words under the guise of a debate, which focuses on existential questions touching the daily lives of citizens, the real experiences of communities, and indirectly, of humanity. The passions it arouses, its vibrant emotions, and its atypical atmospheres are such that they demand time to suspend its flight, at precise moments, to allow the quick pleasures of some of the best days to be savored.[364]

The debate indeed appears as a game with the traits of a combat sport, a bloodthirsty[365] sport, putting actors in opposition[366], who, however, have only words as their weapons, the scent of words, and the revolutionary rhetoric that comes with it. Far from being just a game, the French parliamentary debate has multiple stakes that influence its course and the judges' verdict. It is evident that any debate without a solid architectural and structural foundation would be meaningless. The method suggested by rhetoric requires the orator to adhere to a specific way of reasoning, a certain nomenclature that guides their actions during the speech.

The respect for the structure of the debate is undoubtedly one of the fundamental issues of the parliamentary debate. The structure brings more light, clarity, and readability to the debate, allowing the jury and the audience to better analyze and understand each speaker in detail. Respecting the structure is an oratorical principle, a rule of the game that is imposed on the speakers, at least those who speak in a distinguished manner.

What would a debate be that does not primarily aim to convince its audience? The French parliamentary debate is an excellent exercise in argumentation, where, through the application of multiple logical methods, a jury evaluates which of the speakers, which of the teams, will logically and objectively prevail with the strength of their arguments and the weight of the ideas they support. It is an exercise that could inspire a change of opinion with an impact on the implementation of public policies or community actions. It is also inspired by the traditional debates of deputies in the National Assembly, with the goal of adopting laws that will guide the destinies of French society. As we know, in real debates in the National Assembly, the argument holds a predominant place. A rhetorical exercise inspired directly by such practice would not deviate from the rule that the argument should be the leitmotif of every speech, of every debate.

Therefore, a speaker unable to demonstrate the validity of a position or fact substantially weakens their chances of seeing their cause triumph one day. The speaker must, at all times, gain the assent of their listeners through evidence and testimony highlighted in their speech. The rationality that drives the speaker should not overshadow the fact that the speaker is, above all, a seducer, a charmer who, through a brilliant, flowery, colorful, polite, grand, rich, noble, and flamboyant style, wins the favor of their captivated audience. It is through such a style that the speaker seizes the souls and stirs them. It is through it that the speaker enters the hearts[367] to "plant new ideas and uproot those that were once planted there.[368]" The French debate places immense value on the speaker's ability, in addition to seduction, to stir emotions and passions. It is, in essence, the prime venue for parliamentary rhetoric and the art of eloquent speech. The debater must, therefore, speak not only to the reason of their audience to convince, but most importantly, they must know how to speak to their hearts in order to inspire emotional support for the cause they defend. The art of convincing (A) and persuading (B) form an inseparable pair in French parliamentary debate, guiding the distribution of oratorical glory when the fateful moment arrives, the one in which the winner and the best orator of the debate will be determined.

A - The Art of Convincing

In his memorable work On the Orator, Cicero, as a master of rhetoric, demonstrates that before charming and moving his audience, the orator must first educate them. Every orator must, above all, prove the truth of their claims.[369] French parliamentary debate does not stray far from this art of convincing, theorized by ancient rhetoric for millennia, an art that remains highly relevant today. Like in Canadian debate, the debater must present tangible arguments that prove, beyond any doubt, the thesis they defend. The argument must be related to the motion and can be based on causality or authority. The orator may choose a vivid description or use analogies and comparisons to establish the validity of their thesis. Finally, the argument could be made through hypothesis, induction, abduction, or syllogism, methods that are especially suited to legal reasoning. The art of convincing here does not grant argumentative value to various fallacies and strategies. The orator must differentiate between a substantive argument and a petition of principle, which is an argument based on premises assumed to be true but in need of demonstration.[370] In the same vein, false analogies and sophisms do not necessarily qualify as arguments.

The art of convincing in French parliamentary debate requires that the orator distinguish between the thesis and the statement of their argument, ensuring not to confuse the explanation of the argumentative mechanism, its impact, with an example, a citation, or simply an article of law. They must always challenge the logical link between what they assert and the thesis they defend. The art of convincing ensures that the orator and their team can ultimately achieve rational support for their cause, based on the arguments, relevant evidence, and testimonies they present during their speech.

It goes without saying that the art of persuasion also involves the debater's ability to effectively refute their opponent's argument by logically demonstrating how it suffers from severe deficiencies and, consequently, does not merit serious consideration. It involves directly addressing the opponent's argument and dismantling it to its core based on objective reasoning. The art of persuasion also includes the debater's ability to rehabilitate one of their team's arguments when their opponent has demolished it, an argument that has practically fallen apart due to the multiple blows it received during refutation.

The debater will demonstrate, through various logical methods, how this well-known, overdeveloped refutation could not shake the solid argument presented by their team. It will not be enough to simply assert this in order to earn the favor of the highly intelligent judges; it must be demonstrated through a mechanism derived from the contradictory nature of the debate, akin to reasoning in the court of reason and a dialectical path toward knowledge.

The art of persuasion is also the talent the debater has to summarize the debate, particularly their team's arguments, the mistakes of their adversaries, and, in a solemn tone, tip the balance of the debate in their team's favor by methodically and dialectically demonstrating why and how their team stands out; to show why and how there is no choice but for the judges to allow truth to triumph by granting it the supreme glory of victory in the debate. Debate is undoubtedly a combat[371] sport in which the only weapons are words, and the positions defended by the orators are imposed, not necessarily representing their personal opinions or convictions. The saying that when one drowns, even if on a snake, one must hold on, finds its full meaning in this context. The orator must invoke or summon any author or argument that can help prove the validity of their cause. Furthermore, it must be noted that in France, the ideological division within the elite, both at Sorbonne and Assas, can have either a positive or negative consequence on the final judgment the orator will receive.

As if it were yesterday, I still remember that passionate debate we had at the Sorbonne's management amphitheater, during the World Debate Championship. As a member of the opposition, I was tasked with defending the place of the English language in a France that, if too closed off from the world, would suffocate in an increasingly globalized world, where the English language was gaining prominence both in diplomacy and in international business. In this progressive momentum, I had the opportunity to quote several excerpts from speeches by Nicolas Sarkozy[372] at the United Nations, advocating for a world in the 21st century that takes into account the realities of the century, advocating for the urgency of multilateralism as the foundation for stable international relations. Curiously, during the traditional jury comments, one of its members, a law professor from Assas, in a relaxed and humorous style, didn't hesitate to tell me never to cite such an author or authority again—at least if I wanted to win. Without claiming to judge the validity of such a statement, because in debate the judges are "gods," I still felt that the honorable judge lacked objectivity in evaluating this aspect of my speech.

It seemed to me that he hadn't fully considered the fact that the position I was defending did not necessarily reflect my personal opinion, and that invoking such an authority did not indicate my admiration for it, nor for that line of thought. Lastly, it seemed to me that the judge hadn't fully taken into account that I wasn't French, and that a Franco-French debate mattered little to me. As a debater, it was my responsibility to find the most relevant authorities to support my argument on a motion and position that had been imposed on me just an hour before the debate. It can sometimes be difficult for a judge to maintain perspective during the process that leads to the evaluation of an argument; this is likely why Cicero emphasizes the need, beyond instructing, to charm the jury, but especially to move it.[373]

Following the same thread, Master Marc Bonnant, former President of the Geneva Bar, recognized the delicacy of addressing certain issues during debates in France at the trial of *Les Fleurs du mal* organized by the Lysias Oratorical Society Paris[374] I, in the first chamber of the Paris Court of Appeal on March 14, 2013. On this occasion, as "lawyer for Charles Baudelaire," he opposed "imperial prosecutor Pinard," played by Master Bertrand Périer. As can be seen, this factual description highlights the necessity for speakers to update their criteria related to their art of persuasion in French debates: knowing the positions, the facts of positioning, and previous stances of the jury.

This knowledge helps avoid invoking arguments or authorities that, in truth, could backfire on the speaker simply because these elements oppose the personal conviction of a judge who holds significant discretionary power; this discretionary power determines which of the two teams will win the debate. This aspect, which pertains more to *pathos* than to *logos*, we believe, should also be taken into account by this dimension of rhetoric. This knowledge of the ideological and even political tendencies of the jury would allow for the implementation of the necessary "rhetorical precautions[375]" to inevitably lead to victory based on the power of the arguments, precautions that would also impact the emotional adherence of the jury meant to confirm the final victory.

B - The Art of Persuasion

The orator is certainly an educator who teaches and instructs through his speech, but he is also, above all, a seducer and an actor who, through various rhetorical devices, charms and moves his audience to persuade them. Therefore, the debater must act upon the audience through the powers granted by verbal magic, oratory action, and his ability to highlight pathos. This is something that Jacques Amyot[376] already acknowledged in his 1579 project on royal eloquence, where he made a striking description of persuasive speech: "There is nothing like knowing how to handle a multitude of men with fine speech, tickling their hearts, mastering their wills and passions, even pushing and holding them to your pleasure, and, as it were, carrying the spur and bridle at the tip of the tongue.[377]" This statement continues the path set by Cicero in 46 B.C.: "The eloquent man we seek... will thus be able to... please and move in both a plea and a political speech... To please is a sweetness, and to move is a victory.[378]" French parliamentary debate adheres to these ancient rhetorical principles that place significant emphasis on *ethos* and *pathos*.

Unlike the Canadian style debate, simply having the most relevant arguments is not enough to see one's cause triumph in French style. The debate goes beyond mere argumentation to embrace other aspects that are more subjective but seem impactful in the process that allows for evaluation: beyond the art of convincing, the art of persuading.

Persuasion is the talent that any orator is recognized for who, by using various devices such as style, tone, gestures, facial expressions, and even memorization of the speech, succeeds in eliciting the emotional commitment of the jury and audience to the cause he defends. French debate places as much importance on this aspect. It is sometimes so intertwined with eloquence, that is, the art of speaking well. Here, we find not only debaters but also rhetoricians and even sophists. The jury will not only assess the argumentation but also determine which debater inspires confidence, uses the finest methods of rhetorical persuasion, and skillfully employs rhetorical figures such as embellishment and amplification. Most importantly, the jury will focus on the oratorical performance, specifically the debater's ability to interpret their speech with the appropriate variations in voice, tone, gaze, and overall non-verbal communication. The orator's memory, if utilized, could also help tip the scales in their favor. The art of persuasion also encompasses the ability to stir emotions through rhetorical devices like metaphor, anaphora, suspense, and oxymoron—figures of amplification that evoke emotion in the audience and awaken dormant passions within them.

As we debated in the amphitheaters of the Sorbonne and Sciences Po or in the majestic halls of the Quai d'Orsay, we observed the charm embodied by each orator and each team. Majestically dressed, the arrangement of colors in their attire gave the impression of being in the presence of not only orators but also artists, adherents of a very popular clothing style in Paris: the SAPE[379] (Société des Ambianceurs et des Personnes Élégantes). But we were far from it! The most beautiful suits worn by the orators, the finest dresses of the oratrices, were rather elements of seduction highlighted for persuasive purposes. This is not the seductive sense of the term in a romantic context, but rather the orator's ability to demonstrate credibility and inspire trust during their speech. We have even seen speakers remove their suits to demonstrate the shift in their metaphorically Stance[380], in addition to the spectacle effect that this situation brought to the debate. During the debate, we sometimes felt like we were in a poetry competition. The lyricism that carried the speeches left no one indifferent. I remember, during my final speech, deliberately choosing not to use notes. This situation gave me many moments of grace, often interrupted by the reactions of the fired-up audience, whose applause, shouts, and cheers pushed the speaker to surpass himself and give the best of himself.

The French debate undoubtedly differs from the Canadian debate in its artistic side, the place of honor given to the orator's literary and general culture, their acting talent, their voice, and facial expressions that directly reach the listener's heart, evoking passions that help win the debate. Being a great debater in this style is not limited to the argument, which, although contributing in a more than minor way to winning the cause for which the speaker sacrifices himself, is not sufficient on its own to determine the outcome of the debate; it is understood that it is not only about convincing, but also, and above all, persuading, contrary to an opinion that wrongly believes that all rhetoric is superfluous and thus useless to society. The French parliamentary debate teaches us that speech is action, that speech can have powers, and that rhetoric, just like dialectic (logos), aims to persuade and convince.

The French debate has shown us how rhetoric can be both revolting and revolutionary, depending on the direction in which it is applied.

Greatness And Miseries of The Structured French Debate

Oratory in France has its origins in the revolutionary winds that swept through the country at the dawn of the Enlightenment. The monarchical regime, which consecrated an almost divine absolutism, could not withstand the hurricane and storms of history, driven by speakers fueled by democratic momentum, a sense of revolution, social justice, and civic service.

Oratory, through its history, has served the great republican and democratic transformations; it has been in service to noble causes and to development in general. From this glorious history came a debate format, an oratorical model that, for millennia, has facilitated confrontations and the formation of speakers in France, freed from the remnants of absolutism: the structured parliamentary debate. The French parliamentary debate, as we discovered it, is a rather special system that pits eight speakers against each other with determination, but also with enthusiasm, in front of an audience that is generally animated, even inflamed, and which participates directly or indirectly in the spectacle offered by the speakers. Taking place in venues and amphitheaters steeped in symbolism and history, the clash of ideas sparked by the parliamentary debate, its prestigious jury, and its majestic setting, gives rise to magical moments resembling a game of ping-pong, with actors returning the ball until the final proclamation of victory for one team over the other.

The structured French debate develops skills in the speaker, particularly research abilities when seeking arguments that support their cause. It also nurtures the art of arrangement, strategy, and even acting skills necessary to embody their own speech. The distinguished debater here possesses nearly encyclopedic knowledge, a general culture, a literary background, and exceptional legal expertise, thus rising above the crowd.

The French debater is an architect of discourse, a professional in the art of rhetorical decoration, amplification, and stylistic, semantic, and morphosyntactic techniques that color the speech, illuminating it like a firefly in the heart of the night. Like a musician, the speaker here masters the modulation of their voice tone, diction, pauses, silences, but above all, the rhythm of their speech, which appears highly rhythmic and has the effect of soft music to the ears of the audience, who are glued to the speaker's lips, constantly amazed by their rhetorical turns and mastery of dialectic.[381] Such a debater is a smooth talker, a seducer who uses various elocution and style techniques to charm the audience, making them feel more confident and ready to accept what the speaker calls "truth" in the context of the debate. They will especially know how to play on the emotional fiber of the listener to gently penetrate their heart. The French-style parliamentary debate is not always rosy; at times, it can be grim. The ideological conditioning of some judges can limit the scope of the debate, which is merely an oratorical exercise in which one practices argumentation, where the argument does not always represent the personal opinion of the debater defending it.

This situation can, in some cases, constitute a limitation on freedom of expression, which was one of the founding principles of the French Revolution of 1789. Likewise, it is sometimes difficult for the debater to know exactly what they need to improve after a competition. The result sheets are not available, and the speaker may spend their life wondering about the real reasons for their defeat and how they should proceed in order to improve their shortcomings.

Finally, the French parliamentary debate certainly recognizes the primacy of the argument but does not fully honor the logos in the evaluation process. This situation generates speakers who can be eloquent, making rhetoric for the sake of rhetoric. Rhetoric for the sake of rhetoric is beautiful! But it is not capable of infusing into a free and democratic society the revolution and systemic changes that must guide the destinies of future generations. It may be time for French debating societies to rehabilitate the logos fully. Only then will the triptych logos-ethos-pathos find its full meaning. Only then could we better nurture the dream of seeing rhetoric inspire the revolutions of tomorrow—a revolutionary rhetoric in the service of art, aesthetics, social ethics, and development.

CHAPTER X:
AFRICAN STYLE RHETORIC

Credit: Michael Voinis for Purée Maison

Simplice Zombre is a talented speaker who is revolutionizing the art of rhetoric in Africa. He embodies this African rhetoric, carried by griots since time immemorial. Under his artist name, "Simplice Simply Simple," he dedicates himself to putting rhetoric at the service of social development in Burkina Faso. In this photo, he electrifies an amphitheater at the Sorbonne during the World Debate Championship with an improvised speech.

Oratory is at the heart of Africa's history. "From the heritage of knowledge of all kinds, passed down patiently from mouth to ear and from master to disciple through the ages[382]," as the Malian writer Amadou Ampathé Ba once recognized.

African culture is inherently oral, embodied by the griots[383], who have been its heroes since time immemorial. It would not be unreasonable to think that rhetoric originates in African cultures, which have been largely oral in their essence, substance, and

210

quintessence. This is especially true, given that historically and traditionally, the griot, through their oratory skills, teaches the people about their history and origins. They are peacemakers who use their verbal skills to help resolve misunderstandings between families and communities. They are also artists[384] who, through the mastery of the kora[385] play, sing praises of the powerful and recount the exploits of ancestors. For centuries, griots have passed down marvelous tales of wild animals and powerful warriors who marked their time from father to son. The griot's word is sacred, and not every word is meant to be spoken, as they say in Africa. To respect the sacred power of speech in Africa, griots always use the following formula before speaking in public: "Let what is to be said be said, and let what is to remain silent remain silent.[386]" Oratory is a natural phenomenon in Africa, marked by a culture of orality. This cultural orality has led some thinkers to mistakenly believe that it had neither history nor philosophy.[387]

However, the African is by nature an orator who, through wisdom, tales, and legends passed down from his ancestors, highlights the artifices of rhetoric. It is this oratory art that brought glory to great empires such as the Mali Empire, the Zulu Empire, the Ghana Empire, the Kanem and Congo kingdoms. After centuries of humiliation marked by slavery and Western colonization, it is still rhetoric that restores Africa's honor.

Thus, we saw highly charismatic nationalist leaders fiercely claim their people's independence and sovereignty through a rhetoric with highly revolutionary flavors. This was the era of independence.[388] These independences, gained through numerous *meetings* and heated political debates, gave rise to new problems and challenges: the ignorance of fundamental rights, the contempt for the most basic freedoms, and the emergence of police states with extravagant powers. It is still the public debate, marked by immense internal struggles, that facilitated the rise of the rule of law, at least in theory. To achieve this, intense legal rhetoric was needed, and thus initiatives were born to prepare the African legal professionals of tomorrow for the legal challenges imposed by the realities of the moment. However, although oratory is intrinsic to African culture, Africa still seems to have not developed a debate system true to its cultural identity, like what can be observed in France, England, the United States, or Canada. Influenced institutionally by globalization, its parliamentary debate style would still be searching for its true identity. There is, however, a real desire among African orators to reclaim their rightful place in the world of rhetoric and debate, as evidenced by the proliferation of debate societies and the offensive of their orators during various international meetings. Analyzing oratory in Africa will allow us to see, on one hand, how rhetoric played a major role in liberating this part of the world from colonial rule; on the other hand, it will allow us to explore the development of parliamentary debate, its variations, its façades, but most importantly, it will help us assess the future of oratory in Africa. It is therefore prudent, before analyzing the oratorical style specific to African speakers (II), to first consider the emergence of debate societies (I).

I - The Dawn of Structured Debate in Africa

Although Africa is the birthplace of global oratory, it does not have, strictly speaking, a system of argumentation or an oratory tradition similar to what we see in France, Australia, England, the United States, or Canada. It is only in recent times that we can note the emergence of societal debate on the continent, especially in light of the revolutionary wave that swept across it during the years of turmoil.[389] After the independence movements, political regimes were dominated by the precedence and even preeminence of strong and providential men. Such a context was not conducive to adversarial debate. Following the fall of the Berlin Wall, democracy rapidly spread across the African continent, like a swarm of locusts. Sovereign national conferences were revolutionary founding actors in the debate and freedom of expression. Although it must be acknowledged that revolutions and marches were necessary to pressure some heads of state into declaring democratic openness.

It was the case in former Zaire, now the Democratic Republic of Congo. Mobutu, then the head of state, burst into tears as he proclaimed the change of regime towards multipartism and participatory democracy.[390] It was in this context of openness to political pluralism, but especially freedom of expression, that organizations of speech emerged like mushrooms, with the major goal of using oratory to spark revolution, public debate, and civic engagement, in order to build a more democratic society, one that considers both its particularities and its differences. Marius Binyou,[391] in his notable thesis, established an inventory of oratory organizations worldwide, particularly in Africa. Having interacted with and followed the evolution of some of them, it is necessary to analyze how these debate societies, beyond helping practice African-style rhetoric, contribute to inspiring civil society in their nations. We will examine, in turn, the cases of iDebate Rwanda (A) and the Cameroon Debate Association (B).

213

A - Idebate Rwanda

iDebate Rwanda is undoubtedly one of the leading oratory organizations in Africa. Born after the Rwandan genocide of 1994, which was a difficult trial for the country, this organization, through the art of oratory, tries to give a new face to a country deeply affected. Co-founded by Jean-Michel Habineza, iDebate Rwanda enables many young Rwandans to experience the reality of parliamentary debate in a format similar to the British style.

Covering various topics such as climate change, peace, democracy, and social coexistence, the debate helps young people in this country stay engaged with social issues. More importantly, it shows them the necessity of developing a culture of peace and unity in a country recovering from one of the most devastating genocides in world history. The art of oratory shapes young leaders with strong argumentation skills, eager to help build a Rwandan society free from hatred and promoting healing through the words of this distinguished citizen.

iDebate Rwanda regularly organizes the East Africa Debate Championship, bringing together speakers from the sub-region to meet and debate in a spirit of camaraderie about pressing issues affecting the region. This competition highlights the top speakers in East Africa and ranks among the most significant rhetorical contests in Africa. One of the flagship projects of Rwandan orators is the *Post Genocide Generation US Tour*, which allows the brightest speakers to spend time in the United States, visiting major universities across the country to share their experiences on the genocide. At the same time, they learn about democracy, American culture, the history of the Civil Rights Movement in the United States, and debate techniques specific to that country. Through debate, Rwandan orators acquire tools that will not only enhance their communication skills but also increase their awareness of the issues of their time. The speaker here is able to use rhetoric for revolution, embodying Frantz Fanon's statement: "Each generation must, in relative opacity, discover its mission: to accomplish it or to betray it.[392]"

The orators of iDebate Rwanda have the advantage of mastering oratory at a young age. Often, these are high school students who cultivate a passion for rhetoric and parliamentary debate that can sometimes feel overwhelming. This situation cultivates in them the critical thinking necessary for reasoning and refutation, as well as a clear desire to engage in the community to turn the ideas defended during debates into action. The exuberance and enthusiasm driving these orators suggest that they will become the best leaders of tomorrow's Rwandan society. The *Post Genocide Generation US Tour* is invaluable as it helps the orators become sensitized to the discourse of hate, allowing them to protect society from the scourge of genocide. But more importantly, the exchange with the United States allows the orators not only to share their experiences but also to learn more about the American Revolution, the Civil Rights Movement, American institutions, democracy, and human rights. The experiences gained by these young orators help shape leaders aligned with the republican values that distinguish exceptional speakers. These orators, in a Rwandan society torn by one of the worst genocides in history, will become better ambassadors of peace, multiculturalism, tolerance, and coexistence. Orators who will turn the art of debate into a tool for social development.

iDebate Rwanda is undoubtedly one of the best examples of the emergence of parliamentary debate in Africa. Through structured debate, the organization helps raise awareness among the youth about social issues while simultaneously contributing to healing the wounds of a Rwandan society that has not yet fully come to terms with the painful legacy of the genocide.

However, a parliamentary debate structure that takes into account the continent's institutional history and ancient oral traditions would seem more relevant and authentic for oratory in

Africa and globally. The need to create a debate format that reflects African traditions is a pressing issue. This challenge, it seems to me, must be taken up by the orators and rhetoric professors of Africa. For, as the saying goes: "As long as the lions do not have their historian, the hunting stories will always glorify the hunter."[393]

B - The Cameroon Debate Association

The Cameroon Debate Association was founded in 2009 in the city of Dschang. It trains young people in Cameroon in structured parliamentary debate, eloquence, and leadership. It has trained numerous orators who have won continental and international competitions in both French and English. The Cameroon Debate Association implements a debate system similar to the French system, as practiced by the Fédération francophone de débat, which we have analyzed in depth above.

Marius Binyou, its founder, is working tirelessly to ensure that oratory becomes part of formal education at the primary, secondary, and university levels. In this regard, young people are trained, and competitions are organized at various levels. The organization has proven that debate is not just for the sake of debating; it has shown that An orator must have a social mission, and that rhetoric is not an intellectual exercise, but a true driver of social development with direct impacts on the lives of fellow citizens. The speaker here is a man of conviction who seeks to change his society through social and civic engagement positively. He masters the art of speech, arrangement, and rhetorical devices. But he says to himself, "Yet, it is necessary to implement the convictions that emerge from his speeches." In essence, he is a committed citizen who seamlessly integrates his art with his social missions, utilizing his art to transform his society. To this end, Cameroon has been shaken since 2014 by a social crisis called the "Anglophone crisis," which pits the Anglophone region against the Francophone region. An increase in hate speech and community tensions marks this crisis. In response to this reality, the speakers of the Cameroon Debate Association did not sit idly by. They committed to alleviating the suffering of internally displaced persons. French language classes were organized, as well as speech training courses, and even a competition called *Oratuim*, aimed at restoring confidence to the displaced persons. Through these commendable actions, the organization illustrated that the speaker is not only an agent of change but also a leader attuned to the social issues that hinder his community. The speaker here is a revolutionary capable of grasping the bull by the horns to advance the causes that are dear to him. He is both a man of reason, a man of passion, but above all, a man of action.

In the same spirit, Marius Binyou, during a study trip to Egypt, founded the Society of Oratory at the Senghor University of Alexandria and the International Network for the Promotion of Oratory in Africa, the Caribbean, and the Pacific (RIPAO). The Society of Oratory at Senghor University practices a style of parliamentary debate very similar to the French style.

The International Network for the Promotion of Rhetoric in Africa, the Caribbean, and the Pacific has a mission to popularize rhetoric in Africa, particularly by harmonizing practices. This network organizes oratorical contests largely inspired by the French-style structured debate discussed in the previous chapter.

Like iDebate Rwanda and the Cameroon Debate Association, many other debate societies exist across the continent, Like the Oral debates[394] in Burkina Faso, Mali, Senegal, Ivory Coast, Togo, Ghana, and Nigeria. These societies have developed debate systems generally similar to the French model, while significantly contributing to the dynamization of civil society in their respective countries. Although parliamentary debate has blossomed in Africa over recent years, with numerous debate and eloquence organizations emerging, there still seems to be a lack of authenticity in the debate structure, as seen with iDebate Rwanda.

Additionally, the art of rhetoric appears quite disparate across the continent. Harmonizing oral practices and sharing best practices without any hesitation between debate societies could help restore the reputation of parliamentary debate in Africa and enhance the performance of its debaters on the international stage. There's no doubt that parliamentary debate in Africa has a bright future if efforts continue to be made. After all, the bird doesn't build its nest in a single day. I recall a heated debate at the Louis Liard amphitheater at the Sorbonne, where I had a tête-à-tête with Nyanyui Siliadin from the Togolese debate society. We briefly discussed the question of an authentic debate structure in Africa and even the possibility of a pan-African organization that could govern the operation of oral practices across the continent. Efforts have been made to submit the project to the discernment of national debate societies. Siliadin took on the responsibility of advancing the project, and I made it clear to him that he could count on my collaboration. It was more important than ever that Africa reclaims its rightful place. Yes, it has much to give and teach the world. Such an idea would accelerate the progress of parliamentary debate in Africa, with the hope that the fruits will fulfill the promise of the flowers.

II - The Revolutionary Spirit of Oratory Competitions: The Evolution of Debate in Africa

Photo credit: FFD[395]

In this photo, the charismatic speaker Tracy Ntumba Busanga Munyoka from the Democratic Republic of Congo delivers a speech during the Clash of Champions at the Quai d'Orsay, as part of the week dedicated to Francophonie. Tracy uses her oratory skills to advocate for girls' right to education in Congo. She is a reference that demonstrates trust in women. Her commitment to social justice shows the ability of oratory to spark revolution.

Although African culture is primarily oral, it has not seen structured debate as it developed in Western civilizations and more recently in prestigious American, European, and Australian schools. For a long time, it lived in introspection, and it was only in the early 1990s, thanks to international and continental student mobility, that African rhetoric finally found an international platform for expression. We have seen young African lawyers engage in verbal battles during one of the most prestigious legal events. Organized and supported by the famous Faculty of Law at the University of Pretoria, particularly its Centre for Human Rights, the oratory competition has allowed young lawyers to face off on pressing legal issues in Africa since 1990. In an Africa sometimes ravaged by armed conflicts, the competition serves as a means to combat, through oratory, the ignorance of human rights, which has caused so much suffering on the continent's path.

It is a privilege to advocate in this international competition for human rights and oratory. One must admit that the moot court competition is a major event that helps build tomorrow's leaders and the best lawyers. Beyond that, the competition breaks down the barriers of colonization, transcends linguistic and legal systems, and allows young advocates to work hand in hand for a stronger Africa of tomorrow—an Africa where multiculturalism, co-existence, and human rights will be a reality; in short, a beautiful and diverse Africa.

The advanced dynamics of oratory at prestigious French schools such as Sorbonne and Sciences Po, as well as in the United States and Canada, has inspired great speakers to conquer the world of rhetoric as if they were lords, from Alaska to Argentina, from Cape Town to Cairo, from Dakar to Djibouti, from Paris to Helsinki, from Australia to New Zealand, from Beijing to Moscow... Thanks to these hegemonic trends, and at times even supremacist, African speakers are invited to the table of debates across the Western world to showcase their abilities.

We have seen Senegalese orators shine at the Sorbonne and Sciences Po, Burkinabè speakers excel in France and Lebanon, as well as speakers from Cameroon, Algeria, Congo, Chad, Togo... This was the golden age of parliamentary debate in Africa. Orators, once relegated to the shadows, can now gain notoriety and speak on a global stage before a high-caliber audience. The advent of debate and advocacy competitions has further structured African rhetoric, which had long remained hidden. To better understand this phenomenon, it would first be necessary to examine the contribution of the African moot court competition to this dynamic (A). Only after that will we analyze the international debate and eloquence competitions in detail (B). Indeed, all signs point to these events having somehow fostered the rise of parliamentary debate and rhetoric in Africa, giving birth to a new class of orators capable of making a significant impact through verbal magic and, thus, leading their respective societies toward a brighter future, if not one full of praise.

A - The African Moot Court Competition of The Faculty of Law at The University of Pretoria

Since 1990, the University of Pretoria has organized a moot court competition. This competition allows over one hundred and fifty law schools to send their best advocates accompanied by an international law professor. Before the competition, a hypothetical[396] case is sent to the law schools. It is based on human rights violations occurring between two fictitious states, violations which raise legal questions submitted for review by the African Court on Human and Peoples' Rights. During the competition, students must prepare two pleadings: one as the claimant and another as the defendant. Similarly, they will plead twice as the claimant and twice as the defendant in front of different teams and probably a different jury[397], which will evaluate the advocates based on a pre-established grid. The pleadings take place in English, Portuguese, and French. Once the preliminary rounds are completed, the best Anglophone, Francophone, and Lusophone teams advance to the final, where they form two mixed teams that must work together beyond linguistic, legal, and even academic barriers.[398]

Writing two pleadings for the same case—one for the claim and the other for the defense—helps structure one's thoughts better and allows the student to identify the most relevant legal arguments, both for the claim and for the defense. It is a high-level intellectual exercise that provides mastery over various articles, case law, their relevance, and limitations in relation to the case. Orators find immense joy in arguing both in favor of and against a jury composed of top international law professors, judges, and lawyers. The competition helps to understand the difference between rhetoric and strictly legal argumentation. One might sometimes have too poetic, almost lyrical, a conception of pleading. With the guidance of distinguished judges, it becomes clear that it is primarily a technique.

In this regard, Nelson Mandela said: "Is there a better way to promote human rights than to bring together students, who are the leaders, judges, and professors of tomorrow, from different countries, along with judges from the highest courts and professors to debate the crucial issues of our time in the exciting and stimulating atmosphere of a courtroom where they can confront their arguments and talents in a spirit of fierce, yet friendly, competition?"[399] It is certainly realized after the competition that many things in the world could be accomplished through law, that great battles could be fought, and great victories achieved.

The moot court competition has certainly ignited a flame in Africa: the flame of revolution through the art of pleading, the flame of a certain idea of social justice, the flame of engaging in today's great battles to ensure tomorrow's victories.

B - International Debate and Eloquence Competitions

Simplice Zombre receives an ovation from the audience at the University of Paris-Sorbonne. In a highly proverbial style, infused with African wisdom, this orator leaves no one indifferent. His posture commands respect, his words are sweet, and his memory is vivid.

International debate and eloquence competitions have allowed many aspiring African orators to confront the great arenas of debate. Orators from Africa have been able to demonstrate their capabilities directly. While we were all gathered at Sorbonne, I had the opportunity to see the African teams invited to the World Debate Championship, including teams from Burkina Faso, Senegal, and Algeria. In my opinion, they were the best orators. They were all charismatic and possessed a unique gift: remarkable memory. They were able, while developing an argument, to make very long quotes from memory, peppering their speeches with quotes, proverbs, case law, and even articles of law, where applicable. They are generally very elegant orators, embodying confidence and a sense of honor that leaves no doubt. This is what could be observed in the orator from Burkina Faso, Simplice Zombré, who, dressed in his white gandoura, left no one indifferent when he spoke. With each intervention, Simplice raised the crowd due to the verbal magic he embodied so well; it was a pleasure to listen to him and stay glued to his words. Just by his posture, he made an impression.

This may remind one of the griots from ancient Africa. However, during these events, the African orator often struggles to be effective in winning the debate, with structural issues being the primary challenge. This brings to light the question of a debate structure specific to Africa. Structure is indeed the element without which the orator cannot thrive. Mastering the structure allows the judge to know where the debater is in their reasoning at any given time. Another difficulty is related to the proverbs and quotes that judges do not always understand. But this is a strength for Africa. With time and practice, the methodical use of proverbs and wisdom will eventually be accepted by all. One must not overlook other subjective factors, such as accents, diction, and many others that have remained hidden, which hinder the emergence of African orators on the global stage. In any case, international competitions are a unique moment for African orators who learn from others, build connections with other orators, and develop bilateral relationships with debating societies from other countries, in order to exchange good practices related to debate or rhetoric, as the Oratory Debates of Burkina Faso did with the Canadian Interuniversity Debate Society.

In the background, one can notice a revolutionary momentum in African debate societies after oratory competitions; indeed, these societies seek to modernize in order to align with the international scene. Among the orators, there is a strong will to work harder and even to get involved in society through community projects, or a desire to enter politics or law to live the myth of debate competitions, in which they were honorable members of parliament. Debate competitions ignite a certain flame in the orator—the desire to open up to the world of global rhetoric and to feel useful to their society. An ideal now exists, reflecting Antoine Marie Roger de Saint-Exupéry's statement: "To be a man is precisely to be responsible. It is to know shame in the face of misery that seemed beyond one's control. It is to be proud of a victory that comrades have won. It is to feel, by placing one's stone, that one is contributing to building the world."[400]

Greatness And Misery of Oratory in Africa

Undoubtedly, the art of oratory is intertwined with the history of Africa, whose culture is essentially oral. Embodied for time immemorial by the griots, who were its heroes, the art of oratory in Africa has evolved, like a long and peaceful river, giving rise to atypical orators who master the use of formulas, metaphors, and various rhetorical devices: simply, magicians of speech, with speech being sacred here. The African orator is an artist, a poet who does not simply say certain things but deliberately chooses to say them in a particular way. He naturally masters argumentative techniques and the arrangement of arguments. He is a self-taught rhetorician who works to make his speeches more convincing, more beautiful, and capable of directly reaching the hearts of his listeners.

The speeches of Nelson Mandela, Patrice Lumumba, Thomas Sankara, Sékou Touré, Samora Machel… give us an idea of the African way of argumentation, which is unique in the world. Africa has long been an oral culture, a characteristic that sets it apart. However, global oratory, from Athens to Rome, passing through Paris and London, has undergone developments. Indeed, each civilization has conceived an oratory model based on its cultural model, as seen in France with the structured parliamentary debate, in England, or Canada with their debates.

Africa, however, has not yet developed an oratory model that takes into account its history and its pioneering traditions in rhetoric, which remain underdeveloped, poorly formalized, and underappreciated. Debate societies in Africa, as an exception, apply imported Western debate grids and principles for the training and evaluation of debaters. As a comparative debate system, it is admirable, but it is still these imported grids that regulate many national championships.

However, Africa would benefit from occupying its rightful place in the world of rhetoric and parliamentary debate. The African orator is highly valued for his style, presence, charisma, knowledge of history, proverbs, wisdom, sense of honor, and community commitment. But sometimes, he lacks the structure to support his speech, which is filled with flowers, high intelligence, and wisdom. This is probably why some orators with strong potential struggle to make an impact at global rhetoric events, despite being far above the competition. There is no doubt, however, that sometimes subjective factors related to juries have acted as stumbling blocks for these orators, who use all their resources to carve a path in the world of speech. Ultimately, Africa appears to be the cradle of global oratory. However, other civilizations may have stolen the spotlight by modernizing existing rhetorical practices and utilizing them for revolutionary purposes. Perhaps it is time for the continent that is the birthplace of civilizations to formalize debate techniques and practices that take into account its rich history, carried by the griots, its traditional political system, its ancient civilizations, and the significant developments in parliamentary debate. After the tragic episodes of slavery and colonization, Africa has been the stage for great atrocities.

From coups to various armed conflicts, it has suffered. In recent years, community tensions characterized by the proliferation of hate speech, which continues to grow like a sea mushroom, have been observed at all corners of the continent, becoming a real and persistent issue. Faced with such macabre and almost pitiful situations, the orator plays a crucial role in the dispute resolution process, hanging over Africa like the sword of Damocles. Rhetoric in Africa, since ancient times, has never been a tool of simple pleasure. It has always served as a conduit for development through the griots. Would it not be time to introduce oratory and parliamentary debate in formal education across the continent to train new generations sensitized to the values of peace, democracy, and human rights? Could we, at this point, dare to hope for a future where Africa is free from hate speech, genocides, and armed conflicts? Because oratory would have produced a new type of leader, one concerned with noble values and imbued with a revolutionary spirit that would positively change Africa and the world, for the great happiness of all, with rhetoric simultaneously becoming an instrument for the development of nations.

FIFTH PART:
THE ORATOR FACING THE LEGAL AND ETHICAL CHALLENGES OF SPEECH

The orator is, by nature, a good man, a noble who does not resort to deceitful methods to achieve the goals sought in a debate. Above all, he is a man of value entrusted with a very particular mission at a very particular time, and he wishes that the values he embodies become the values of everyone. As we can easily see, these values must be healthy. The orator must uphold ethical standards in their speech, avoiding any content that contradicts morality and social decorum rules. The orator must be honest in the statements he makes during his speech, and he must ensure that he presents the most realistic vocabulary, thus avoiding abuses that, in truth, could compromise the audience's[401] appreciation of his words; and, of course, he must defend morally acceptable causes in order to increase his credibility. Moreover, he must know how to distinguish between a quote, a proverb, the ideas of another orator or author, and his own thoughts. To pass off someone else's ideas as one's own is to commit plagiarism. Such a situation permanently damages the orator's credibility and, worse, his reputation, when he engages in such low tactics. In reality, it would not be worthy claiming the shining nobility that is recognized in orators.

The orator is certainly an ambassador of freedom of speech, with the right to express himself freely in a free and democratic society. But does he have the right to say whatever he wants? The orator must imperatively avoid hate speech in his oration, which, in truth, does not enjoy legal protection. Hate speech has been the origin of many hate crimes that have already destroyed too many lives. As a peacemaker and ambassador of coexistence, it is important that the orator contributes to writing the bright moments of human history. In this perspective, it goes without saying that the orator must avoid in his speech any racist, sexist remarks, or those inciting hatred against a particular group.

He must refrain from glorifying terrorism, inciting genocide or tribalism, among others. These serious offenses for oratory fall under the jurisdiction of national, community, international, and transnational law. Overall, the law is quite strict and generally proposes exemplary punishment in order to limit the effects of hate in the world. In such cases, the orator must know how to hold his tongue. Though speech is powerful and represents a share of power, it can under specific conditions both create and dismantle society. This is why the law regulates this exciting exercise of speech to limit the potential excesses that may arise. It becomes essential that the orator is sensitized to the general legal provisions and the consistent case law that governs speech. In this way, he will better understand the red line that he should not cross in any speech. He will know the sanctions to which he may be exposed depending on his geographical location, as no one is supposed to ignore the law, and the law is only valid if its violation leads to a sanction.

The legal framework of oratory undoubtedly promises a society crowned with noble orators who, in various speeches, uphold the weight of ideas and the strength of arguments, as well as the cardinal values of peace, coexistence, and multiculturalism. We will therefore focus on this dimension of oratory that emphasizes the legal framework of speech (Chapter XI), which will show how law governs rhetoric and various communication practices. In other words, how the orator can be exposed to the law due to a compromising speech that undermines the sacred foundations of society.

CHAPTER XI:
THE ORATOR BETWEEN THE RIGHT OF SPEECH AND THE SPEECH OF LAW

The art of oratory is noble. This nobility comes from the fact that throughout history, the orator has been at the center of great revolutions that have positively improved the world. We saw this with the French Revolution, the American Revolution, and the independence movements in Africa, Asia, and Latin America. Orators were at the heart of these changes. While rhetoric can build, it can also sometimes harm humanity, as we saw with the rhetoric of hate propagated by Radio Mille Collines during the tragic Rwandan genocide. A radio station that, through its rhetoric, ignited violence when it should have returned to the nobility embodied by rhetoric. This rhetoric of hate caused so much harm to humanity! We also saw it during apartheid in South Africa, where orators incited and pitted one community against another. We saw it again during the Armenian genocide and the painful memory of the Holocaust.[402] Hate speech is a virus that undermines oratory, and the orator, from his elevated position, should avoid it, ensuring that rhetoric can return to its true purpose: to build and revolutionize the world, to promote peace, and the values of coexistence.

In his memorable work *On the Art of Oratory*, Cicero did not hesitate to assert: "... to arm oneself with eloquence to defend, and not to attack, the interests of the State, is to make oneself as useful to oneself as to one's country, and to deserve the love of one's fellow citizens."[403] According to the Council of Europe, specifically its Committee of Ministers in its recommendation number 97, "hate speech" "should be understood as covering all forms of expression that spread, incite, promote, or justify racial hatred, xenophobia, anti-Semitism, or other forms of hatred based on intolerance, including intolerance expressed in the form of aggressive nationalism and ethnocentrism, discrimination, and hostility towards minorities, immigrants, and people of immigrant origin."[404] As we can see, the orator must exercise caution, for "hate speech is not a speech that enjoys protection."[405] Therefore, the orator must ensure, in any oration, that they respect the law, depending on their geographical location.

International law, as well as the consistent case law of international tribunals, condemns with the greatest vigor the hate speech that has marked the darker periods of human history. This is the same in Canadian law and the law of various countries worldwide. The international community is unanimous in its belief that hate speech is a flaw in rhetoric that requires sanctions commensurate with the danger of the offense, in order to allow rhetoric to serve development, the rapprochement of peoples and nations, and to provoke just revolutions when the circumstances demand it. It would therefore be wise that, although motivated by good intentions, the orator should be sensitized to the limits of his speech, limits imposed by the law. The orator is certainly an infinitely cultured man who knows how far he should not go in his oration; but since one cannot spend a day dismantling clocks without wondering, even slightly, what time it is, it is imperative that the law and its consequences be known so that, in the end, no one is ignorant of it and acts accordingly. Following this thread, it would be entirely sensible to analyze the consistent case law of the European Court of Human Rights on the issue of hate speech (I) before delving into an analysis of some elements of Canadian law, international and transnational law, regarding hate speech (II).

I - The State of International Case Law On Speech

The European Court of Human Rights has ruled on cases highlighting the issue of hate speech. Based on this case law, the orator should refrain from engaging in various aspects of hate speech. Such behavior would be contrary to the law and certainly to the noble values conveyed by rhetoric. Whether it is hatred against an ethnic group[406], hatred against a racial group[407], hatred against a religious group[408], or incitement to violence and support for terrorist[409] activities, the European Court of Human Rights believes that these behaviors have no place in speech, much less in a free and democratic society adorned with the vibrant colors of the rule of law. In this context, the orator should adopt a republican attitude that calls for respecting the law and social specificities, the values of tolerance, social peace, and non-discrimination.

The European Court of Human Rights has also ruled that threats to democratic order[410], denialist and revisionist theses, glorification of war crimes, glorification of violence, incitement to hostility, and incitement to discrimination or racial hatred are forms of hate speech subject to sanction, just like ethnic and religious hatred. As we can see, as an ambassador of freedom of speech, the orator cannot afford to cross red lines. Freedom of speech is certainly a fundamental right, but in its exercise, the orator must face clearly established obligations and responsibilities; one of its major limits is hate speech, which, of course, does not enjoy any legal protection. To better raise the orator's awareness of the legal framework of speech by law, we will analyze some aspects of the decisions of the European Court of Human Rights to determine their implications for the orator. Specifically, we will look at the Court's position on: incitement to discrimination or racial hatred (A), and denialism and revisionism (B). The analysis will allow us to better understand these concepts, but more importantly, it will enable any orator to know the current state of the law in this matter, so that they can always advocate for the values of tolerance, social peace, and the republican and democratic values that form the foundation of civilized societies.

A - The Prohibition of Incitement to Discrimination or Racial Hatred

In his speech, the orator must exercise caution. His address must always promote the democratic values of the rule of law and, when necessary, democratic revolution, especially when facing social injustices. He must refrain from inciting discrimination or racial hatred, as was seen during the dark periods of human history. Incitement to discrimination or racial hatred is when an orator makes statements in a speech to encourage others to express hatred, violence, or discrimination against a particular group, based on their religion, national origin, or ethnicity.

The European Court of Human Rights, in the case *Le Pen v. France*, ruled on the issue of incitement to discrimination or racial hatred. In this case, the applicant, Le Pen, was, at the time of the events, the president of the National Front, a political party in France. He specifically argued that his conviction for "provocation to discrimination, hatred, or violence towards a group of people based on their origin, membership, or non-membership of an ethnicity, nation, race, or religion" for remarks he made about Muslims in France in an interview with *Le Monde* in which he stated: "The day when we no longer have 5 million, but 25 million Muslims, they will be the ones in charge," violated his freedom of expression.

The European Court, before any substantive debate, declared the application inadmissible. It then continued by stating that, although the applicant's remarks were part of a general public debate related to the issues of immigrant settlement in host countries: "the applicant's comments, however, were certainly likely to give a troubling image of the Muslim community as a whole, potentially sparking feelings of rejection and hostility. He contrasted, on the one hand, the French people with, on the other hand, a community whose religious affiliation was expressly mentioned, and whose rapid growth was presented as an already existing threat to the dignity and safety of the French." The European Court ultimately concluded that the grounds for the applicant's conviction as determined by the domestic courts were relevant and sufficient. "Furthermore, the conviction was not disproportionate," stated the highly intelligent judges of the European Court of Human Rights. The Court, therefore, concluded that: "The interference with the applicant's exercise of his right to freedom of expression had been necessary in a democratic society."[411]

As seen in this decision of the European Court, by making such a statement about Muslims in France, the applicant incited the French to discrimination and hatred against the Muslim community: it was hate speech. This is certainly why the highly intelligent judges of the Court sided with the domestic courts, justifying the state's interference in the applicant's exercise of his freedom of expression on the grounds of necessity in a democratic society, as hate speech itself does not enjoy any legal protection.

The orator, in every circumstance, should take this jurisprudential precedent into account in order to deliver speeches that contribute to the unity of peoples, coexistence, the promotion of peace, multiculturalism, and republican values. As the European Court of Human Rights has rightly acknowledged in several cases, the orator will ensure that his interventions promote the values of tolerance, social peace, and inclusion, which form the foundation of democratic societies. From a strictly legal perspective, the decision is essentially European, meaning it does not apply to non-European orators.

However, it may still hold a moral, symbolic, and even pedagogical value for other continents, and this will certainly resonate favorably in other parts of the world. The history of humanity has given us orators like Nelson Mandela, Barack Obama, and Martin Luther King... They never delivered hate speeches, but had the ability to develop a sense of coexistence.

While it is true that the orator should refrain from delivering any speech aimed at inciting the people to discrimination and racial hatred, it is also true that the orator should not remain passive in the face of acts of discrimination and racial hatred. It is by denouncing such attitudes through revolutionary rhetoric that the orator sets in motion a revolution capable of ensuring a high-quality systemic change. In fact, it would be to fail in his historical mission to remain silent when the most glaring social injustices continue to gain ground. One can note, with joy, such revolutionary rhetoric in the intervention of the Congolese nationalist Patrice Lumumba, who in a memorable speech vigorously denounces racial hatred and discrimination that marked the colonization of the Congo by Belgium.

In his struggle for freedom, he uses highly revolutionary rhetoric to denounce the contempt shown toward his people because of their skin color. This can be seen in his historic speech of June 30, 1960: "This struggle, which was one of tears, fire, and blood, we are proud of it to the deepest part of ourselves, for it was a noble and just struggle, an essential struggle to put an end to the humiliating slavery that was imposed upon us by force... Who will forget that a Black person was addressed as 'You,' not, of course, as a friend, but because the honorable 'You' was reserved for only the Whites? ... We knew that the law was never the same, depending on whether it concerned a White or a Black: accommodating for some, cruel and inhuman for others... We knew that in the cities, there were magnificent houses for the Whites, and dilapidated huts for the Blacks, that a Black person was not allowed in cinemas, restaurants, or stores called 'European,' that a Black person traveled in the hull of barges, at the feet of the White in his luxury cabin..."[412]

The revolutionary orator Lumumba, in this iconic speech, denounces racial hatred and discrimination, which were the foundations of the Belgian colonial system. However, he does not incite the Congolese people to discriminate against the Belgians. He refrains from using hate rhetoric, which would be contrary to the ideals of social justice and freedom so strongly advocated by the nationalists. Nevertheless, and fortunately, he envisions better days for his fellow citizens. Days strongly marked by the triumph of the rule of law in Congo, despite the wounds of a past still very fresh in people's memories: "We will effectively eliminate all forms of discrimination and give each person the proper place that will be due to their human dignity, their work, and their dedication to the country. We will not impose peace through the force of guns (...), but peace through hearts and goodwill (...)."[413] One can see a prime minister who, although recognizing the atrocities of colonization and its racist tendencies, calls on his people to reconciliation, to coexistence, and not to revenge against their former oppressors. In a peaceful rhetoric, he expresses his hope of building a nation in the near future that respects the rights and freedoms of its citizens and friends, regardless of their ethnic origin, color, or political allegiance. The revolutionary Lumumba went so far as to make the ultimate sacrifice in the hope of seeing this cause triumph for the happiness of the Congolese and Africans. He embodied the social commitment and sense of sacrifice that every revolutionary orator should possess. Through his words, Lumumba turned the beauty of speech into a tool for fighting against injustices and various forms of discrimination. This sense of sacrifice can also be seen in his final letter to his wife, Pauline, written from the depths of his dark prison in Katanga[414], where, despite the physical and psychological torture from his tormentors, the orator never once gave up on his sacred convictions. Convictions that he always defended on the high plateaus of discipline, without ever drinking from the cup of bitterness and hatred.

Lumumba undoubtedly embodies the nobility sought in a distinguished orator. An orator at the service of social justice, an orator at the service of peace and national cohesion. An orator, finally, who does not hide behind a velvet glove to denounce human rights violations and the degradation of human dignity. It is therefore clear that the revolutionary orator, like Lumumba, must denounce any injustice based on discrimination, while opposing injustice with the law, and if necessary, with the justice system. Opposed to injustice, peace and the law belong to intellectual elegance, the nobility that characterizes great orators and great revolutionaries.

Photo credit: Michael Vionis for Purée Maison

Debate brings people together by creating an atmosphere of conviviality in which orators from all nations walk hand in hand in a harmonious spirit, without distinction of nationality, religion, or social class. Debate, in this sense, should be viewed as a method of conflict resolution, a vector of peace between people. As seen in the faces of these orators united by debate, they happily savor the delights of rhetoric.

B - The Prohibition of Denialism and Revisionism

There are historical events, such as the Holocaust and many others, that the orator will never question. In Belgium and Europe, this is considered a serious offense because the orator is, above all, a man of honor. It is his duty to present history, especially the serious events that occurred in it. Denialism is the denial of historical facts, despite the presence of overwhelming evidence reported by historians, and is done for racist and political purposes. Revisionism, on the other hand, is when an orator seeks to reinterpret or reframe facts in line with objective data without making real selections.

The European Court of Human Rights ruled on a case of denialism and revisionism in the case: *M'bala M'bala v. France*. In this case, Dieudonné M'bala M'bala, an engaged comedian, had been convicted for public insult against a person or group of people based on their origin or membership in a specific ethnic, national, racial, or religious group, in this case, people of Jewish origin or faith. At the end of a performance given at the Zénith theater in Paris in 2008, the defendant invited Robert Faurisson—a scholar repeatedly convicted in France due to his denialist and revisionist theses[415], which involved denying the existence of gas chambers in concentration camps—to join him on stage to receive the applause of the audience and be awarded the "Unapproachable and Insolent" prize. This prize, symbolized by a three-branched candelabrum topped with three apples, was presented to him by an extra dressed in striped pajamas with a yellow star sewn onto it that read "Jew," qualifying him as a representation of a deportee from the concentration camps.

The European Court of Human Rights declared the application inadmissible before any substantive debate. It ruled that the applicant could not benefit from the protection of Article 10 (freedom of expression) of the Convention. The Court considered that during the contested passage, the evening had lost its character as an entertainment show and had become a meeting that, under the guise of a humorous performance, promoted denialism due to the central role given to Robert Faurisson's intervention, and the humiliating positioning of the Jewish victims of deportation, in contrast to the person who denied their extermination. In the Court's view, this was not a show, even if satirical or provocative, that would fall under the protection of Article 10 of the Convention; but, in reality, in the circumstances of this case, it was a demonstration of hate and anti-Semitism, as well as a denial of the Holocaust. Disguised as an artistic production, it was as dangerous as a direct and abrupt attack, while representing the expression of an ideology that goes against the values of the Convention. However, the Court considered that in this case: "the applicant had attempted to distort Article 10 from its intended purpose by using his right to freedom of expression for purposes contrary to the text and spirit of the Convention, and which, if accepted, would contribute to the destruction of the rights and freedoms guaranteed by the Convention."[416]

In light of this precedent, it is clear that the orator, at all times, must exercise caution, regardless of the context of his speech. There are events in history that cannot be denied or simply questioned in a speech, as doing so would indirectly manifest hatred against a community. The orator must always rise above the fray. Denialist and revisionist theses should be completely eradicated from speeches. They do not respect history, and they contribute to hatred and discrimination against a community: the Jewish community that lived through these atrocities.

These theses can in no way benefit from the protection of Article 10 of the European Convention on Human Rights; they are, in fact, hate speech, which is not protected, creating tensions and acute social unrest, as revealed in the case *M'bala M'bala v. France*. However, the orator is a man of knowledge, a social pacifier, a republican who, through his speech, positively influences his society, without suffocating or asphyxiating it with hate speech tinged with anti-Semitism.

II - The State of The Rule of Law On Speech

Various legal frameworks have addressed the issue of hate speech in recent years. Hate orators have caused too much harm to humanity. They have triggered wars, genocides, and tribal and community tensions. In such a context, the law cannot remain indifferent, especially since it is called to adapt to the evolution of society, to its problems, and its deepest flaws.

Each time an orator delivers a speech, the law will be nearby to remind him that, although he is an ambassador of freedom of speech, it indeed has its limits. The orator will never use his right to freedom of expression for purposes contrary to the texts and spirit of the laws. The orator will refrain from using words of hatred in his speech which could lead to real hate crimes, which have caused so many victims in the past.

Canadian law seems quite generous in terms of relevant provisions aimed at combating hate speakers and hate speech. Whether it is the Criminal Code, the Canadian Human Rights Act, or provincial laws, there is a clear unanimity that hate speech has no place and should be fought with all necessary rigor. This is almost the same stance noted in international law, where hate speech is combated by force. This is what some provisions of the International Covenant on Civil and Political Rights[417] reveal, as well as the International Convention on the Elimination of All Forms of Racial Discrimination. In some countries, the rhetoric of hate is experiencing a rapid and worrying rise.

It is hate that inspires certain orators who engage in speeches capable of hindering national cohesion and the stability of the state. This is why many countries have either passed and enacted special laws against hate speech or adapted their internal legal frameworks to include anti-hate speech provisions, as Cameroon and South Africa have done.[418] The national and international legislations highlighted here are for informational purposes. It would be wise for every orator, beyond the international law ratified by their country, to review their country's relevant positive law on the issue of hate speech, because after all, "No one is supposed to ignore the law."

Generally speaking, the laws of various countries are extremely strict regarding the handling of hate speech. This situation, of course, aims to make rhetoric a vehicle for development, not an acute social problem.

There is no doubt that the orator who steps onto the podium to deliver a speech has a historical responsibility: that of revolutionizing his society in a democratic and republican spirit, highlighting values close to the letter and spirit of the laws. He must understand the limits of his rhetoric and the potential legal consequences that could arise if he ultimately engages in an escalation of verbal violence, which recalls the less glorious moments of human history. It would be appropriate for the orator, this magician of words, to be made aware of what various legal frameworks provide concerning hate speech, so that he can act or adjust accordingly, for a world that is even brighter and spared from hate speech and its disastrous consequences.

Thus, on one hand, we will lift the veil on Canadian law and hate speech (A). On the other hand, we will examine some articles of international law concerning hate speech (B). Finally, we will analyze the provisions of Cameroonian and South African law on hate speech (C).

A - Canadian Law and Hate Speech

Canadian law appears to be quite generous in terms of relevant provisions aimed at fighting hate speech, as can be noted through its Criminal Code, the Canadian Human Rights Act, and its numerous provincial laws on the matter.

The Criminal Code of Canada, in section 319, states: "(1) Everyone who, by communicating statements in a public place, incites hatred against an identifiable group, where such incitement is likely to lead to a breach of the peace, is guilty: a) either of a criminal act and liable to imprisonment for up to two years; b) or of an offense

241

punishable on summary conviction..." The orator must therefore not incite hatred against an identifiable group. He must avoid any form of expression in his speech that incites, promotes, or justifies racial hatred, xenophobia, anti-Semitism, or other forms of hatred based on intolerance, including intolerance expressed in the form of aggressive nationalism and ethnocentrism, discrimination, and hostility towards minorities, immigrants, and people of immigrant origin.[419]

But above all, the orator should know the sanctions that apply to him under the Criminal Code in case of violation of Section 319. Through this article, the legislator seeks to encourage communications and statements that are more grounded in tolerance and multiculturalism, which are sacred Canadian values that should inspire the orator. The purpose of rhetoric is to serve society, to contribute to revolutionizing society in various dimensions; it is supposed to serve social development, as demonstrated by Cicero in the past, through his social and community engagement. The orator who resorts to hate rhetoric is a pseudo-orator, useless to society. He naturally falls under the influence of Section 319 of the Criminal Code.

It's almost the same reasoning found in Articles 12 and 13 of the Canadian Human Rights Act. The Supreme Court of Canada, in the case *Canadian Human Rights Commission v. Taylor*, outlines the content of these provisions while explaining why we should fight against hate speech in Canadian society, adorned with the bright rays of the rule of law and democracy: "... hate propaganda presents a serious threat to society." It harms the dignity and self-esteem of the members of the target group and, more generally, contributes to sowing discord between different racial, cultural, and religious groups, thereby undermining the tolerance and open-mindedness that should flourish in a multicultural society dedicated to achieving equality... Since its inception, rhetoric has never aimed to sow discord between groups in society; it is a revolutionary tool, and the orator is a peacemaker and unifier. Hate speech is not a speech that rhetoric itself can exalt; it is a colorless, odorless, and tasteless speech, a speech that presents itself by opposing the noble values of tolerance and multiculturalism highlighted by the highly intelligent judges of the Supreme Court of Canada in the aforementioned case. The pedagogical value of this case law is likely to inspire many orators and hinder pseudo-orators whose only credo and argument is hate speech.

The orator will thus make a methodical use of the art of oratory to fight for just causes, to inspire peace and harmony when cacophony reigns. He is a social actor who uses oratorical seduction as a tool to awaken consciences and bring about the necessary revolutions.

When social justice is threatened, rhetoric is called upon. When social peace is disturbed, the art of oratory must restore it in order to facilitate greater cohesion in society and a march towards democratic ideals. The speech by Barack Obama during the fiftieth anniversary of the Selma march is a living example.[420] In an America marked by police brutality and racism, President Obama denounces a festering wound that shames democracy and the ideals held by the founding fathers. He suggests instead the advent of a society in which diversity is valued, fundamental rights are revered, a society in which young and old, rich and poor, Democrats and Republicans, Black and White, Hispanics, Asians, and Native Americans[421] will smoke the peace pipe for an America that is even stronger, even more united. In an upward tone, President Obama – in this speech at Selma – declares: "We will make a mistake if we suggest that racism has been banished, that the work undertaken by the men and women of Selma is finished, and that the racial tensions that persist are the result of those who use race for their own purposes [...]

We must open our eyes, our ears, and our hearts to see that this racial history still casts its shadow today. We know that this march is

243

not over."[422] In the image and likeness of orator Obama, our revolutionary orator should fight for social justice when it is despised, and advocate for peace when it is threatened. This is also what it means to be a revolutionary orator, in the image of Barack Obama.

The law of the Canadian provinces and territories is broad in provisions that condemn hate speech and discrimination. This is the case with the Quebec Charter of Human Rights and Freedoms[423], the *Saskatchewan Human Rights Code*[424], particularly in Section 14, and the *British Columbia Civil Rights Protection Act*[425], particularly in Section 1.[426] These various provisions aim to spare society from the scourge of hate speech. They ultimately aim to give more space to speeches capable of leading society toward its glorious destiny.

B - International Law and Hate Speech

Various international legal instruments address the issue of hate speech. These pacts, treaties, and conventions have been ratified by numerous states and thus incorporated into domestic legal systems. Ratification gives a litigant the right to invoke the international text before common law courts. A victim of hate speech or hate crimes could therefore plead an international text ratified by their country, addressing the issue of hate speech before ordinary courts.

The International Covenant on Civil and Political Rights, ratified by the majority of states, states in Article 20: "1. Any propaganda for war shall be prohibited by law. 2. Any advocacy of national, racial, or religious hatred that constitutes incitement to discrimination, hostility, or violence shall be prohibited by law." Paragraph 1 formally prohibits war propaganda. The international community still remembers the painful and disastrous trials of World War I and II. It also remembers the liberation wars in Africa and the multitude of deaths that were caused. This justifies the adoption of preventive measures to spare humanity from the scourge of war: the orator has a historical responsibility in this regard.

Wartime rhetoric should have no place in speech. The orator must at all times advocate for peace and, when it is threatened, must promote dialogue, mediation, and even conciliation between nations. In paragraph 2, Article 20 prohibits calls to hatred or incitement to discrimination. This is a clear warning to any orator who makes incitement to hatred the foundation of their argument. The Covenant on Civil and Political Rights clearly tells us that the freedom of speech enshrined in various human rights texts has a limit. This limit is wartime rhetoric, and this limit is also, and especially, hate speech, which does not deserve to be protected but should be sanctioned with the utmost force.

The International Convention on the Elimination of All Forms of Racial Discrimination, ratified by the majority of states[427], states in Article 4:

"The States Parties condemn all propaganda and organizations that are inspired by ideas or theories based on the superiority of one race or group of people of a certain color or ethnic origin, or that claim to justify or encourage any form of racial hatred and discrimination..." This is the same spirit as Article 20 of the International Covenant on Civil and Political Rights, which can be seen in Article 4: the prohibition of hate speech in all its forms. Instead, rhetoric should be used to achieve progress in social peace and cohesion between communities.

Rhetoric, we cannot say it enough, embodies a certain dignity, a certain elegance, a certain nobility. The revolutionary orator we envision will not engage in war propaganda, much less in the propaganda of hate speech. He is a committed citizen who fights his battles on the high plateaus of dignity and discipline.[428]

In an America deeply marked by racial discrimination, the Reverend Martin Luther King, the distinguished orator of his time, engaged in the fight for civil rights through speeches widely listened to by the American public. In a context of the most flagrant social injustice, the eminent orator declared in a very committed rhetoric: "... The time has now come to realize the promises of democracy; the time has come to emerge from the dark and desolate valleys of segregation and walk the sunny path of racial justice; the time has come to lift our nation from the quicksands of racial injustice and place it on the solid rock of brotherhood; the time has come to realize justice for all of God's children[429]..." Orator King, in a situation of social tension, favors a democratic, fraternal, and legal approach that would allow his nation to experience the long-awaited spring of freedom and equality in the United States, deeply marked by racism in the 1960s.

A rhetoric of hate in such a socially tense climate would have plunged the country into one of the bloodiest civil wars in U.S. history. Our revolutionary orator has used the beauty of oratory in the service of truth, in the service of democratic institutions, and in the service of racial and social justice. This is especially true because, in his speech, he calls on his people to uphold dignity in the battle against their adversaries: "But there is one thing I must say to my people, standing on the welcoming threshold that leads to the palace of justice: in securing our rightful place, let us not become guilty of reprehensible actions. Let us not seek to quench our thirst for freedom by drinking from the cup of bitterness and hatred. Let us always fight our battles on the high plateaus of dignity and discipline. Our creative claim must not degenerate into physical violence. Again and again, we must stand on the majestic heights where we will oppose the forces of the soul to material force..."[430]

It is clear from this excerpt that Orator King embodies the values of dignity, discipline, tolerance, and coexistence; in short, noble and wise values that make rhetoric and orators key actors in social development. Our revolutionary orator will draw inspiration from Martin Luther King, from his beautiful anaphora and his art of using the beauty of oratory to serve noble causes. Thus, we could have a society in which the law is no longer simply a truth on this side of the Pyrenees and a mistake beyond, but also a society that sanctifies and glorifies oratory for its beauty and social utility. Using the beauty of rhetoric to defend highly noble causes seems to be the primary mission of the revolutionary orator. The art of oratory should in no way stray from the republican and democratic spirit, from the letter and spirit of international laws.

C - National Legislations and Hate Speech

In order to address the steep rise of hate speech and orators who, through their interventions, stir up community and identity tensions, Cameroon's national legislature has amended the Penal Code to include provisions against hate speech[431]. Law 2019/020 of December 24, 2019, amending and supplementing certain provisions of Law 2016/007 of July 12, 2016, which governs the Penal Code, was thus passed following the promulgation by the President of the Republic, allowing the Penal Code to be adapted to the realities of the time. Following a highly contested election, the escalation of verbal violence had become the favorite sport of many Cameroonians.

Article 241 – (new) reads: "Outrage against races and religions. (1) Anyone who commits an outrage, as defined in Article 152 of this code, against a race or religion to which one or more citizens or residents belong, is punishable by imprisonment for six days to six months and a fine ranging from five thousand to five hundred thousand francs." The legislator seeks, through such a provision, to protect religious communities coexisting in the country. In this context, the orator will always ensure that his speech aligns with the letter and spirit of the laws. Article 241-1 (new) deals with insults against tribes or ethnic groups. Severe sanctions are reserved for offenders. In such a diverse country, built around more than 250 ethnic groups, it is necessary for the orator to exercise caution when delivering his speech. Values such as tolerance, multiculturalism, and coexistence should always be praised, to foster the emergence of a highly favorable social climate.

South Africa, for its part, after years of policy based on hatred, has finally developed one of the most modern texts regarding the repression and prevention of hate speech. In its *Prevention and Combating of Hate Crime and Hate Speech Bill*, South Africa expands the cases of hate speech. Reading Article 3 allows us to understand that any speech aiming to discriminate against a person due to albinism, disability, HIV, can be classified as hate speech, beyond the other generally accepted criteria. Heavy sanctions are provided, ranging from imprisonment to hefty fines.

The orator, as demonstrated by Cicero, should be useful to society through his revolutionary and unifying speeches, but especially through his social and community engagement, aligning words with action. He will not discriminate, will respect the law, and uphold the values of the Republic. He will always be at the service of the nation, helping to write the most beautiful pages in the history of his country.

In a South Africa that endured the odious system of apartheid for centuries, in a multi-ethnic Cameroon that has known the most extreme community tensions, oratory can still provide solutions for the process of a peaceful revolution. Orators will favor a rhetoric of tolerance and peace that avoids adding fuel to the fire, creating further escalation of the situation. As Nelson Mandela, the orator of orators in Africa, demonstrated despite over twenty-five years of imprisonment under apartheid, when his fellow countrymen and comrades in the African National Congress called for revenge and armed resistance, our orator Mandela, in revolutionary and peaceful rhetoric, urged his comrades to favor peaceful options, including believing in the imminent democracy in the country, materialized by the forthcoming first free elections. Mandela always advocated for peace and love for his fellow citizens, as shown in this excerpt:

"Nobody is born hating another person because of the color of their skin,[432] or their background, or their religion. People must learn to hate. And if they can learn to hate, they can be taught to love, for love comes more naturally to the human heart than its opposite." Through his speeches and actions, Mandela provides one of the brightest examples of what a revolutionary orator should be, a charismatic leader: he is at the service of democracy, the republic, and the ideal of justice. He is a man of speech, certainly, but also a man of action, a role model for the rising generation. In this context, Mandela used his rhetorical skills to spare his country, South Africa, from bloodshed by making democracy triumph through peaceful maneuvers. This is what our revolutionary orator should be.

The Law Holds the Orator Accountable

Despite the multiple rhetorical tricks he masters to always be right against his opponent, the distinguished orator must still observe certain basic ethical rules in order to give more credibility to his speech and even to his own person. The ethics of speech consist, among other things, in making statements that can be proven during a debate in which the strength of arguments takes precedence. The ethics of speech also involve the orator's ability to avoid plagiarism in an intervention, so that one can easily distinguish the arguments he presents and the authorities he invokes to support those arguments. By nature, the orator embodies the values of high society; he is a distinguished person who, through the mechanisms of speech, seeks to etch his name in golden letters in the history of his society. This highly commendable aim cannot be achieved if the man of words does not make ethics a sacred rule in his approach to various platforms in order to convince his audience of the legitimacy or illegitimacy of a cause. Thus, the rhetoric embodied by the orator proves to be the most expressive form of freedom of speech.

According to a certain belief, at the beginning of the world was the word, and the word was made real. Speaking is undoubtedly one of the great privileges of life. Words can build a truly marvelous world, much like Alice's wonderland. In the same way, words can also incite wars, genocides, community and ethnic tensions; they can destroy the world. It is in this spirit that the griots, in ancient Africa, considered speech sacred, believing that not all words should be spoken. And to demonstrate the sacred nature of speech, before speaking, a tradition would have him say: "Let what is said be said, and let what is silent remain silent." The orator must know how to hold his tongue and avoid rhetoric that could inflame his society. It is a historical responsibility to be able to deliver a speech. A speech can both build and destroy, which is why it is urgent to respect the law that applies to speeches. This law formally prohibits hate speech, which appears as a real social cancer, overturning the foundations of society at lightning speed. World War I, World War II, the Rwandan genocide, the Armenian genocide, the Holocaust, community tensions in Africa and Latin America were caused by the rhetoric of hate, war rhetoric, and hate speech.

Since Cicero, the art of oratory has never aimed to destroy society, but to improve it for an even brighter future. The orator is a pacifier, a man of honor who should embody the values of multiculturalism, tolerance, coexistence, and community engagement. He is a revolutionary embodying republican values, with the ultimate goal of putting rhetoric at the service of democracy and the integral development of his society. So many people have lost their lives because of hate speech, so much blood has been shed due to war rhetoric, so many rights have been trampled because individuals thought that hate speech was a rhetorical weapon. The orator we envision should work to spare the world of tomorrow from the scourge of war, genocide, and the rhetoric of hate.

Therefore, any orator who encourages or delivers hate speeches at the expense of the weight of ideas and the power of arguments is a pseudo-orator, useless to society. He will answer for his actions before the competent judicial authorities. The world's states have adopted quite severe laws aimed at sanctioning those who deliver hate speeches. Positive international law is quite generous with relevant provisions that rigorously condemn hate speech. International courts, particularly the European Court of Human Rights and the International Criminal Court, have produced abundant case law condemning the rhetoric of hate in all its forms. It is therefore up to the contemporary orator, depending on his country and continent, to seek the relevant laws and case law that may apply to him if ever he falls under the scope of the law.

The goal of such curiosity is not only to ensure eventual defense but also to prevent the occurrence of inappropriate words or expressions in a speech and to ensure that these speeches and actions align with the noble missions of rhetoric: to promote social emergence! Otherwise, one is not an orator, but a propagator of hate! An attitude that naturally falls under the scope of the law. The distinguished orator must, at all times, demonstrate wisdom. Such wisdom would be likely to spare his speeches from a hateful rhetoric that is essentially harmful to society. And, as Cicero already acknowledged: "Eloquence without wisdom is often too disastrous, and can never be useful. Therefore, the man who, forgetting wisdom and duty, strays from the paths of honor and virtue to give all his attention to the study of eloquence, can only be a citizen useless to himself and dangerous to his country[433]."

CONCLUSION

Rhetoric, in essence, is of crucial importance for the construction of societies. The recent and distant history of humanity shows us that rhetoric has founded cities, ended wars, and resolved community tensions. It has been the origin of peace treaties and armistices that spared humanity from extremely grave humanitarian catastrophes.

When the orator, with mastery, manages to place all the beauty and splendor of the art of oratory at the service of noble and honorable causes, he simultaneously sparks a revolution that will be written in golden letters in the memories of both present and future generations. There are speeches that have changed the course of history while leaving a mark on individual and collective consciousness. We will always remember General de Gaulle's "Je vous ai compris," Kennedy's *"Ich bin ein Berliner,"* Martin Luther King Jr.'s *"I have a dream,"* or Patrice Lumumba's "Congolais" during the proclamation of his country's independence. Thus, rhetoric would be at the service of wisdom. Rhetoric that distances itself from wisdom and its noble values would simply be superfluous and of little use for "revolutions." The distinguished orator will never stray from the "paths of honor" and the sense of duty; otherwise, he would be dangerous for his country[434].

A well-mastered rhetoric allows one to revolutionize, in a progressive direction, his homeland. As we have seen in the cities of Athens and Rome, as we have seen during the great enlightening revolutions that have marked the history of the Americas, Europe, Africa, Asia, and Australia. The art of oratory has always been at the beginning and at the end of various revolutionary movements. It is therefore evident that it is called to play a major role in the future of peoples, individuals, and states in the contemporary world. However, it is necessary for the orator to master, in the smallest details, the missions of rhetoric, which are: to prove, to please, and to move

(*Docere, delectare, movere*) in a plea, in a political speech, or even in commercial negotiations.[435] Above all, the orator is a pedagogue, who will teach new things through his speech. He can only fulfill this pedagogical mission, recognized by ancient rhetoric, if he adopts a scientific reasoning mode that allows the truth to triumph logically, naturally.

Our revolutionary orator must possess the qualities of a researcher. Thus, he will know how to find arguments or how to uncover them; he will distinguish commonplaces from proper places. The distinguished orator cannot do without high strategy: once the relevant arguments are found, he will show discernment and method in the process of choosing arrangement, but especially in the disposition of the said arguments, which will serve to plead his case with the greatest objectivity. Mastery of logos allows the orator to convince his audience by speaking to their mind, to their reason, to demonstrate the validity of the change he wishes to bring about in the city. Next, our revolutionary orator will primarily present himself as a charmer, an exceptional "player." His elocution and oratorical action will caress his audience in the right way, with the goal of subtly making the cause he defends resonate favorably with them. Finally, through decorative figures of speech and the amplification of the discourse, through various rhetorical devices, our orator will succeed in delivering a speech that will directly touch the hearts of the listeners.

This incitement of passions and emotions aims to move the audience, in the hope of achieving victory, in the hope of seeing the cause that is defended so vigorously triumph while implementing the desired changes. Structured parliamentary debate has emerged in recent years as the contemporary form of learning the art of oratory. It is essential to know how each system works in theory, but especially in practice. Mastery of various systems, including French, British, Canadian, or American, would help develop various aspects of rhetoric and strive for oratorical improvement. The world in which we live has been marked by various identity conflicts. As a man of honor, the orator should be aware of the legal and ethical issues of speech because it is crucial to spare rhetoric from an unease that devalues it: hate speech, disregard for the basic rules of the ethics of speech. Such an attitude would destroy the unity of the city, just as hail destroys a flower. This attitude would spare the city from the disasters that occur when it experiences its most flourishing moments.

At the dawn of the year 2000, there was a revival of rhetoric in the world, which seems to be gradually regaining its nobility. More and more, individuals and institutions realize that the art of oratory is the cornerstone of social ascension, the construction, and even the consolidation of the rule of law and democracy. The world of high finance and business is increasingly interested in it for the added value that rhetoric can bring, not only to businesses but also to the development of trade.

Eloquence and pleading competitions are no longer the monopoly of law students at the Sorbonne and elsewhere around the world. Since 2012, the University of Paris-Sorbonne has offered a training course called *Fleurs d'éloquence*, which culminates in a competition. Political science institutes, business and engineering schools have developed similar approaches; debate societies are emerging in faculties like mushrooms, and they participate in numerous eloquence competitions.[436] The practice of eloquence is clearly a way for students to highlight their skills, demonstrating to recruiters that a candidate is determined and ready to face any challenge. The social and professional integration of a young person usually begins with an interview: either for a job or for entrance into a prestigious school. Therefore, mastering the art of oratory allows any candidate to demonstrate what they are capable of. Although the candidate may be specialized and focused on technical skills, these highly commendable skills would not be known if they did not master the art of speech, according to Camille Wallecan.[437]

This is why, regardless of the field or specialization of the citizen, it is everyone's responsibility to attend the school of rhetoric, as it allows one to benefit, in a free and democratic society, from equal opportunities.[438] Rhetoric is part of the official curriculum of many American and Asian universities, a situation that suggests we are witnessing a gradual resurrection of an art that has made the greatness of great nations and democracies. This is all the more true as a recent decision by the French government has reintroduced the oral exam in the French Baccalaureate starting in 2021. It is a real moment of glory for rhetoric, which certainly, we hope, will soon reintegrate formal education in this country, deeply marked by the Age of Enlightenment and its revolutionary ideas. In Africa, in recent years, oratory and debate societies have been training young people, oratory schools for professionals and politicians have emerged, but rhetoric is still not widely popularized.

At the invitation of Africa3535 in Côte d'Ivoire, while receiving a youth award for advocacy and civil society, I spoke at the French Cultural Center in Abidjan in front of entrepreneurs and civil society actors. On this occasion, we recognized that oratory is an essential skill for business development. A good mastery of rhetoric would allow one to succeed in business negotiations, marketing, advertising, or even conquering new markets. Beyond everything, oratory develops leadership skills in the entrepreneur or businessman, which we consider essential to ensure the success of a respected company. On a different level, in Africa, historically marked by community tensions, wars, genocides, corruption, and social injustices of all kinds, I demonstrated how mastering rhetoric could help build an Africa spared from the scourge of hate speech. I shared the dream of seeing a more peaceful Africa, with Africans walking hand in hand to build a promising future, thanks to the practice of oratory, which installs the critical spirit necessary for the flourishing of republican and democratic values carried by rhetoric. As we have mentioned, rhetoric is a noble art that brings with it noble values such as multiculturalism, tolerance, coexistence, social justice, forgiveness, reconciliation, as well as a sense of public service, civic duty, and community engagement. We were able to conclude with the actors of African civil society that it is indeed possible to heal one's ills with words[439], but also with concrete actions that take into account a number of commendable values. In this movement, I recall that during my engagement with the American advocacy foundation ONE, I noted how the strength of convictions and social commitment could influence decisions from high institutions on international development issues, including the fight against preventable diseases, corruption, major financial crimes, the promotion of good environmental governance, equality before the law, and equal opportunities for all in a free and democratic society. We have always been driven by the desire to see our values and convictions bloom through concrete actions and thus bring about the necessary social change. This sense of social responsibility stems from the methodical practice of rhetoric, which reveals our mission while enabling us to see how to accomplish it. The orator is therefore an agent of change who, driven by convictions, is ready to make the necessary sacrifices to lead the revolutions imposed by the social and economic realities of his time.

It thus becomes crucial, given that rhetoric is noble and does not stray from the "paths of honor" or virtue or wisdom, to democratize it, to ensure that everyone has access to oratory for equal opportunities in society, to make rhetoric more widespread in order to train the young leaders who will lead tomorrow's revolutions. But above all, may rhetoric be rehabilitated by reintegrating it into the formal curriculum, from primary and secondary school to university or prestigious schools such as law schools, political science institutes, engineering or business schools. Such options would guarantee the emergence of a society characterized by the consolidation of democracy, republican values, and the rule of law. A society where the clash of ideas regularly takes place without being judged based on other considerations, but solely on the weight of ideas and the strength of arguments. A society with more equality, social justice, and ethics in business. A society where it is a pleasure to congratulate an ideological or political opponent when their ideas triumph over ours. A society in which, in an atmosphere of conviviality, the fragrance of words rises above the fray.

ACKNOWLEDGMENTS

To Gabriel Meunier, Sabrina Fauteux, Yrech Chery, Isabelle Jallifier-Verne, Marianne Amar, Patrice César, Olivier Coulombe, Élisabeth Arsenault, Eugène Aferin, Simplice Zombre, Marius Binyou, Ernest Folefack, Marie-Hélène Haché, Sylvie Bollini, Amanda Carrasco, Christian Charlot, Évariste Manene, Nathan FW, Tracy Ntumba Busanga Munyoka, the debate team at the University of Montreal, the International Youth Offices of Quebec.

And to Nadine Yanmo, Hilaire Pierre Lekeufack, Anatole Mendou, Sabine Mendou, Polycarpe Nawessi, Claude Gilles Djoumessi, Andrée Ngongang, Jean Yemene Kenne, Jean-Marie Mekontchou, Francois Nokam, Ariane, Euloge Pascale, Boniface, Sorel, and Crysologue Mendou.

INDEX OF PLATES

BIBLIOGRAPHY:

Books

1. Ahmadou Kourouma. *Soleil des indépendances*, Presses de l'Université de Montréal, 1968.

2. Alessandro Traversi. *La défense pénale, Techniques de l'argumentation et de l'art oratoire*, Éditions Bruylant.

3. André Lalande. *Vocabulaire technique et critique de la philosophie*, PUF.

4. Aristotle. *Organon, Topiques*, Paris, Éditions Les Belles Lettres.

5. Aristotle. *Rhétorique*, Le Livre de Poche, collection "Classiques de la philosophie."

6. Arthur Schopenhauer. *L'art d'avoir toujours raison*, Éditions Mille et Une Nuits.

7. Bertrand Perrier. *La parole est un sport de combat*, Éditions JC Lattès.

8. C. Perelman. *L'empire rhétorique, rhétorique et argumentation*, Éditions Vrin, 1997.

9. Christophe Boutin. *Les grands discours du XXe siècle*, Éditions Flammarion.

10. Cicero. *De l'invention oratoire*, Ancient Rome, 84/83 BC.

11. Cicero. *L'orateur idéal / orator ad Brutum*, Ancient Rome, 46 BC.

12. Cicero. *Les Catilinaires*, Ancient Rome, 63 BC.

13. Cicero. *Pro-Caelio*, Ancient Rome, 56 BC.

14. Cicero. Rhétorique à Hérennuis, Ancient Rome, 86/82 BC.

15. Cicero. Trois dialogues à propos de l'orateur, Ancient Rome, 55 BC.

16. C. Perelman and Lucie Olbrechts-Tyteca. Traité de l'argumentation, la nouvelle rhétorique, Editions de l'Université de Bruxelles.

17. Demosthenes. L'orateur de la liberté, Editions de l'Épervier.

18. Frantz Fanon. Les damnées de la terre, Editions François Maspero, 1961.

19. Grégoire Schmitzberger and Arnaud Sorosina. Les pouvoirs de la parole, Editions Flammarion.

20. Hélène Tronc. L'art du discours, Editions Gallimard.

21. Jacques Amyot. Projet d'éloquence royal, Editions Les Belles Lettres.

22. James Gasser. La syllogistique d'Aristote à nos jours, University of Neuchâtel, 1987.

23. Jean-Louis Bergel. Méthodologie juridique, PUF.

24. John Locke. Traité du gouvernement civil, Editions Flammarion, 1690.

25. Kévin Labiausse. Les grands discours de l'histoire : de Moïse à George W. Bush, Editions J'ai Lu, 2016.

26. Council of Europe. Manual for Combating Hate Speech Online through Human Rights Education.

27. Marcien Towa. Essai sur la problématique philosophique dans l'Afrique actuelle, Editions Clé Yaoundé, 1971.

28. Montesquieu. De l'esprit des lois, FB Editions.

29. Nicolas Boileau. Art poétique, Hachette Livre.

30. Normand Ballargeon. Petit cours d'autodéfense intellectuelle, Lux Éditeur, 2005.

31. Plato. Apologie de Socrate, Le Livre de Poche.

32. Quintilian. Institutions oratoires, Paris, Éditions Les Belles Lettres.

33. Saint-Exupéry. Terre des hommes, Éditions Gallimard.

34. Stephen E. Lucas. The Art of Public Speaking, Tenth Edition.

35. Trudy Govier. A Practical Study of Argument, Seventh Edition.

THESES AND ARTICLES

1. Boumediene Abed. L'oralité dans la culture traditionnelle africaine, 2014.

2. Commission des droits de la personne et des droits de la jeunesse du Québec. L'incitation à la discrimination ou à la haine, texts compiled by Me Pierre Bosset, legal advisor.

3. European Court of Human Rights. Jurisprudence on hate speech.

4. Le Monde. "L'oral fait sa grande entrée au baccalauréat," February 2020.

5. Les Echos Start. "L'éloquence, une compétence qui fait la différence dans la vie pro."

6. Marius Yannick Binyou-Bi-Homb. Pratique orale et média culture en Afrique contemporaine, Master's thesis presented at the Senghor University of Alexandria.

7. Maxime Bélanger. La rhétorique des passions : le problème du pathos, Master's thesis in philosophy from Laval University.

8. Mélanie Samson and Marianne Perreault. Le raisonnement par analogie, l'argument à pari, Faculty of Law, Laval University, Louis-Philippe-Pigeon Chair of Legal Writing.

9. More Dieye. L'oralité en Afrique, 2012.

10. Par analogie, l'argument à pari, Faculty of Law, Laval University, Louis-Philippe-Pigeon Chair of Legal Writing.

11. Patrick Charraudeau. Pathos et discours politique.

12. Philippe Lemay. Guide du juge, Canadian University Society of Intercollegiate Debate.

13. French Debate Society, University of Ottawa. La cristallisation : l'importance de la synthèse, 2011.

14. French Debate Society, University of Ottawa. La structure : la base d'un discours clair et précis, 2011.

15. French Debate Society, University of Ottawa. Les rôles du débat parlementaire canadien : structure et astuce, 2011.

16. French Debate Society, University of Ottawa. Un bon argument, un bon titre, 2011.

17. French Debate Society, University of Ottawa. Un argument est plus qu'un énoncé, 2011.

18. 12. Société étudiante de débat français de l'Université

19. d'Ottawa : http://sedfuo.blogspot.com

TV5 Monde Afrique/animation : https://afrique.tv5monde. com/videos/animation/kassa-le-messager

FILMS ET DOCUMENTAIRES

1. Aequivox (Le chois des armes) : *Rhétoriques croisées : Hollande-Sarkozy*, 2012.
2. Conférence du stage (Barreau de Paris) : *Maître Denis AGBOTON-1er Prix d'Éloquence 1999 (Robert Badinter)*.
3. Denzel Washington. *Les grands débatteurs (The Great Debaters)*, 2007.
4. IESEG. *L'art oratoire du leader*, 2016.
5. Ladj Ly et Stéphane De Freitas. *À voix haute : La force de la parole*, 2017.
6. Le Club des juristes. *4e Nuit de l'éloquence*, 2014.
7. Lysias Paris-I. *Le procès de Socrate, plaidé par maîtres Bonnant et Trémolet de Villers*, 2016.
8. Lysias Paris-I. *Le procès des Fleurs du Mal par maître Bonnant, maître Périer et maître Schnerb*, 2013.
9. Métropole Rouen Normandie. *Concours d'éloquence 2017 : Fatima Aidara*.
10. Yvan Attal. *LE BRIO*, 2017.

[1] *Nicolas Waquet dans L'orateur idéal, p. 15.*

[2] *Cicéron, De l'invention oratoire, livre premier, p. 7.*

[3] *Grégoire Schmitzberger et Arnaud Sorosina, Les pouvoirs de la parole, Éditions Flammarion.*

[4] *Bene dicendi scientia.*

[5] *Laurent Pernot, La rhétorique dans l'Antiquité.*

[6] *Maître de la rhétorique.*

[7] *This Platonic criticism does not seem objective to us. It is motivated by political considerations. Plato, who never defended the democratic regime that inspires orators, naturally condemns rhetoric that is based on democracy. From a strictly personal point of view, Plato has a vendetta against rhetoric. In reality, it was during a trial that highlighted the pleaders that Socrates, his teacher, was condemned. It is a mistake to criticize a phenomenon for reasons other than objective ones.*

[8] *Laurent Pernot, Rhetoric in Antiquity, p. 68.*

[9] *Gorgias dans Les présocratiques, Bibliothèque de la Pléiade.*

[10] *Hélène Tronc, L'art du discours, Gallimard, p. 13.*

[11] *Ibid.*

[12] *Ibid., p. 8.*

[13] *Pericles, 5th century BC.*

[14] *Albert Camus was a French writer, playwright, essayist, and philosopher. He was also a journalist involved in the resistance and the moral struggles of the post-war period.*

[15] *Montesquieu, De l'esprit des lois, 1748.*

[16] *Hélène Tronc, L'art du discours, Gallimard, p. 97.*

[17] *Frantz Fanon, Les damnés de la terre, 1961 : « chaque génération doit, dans une relative opacité, affronter sa mission : la remplir ou la trahir ».*

[18] *Cicéron : « on naît poète, on devient orateur ».*

[19] *In Greek, speech, thought, reason; "it is the logical form of reasoning." See in this regard Grégoire Schmitzberger and Arnaud Sorosina, Les pouvoirs de la parole, p. 220.*

[20] *Laurent Pernot, La rhétorique dans l'Antiquité, p. 283.*

[21] *Cicero, The Orator, II, XXVII: "The rules of the art of oratory are based on these three principles of persuasion: proving the truth of what one asserts, gaining the goodwill of the listeners, and awakening in them all the emotions useful to the cause."*

[22] *Cicero, The Ideal Orator, p. 67."*

[23] *Cicéron, L'orateur idéal, p. 67.*

[24] *Vocabulaire technique et critique de la philosophie.*

[25] *Aristote, Organon : les topiques, liv. V, p. 1.*

[26] *Dictionnaire Larousse.*

[27] *Dictionnaire Larousse.*

[28] *Voir dans ce sens Techniques de l'argumentation et de l'art oratoire, p. 73.*

[29] *Trudy Govier (2007), A practical study of argument.*

[30] *Plausible" here means what is "rightfully considered true" (Robert).*

[31] *In his manual A Practical Study of Argument, on pages 128 to 135 of the 2010 edition, Govier proposes to orators a set of questions to ask themselves in order to verify the acceptability of a premise:"1: the premise is true! 2: Is the premise classically accepted by competent persons or institutions? 3: Is the premise the conclusion of a solid argument? 4: Is the premise stated by an authoritative source? 5: Has the premise been stated by a trustworthy witness?"*

[32] *"Some people live in solitude, which justifies that we can help them die." In this argument, the premise is true within the context of a debate on the social treatment of the issue. But does this necessarily mean that death should be given because of the existence of this problem? Would solitude justify euthanasia?*

[33] *According to Govier in A Practical Study of Argument: a set of premises solely based on emotions remains insufficient to justify a conclusion.*

[34] *Techniques of Argumentation and Oratory, 4th edition.*

[35] *See in this regard the indicators of strength adopted in the medieval period by the scholastics, especially the works of Thomas Aquinas.*

[36] *Definition from the Dictionary of Philosophy.*

[37] It was a method used by Socrates with his disciples. It aimed to "midwife" the minds by referencing his mother's profession, who was a midwife. Through progressive questioning, he led his disciples to discover the truth they already knew without realizing it.

[38] It is a method put forward by Socrates against the sophists. He gives the impression of asking lessons from the sophists, but leads them to contradict themselves while admitting their ignorance.

[39] James Gaser, La syllogistique d'Aristote à nos jours, June 1987, University of Neuchâtel (Switzerland).

[40] Maritain (1882-1973).

[41] Based on premises that are certainly true.

[42] Based on acceptable elements, not necessarily true.

[43] Based on opinion.

[44] This is Aristotle's move from the particular to the universal.

[45] Aristotle, Organon: The Topics.

[46] Alessandro Traversi, Techniques de l'argumentation et de l'art oratoire, p. 82.

[47] Dictionary of Politics.

[48] In this regard, E. Naville, The Logic of Hypothesis or Alessandro Traversi in Criminal Defense, p. 83.

[49] Apology of Socrates by Plato.

[50] Peirce, the American philosopher and founder of pragmatism and semiotics, defined abduction as a kind of: "suggestion that comes to us like a flash, an act of intimate clairvoyance, though extremely fallible."

[51] Machiavelli.

[52] Kant, Logic, chap. II.

[53] See in this regard, The Art of Always Being Right by Arthur Schopenhauer.

[54] Here, the orator extends the adversary's statement beyond its natural limits, giving it a very broad interpretation.

[55] Focuses exclusively against the opponent and not the subject of the debate.

[56] See in this regard, Socratic maieutics in Apology of Socrates.

[57] Example: "Is it true that you keep everything you haven't lost?"

"Yes."

"Have you lost a pair of horns?""

Well... no, not really."

"Then you are cuckolded." See Diogenes quoted by Alessandro Traversi in Techniques of Argumentation and the Art of Oratory.

[58] *The sophism of the false dilemma consists of arguing that we are faced with two possibilities, one of which is undesirable, and therefore the other must be chosen. However, other possibilities exist. Example: "Either we increase the fees related to the university, or we require high admission fees."*

[59] *Here, the orator moves from a judgment about one or a few particular cases to a general judgment without having analyzed all the cases or a representative sample. Example: "All men are the same."*

[60] *Through this sophism, the orator creates fear, whether by threatening to use force or other means, in order to assert a position. Instead of considering the subject being discussed and weighing the arguments presented, the discussion is shifted to the consequences of adopting such a position.*

[61] *Calling upon the crowd, as it is enough to appeal to its authority. It is obvious that the fact that everyone thinks so is not in itself an argument to conclude that it is right, true, or good.*

[62] *Latin expression meaning: "argument against the person."*

[63] *As the actual or potential listeners will tend to perceive the entire water in the well (the entirety of the arguments) as poisoned.*

[64] *We refer here to a certain context in human history, strongly marked by the Cold War, the division of the world into a communist camp and another, essentially capitalist.*

[65] *For more information, read: Petit cours d'autodéfense intellectuelle, Luxe, Montreal, 2005.*

[66] *Appeal to ignorance.*

[67] *Petit cours d'autodéfense intellectuelle.*

[68] *"It would have severely damaged the glory and divinity of the Pharaoh to write down the fact that Jewish slaves had eventually escaped Egypt or to keep the memory of it alive. That is why only the Bible speaks of it, and there is no other archaeological, historical, or other trace of this event."*

[69] *"Appeal to ignorance."*

[70] *See in this regard, Cicero in his book The Ideal Orator, an epistolary treatise composed at the request of the famous Brutus in 46 BC, which highlights the different elements of eloquence through the figure of an ideal orator.*

[71] *Bonald.*

[72] *Here, according to the manual L'art du discours, it refers to "the search for arguments that will advance the cause." This definition comes from rhetorical treatises, notably Rhetorica ad C. Herennium by Cicero.*

[73] *In the 17th century, René Descartes compared the philosopher to a tree, where the roots are metaphysics, the trunk is physics, and the branches are mechanics. It is this division of Descartes that inspires the scientific posture of the orator. A cultivated man, with diverse knowledge.*

[74] *That is, a specialist in the art of discussion who, as Aristotle said, draws deductions from uncertain opinions or, as Hegel put it, a specialist in affirming a thesis, negating the thesis, and then overcoming the contradiction.*

[75] *See in this regard, Diogenes Laertius, Lives of the Philosophers.*

[76] *See in this regard, Les grands discours du XXe siècle by Professor Christophe Boutin, page 5.*

[77] *Cicero, The Ideal Orator.*

[78] *See in this regard, Alessandro Traversi, Techniques of Argumentation and the Art of Oratory, p. 91*

[79] *According to Quintilian, the argumentative place is the seat where arguments should be stored and from which they should be drawn. In Institutio oratoria.*

[80] *In quibus latent argumenta.*

[81] *Quoted by Alessandro Traversi, in Criminal Defense, Techniques of Argumentation and the Art of Oratory.*

[82] *See in this regard Cicero, in his work De Inventione.*

[83] *Cicero, The Ideal Orator.*

[84] *See Techniques of Argumentation and the Art of Oratory, p. 94.*

[85] *For example, the orator will prove, in a clash of ideas where they are opposed, the opinion of a less famous expert's council, compared to the opinion of a well-established expert with a reputation attested by various authorities.*

[86] *Cicero, The Ideal Orator.*

[87] *The rule of precedent in law. Stare decisis. According to this rule, the solution to a dispute depends on previous decisions based on similar facts.*

[88] *"Based on the frequency with which a given phenomenon is verified and the expectation that this phenomenon will repeat itself under certain conditions." Alessandro Traversi, the criminal defense lawyer from Florence, demonstrates that the place of probability allows the orator to demonstrate the most probable cause in a similar case, based on the principle of probability.*

[89] *"It finds its reason for being in conviction," according to Alessandro Traversi.*

[90] *Also called locus a fictione, it is based on the premise that all reasoning is founded on premises that may be true or false. Such reasoning draws its logical conclusions from its premises. This is why, when a notable contradiction is found between a conclusion and its premise, one will naturally assume the opposite thesis to be true, based on the lack of foundation in the previous reasoning.*

[91] *Cicero, The Ideal Orator, p. 66.*

[92] *"Arguments ad persona," see in this regard Criminal Defense by Alessandro Traversi, p. 97.*

[93] *Quintilian in Institutio Oratoria, Book V, Chapter X, p. 24-30, established a list of multiple places from which the orator could draw this particular form of argument. He mentions, among others: patria (nationality), sexus (gender), habitus corporis (physical appearance), animi natura (character), studia (occupation), fortuna (economic conditions), ante acta dictaque (previous statements or actions). See also Techniques of Argumentation and the Art of Oratory by Alessandro Traversi, criminal law expert.*

[94] *Nicolas Boileau, Art Poétique, Chant 1, V -147-207.*

[95] *"In this temple of the United Nations, we are the guardians of an ideal, we are the guardians of a conscience. The heavy responsibility and immense honor that are ours must lead us to prioritize disarmament in peace."*

[96] *Kévin Labiausse, Les grands discours de l'histoire, de Moïse à George W. Bush, p. 89-90.*

[97] *"We have endured irony, insults, blows that we had to suffer morning, noon, and night, simply because we were black... We have seen our lands plundered in the name of so-called legal texts that only recognized the right of the stronger."*

[98] *Cicéron, L'orateur idéal.*

[99] *C. Perelman, in L'Empire rhétorique: rhétorique et argumentation, affirms:*
"The argument of authority primarily serves to support other arguments and... except when it comes to absolute authority... the conflict of authorities requires a discriminating criterion... Most often represented by competence."

[100] *This involves citing cases similar to those under discussion, with the aim of developing universal maxims.*

[101] *Also called ab absurdo sensu, "it consists of making manifest the violation of the principle mentioned in a system of propositions..."*

[102] *This category and technique is typical of judicial argumentation and rhetoric. Essentially based on a logical principle, it consists, according to the criminal defense manual, of verifying whether there is a coincidence between one concept and another. It involves comparing a fact with a general, abstract concept of wide normative and conventional scope.*

[103] *Jean-Louis Bergel, Méthodologie juridique, Paris, PUF, 2016, p. 263.*

[104] *Introduction générale au droit, 7th edition, Grenoble, Presse universitaire de Grenoble, 2008, p. 61. See also Mélanie Samson and Marianne Perreault: Le raisonnement par analogie, l'argument à pari, in the Louis-Philippe-Pigeon Chair of Legal Writing at the Faculty of Law, Laval University.*

[105] *Known as ductus simplex in the Middle Ages.*

[106] *For example, if a law specifies that the time minors take to shower is considered part of working time, à pari, the orator could demonstrate that the time artists spend applying and removing makeup should also be considered part of their working time.*

[107] *Cicero, De oratore, Book II, p. 172.*

[108] *Alessandro Traversi defines it as: "The argument that allows the extension of this treatment to situations that follow one another gradually, taking advantage of the partial identity relationships that connect the propositions and form the reasoning, as in the case of the sorites."*

[109] *Aristote, Rhétorique, livre II, chapitre 23.*

[110] *Voir dans ce sens, Techniques de l'argumentation et de l'art oratoire, p. 108.*

[111] *Matthieu, Évangile selon Matthieu, 6, versets 25-30 : "La vie n'est-elle pas plus que la nourriture, et le corps plus que le vêtement ! Regardez les oiseaux du ciel : ils ne sèment ni ne moissonnent, ils n'amassent rien dans des greniers, mais votre Père céleste les nourrit. Ne valez-vous pas plus qu'eux ! Pourquoi vous inquiéter aussi du vêtement ? Regardez les lis des champs, comment ils croissent : ils ne travaillent ni ne filent... Si Dieu habille ainsi l'herbe des champs, qui est aujourd'hui et qui demain sera jetée au feu, ne sera-t-elle pas beaucoup plus pour vous, gens de peu de foi !"*

[112] *Francophone Debate Federation*

[113] *Cicero, De Oratore, Book II, pp. 292-294: 'When speaking, I follow the method of sticking to favorable elements, embellishing and amplifying them, slowing them down and dwelling within them, attaching myself to them; as for disadvantageous and unfavorable elements, I move away from them, but not in such a way that it seems like I am fleeing from them. Rather, I make them go completely unnoticed... In short, the essence of the method is this: if I feel stronger in refuting the opponent than in supporting my own arguments, I direct my entire attack against my opponent; if it is easier for me to defend my thesis than to refute my opponent's, I do everything in my power to detach the listeners' minds from defending the opponent's position. I then address my own. And I admit that, if some argument presses too strongly against me, I have the habit of withdrawing, but in such a way that I give the impression not of fleeing after throwing down my shield or putting it behind my shoulders, but rather of making a retreat while speaking that resembles a battle (adhibere quandam in dicendo pugnae similem fugam).'"*

[114] *Quintilian, Institutio oratoria, Book VII, p. 3. Cited by Traversi.*

[115] *Quintilian, Institutio oratoria, Book VII, p. 1. See also La défense pénale, p. 118.*

[116] *Cicero, De oratore, Book II, p. 76.*

[117] *Cicero, The Ideal Orator.*

[118] *Quintilian, Institutio Oratoria.*

[119] *Cicero, De Oratore ad Quintum Fratrem, Book II, p. 321.*

[120] *"I do not want, my friends, to steal your hearts. I am not an orator like Brutus, I am, as you all know, just a rough and straightforward man, loving those who love me, and they know it well, those who gave me permission to speak*

about Caesar, for I do not have the mind, the courage, the speech, the gesture, or the accent, nor the eloquence that stirs the blood. I speak plainly, I tell you only what you know, I show you the wounds of my dear Caesar, poor mute mouths, and ask them to speak for me..."

[121] *See Hélène Tronc, L'art du discours, Gallimard, p. 50-51.*

[122] *Adrien Rivierre, L'homme est un conteur d'histoire, Éditions Marabout.*

[123] *Quintilien, Institutio Oratoria, Book IV.*

[124] *Alessandro Traversi, Techniques de l'argumentation et de l'art oratoire, Chapter VI.*

[125] *Quintilian, Institutio Oratoria, Book II.*

[126] *Aristote, Rhétorique, liv. III, chap. 17.*

[127] *Voir Hélène Tronc, L'art du discours, p. 156.*

[128] *Émile Zola, accused of defamation against the army, could not provide material evidence to demonstrate the innocence of Captain Dreyfus. However, he chose to end his speech by repeatedly stating, "Dreyfus is innocent." He emphasized his honor, his work, and his authority as a writer before the jury. Zola, as we can see, pulls out all the stops to tip the scales in his favor. The rhythmic figures, the anaphora, in short, the style, add power to this final stage of the speech before the jury. See in this regard: Hélène Tronc, The Art of Speech, p. 55.*

[129] *"I decided not to exceed a jar of water with my speech, so I don't intend to dwell on the details..." Hypereides, against Philippides, p. 13.*

[130] *See in this regard Hélène Tronc, L'art du discours, Gallimard, p. 55.*

[131] *Cicero, Pro Caelio, p. 79-80, cited by Alessandro Traversi in La défense pénale.*

[132] *C. Perelman, L'empire rhétorique: rhétorique et argumentation, Paris, Librairie philosophique J. Vrin, 1977, translated by Id. Botto and D. Gibelli, Il domino retorico. Retorica e argomentazione.*

[133] *In reference to the arrangement with which the Greek general Nestor, immortalized in The Iliad, arranged his troops.*

[134] *The secret, according to Quintilian, is to always keep the end of the speech in mind in order to guide and animate all parts of it.*

[135] *In memory of the arrangement with which the Greek general Nestor arranged his troops.*

[136] *See in this regard, Hélène Tronc, L'art du discours, Anthology collection, Gallimard Library, p. 106.*

[137] *See in this regard, Seneca in Epistolarum moralium ad Lucilius. Also see Traversi in La défense pénale, techniques de l'argumentation et de l'art oratoire, p. 131.*

[138] *Cicero, De Oratore ad Quintum Fratrem, Book I*

[139] *In Greek, it refers to everything determined by habit. "It designates the moral credibility of the orator and the trust they inspire, often depending on the proximity they manage to create and maintain with their audience." Grégoire Schmtzberger and Arnaud Sorosina in Les pouvoirs de la parole, p. 219.*

[140] *Michel Meyer, La rhétorique, p. 20.*

[141] *Ibid., p. 21.*

[142] *Cicero, De Oratore.*

[143] *Elocutio or eloquence is the "third stage in the development of a speech, which consists of 'putting into words.'" This involves choosing phrases, vocabulary, and the style to adopt. See Les pouvoirs de la parole, p. 218.*

[144] *Cicero, The Ideal Orator, p. 39.*

[145] *Aristotle, Rhetoric, Book III.*

[146] *Cicero, Orator ad M. Brutum, p. 61.*

[147] *Quintilian, Institutio Oratoria, Book III.*

[148] *"I also studied the precepts given on elocution, which are: first, the purity and correctness of language, clarity, neatness, elegance, and finally, the propriety and suitability of the style with the subject. I learned everything taught about each of these qualities, I even saw that the art sought to regulate what depends most on nature, I retained some principles on pronunciation and memory, and I practiced applying them." Cicero, Dialogue on Eloquence: De Oratore, Brutus, Orator. Of the Academics, Book I. On Old Age, trans. P-L, Paris, Didot, 1866, p. 56-58 in Power of Speech.*

[149] *Laurent Pernot, La rhétorique dans l'Antiquité, p. 295*

[150] *Cicero, Rhetorica, Book IV.*

[151] *Cicero, Orator ad M. Brutum, p. 78, cited by Alessandro Traversi.*

[152] *Cicero, Orator ad M. Brutum, p. 86.*

[153] *Cicero, Oratore ad Brutum.*

[154] *Ibid.*

[155] *Alessandro Traversi, La défense pénale, techniques de l'argumentation et de l'art oratoire, p. 144.*

[156] *"For a long time now, not only among us but also among other peoples, the opinion has spread, disastrous for the republic and dangerous for you, that with the current judicial system, a wealthy man, even though guilty, can escape justice. Now, at such a delicate moment and precisely for the judiciary..."*

[157] *Office québécois de la langue française, Barbarismes lexicaux, November 2019.*

[158] *Examples of solecisms: "échouer un examen" instead of "échouer à un examen," "se rappeler des bons moments" instead of "se rappeler les bons moments"...*

[159] *Nicolas Boileau, Art poétique, chant IV, p. 147-207.*

[160] *Aristote, Rhétorique, liv. III.*

[161] *Cicéron, De l'orateur, liv. I.*

[162] *Cicero, De oratore, Book I.*

[163] *Quoted by Traversi.*

[164] *Quintilian, Institutio Oratoria, Book XI, Chapter III.*

[165] *Cicero, On the Orator, p. 59.*

[166] *Alessandro Traversi, Criminal Defense, Techniques of Argumentation and Rhetorical Art, p. 148.*

[167] *Cicero, De Oratore, p. 228.*

[168] *Cicero, Rhetorica ad C. Herennuim, Book III.*

[169] *Cicero, On the Orator, p. 183.*

[170] *See also in this regard, Alessandro Traversi, Criminal Defense, Techniques of Argumentation and Oratory Art, p. 150.*

[171] *Quintilian, Institutio Oratoria, Book XI, Chapter II, p. 47.*

[172] *Alessandro Traversi, La défense pénale, techniques de l'argumentation et de l'art oratoire, p. 158.*

[173] *Quintilian, Institution oratoire.*

[174] Cicero, *De Oratore*, Book I, p. 260-261.

[175] Cicero, *The Ideal Orator*, p. 41.

[176] Hélène Tronc, *L'art du discours*, Gallimard, p. 53.

[177] Cicero, *The Ideal Orator*, p. 42.

[178] Quintilian, *Institutio Oratoria*, Book XI, Chapter III.

[179] Hélène Tronc, *The Art of Speech*, Gallimard, p. 56.

[180] Alessandro Traversi, *La défense pénale, techniques de l'argumentation et de l'art oratoire*, p. 183.

[181] In this regard, Erasmus (1467-1536) in *The Praise of Folly* expresses concern about the orators of his time who try to impress the audience indiscriminately through varying tonalities: "They have taken, I don't know where, that the exordium should be delivered slowly and without éclat. What do our people do? They begin in such a way that they cannot hear themselves, an excellent method for not being understood by anyone. They have been told that, to stir passions, one must raise the tone; to obey the precepts, at the moment least expected, they suddenly burst into furious outbursts. It is still traditional for them that the orator must warm up gradually. Thus, after beginning haltingly, they suddenly start to shout, even in the coldest place, and then they end so low that one would think they were about to breathe their last."

[182] Cicero, *Orator ad M. Brutum*, cited by Traversi.

[183] Laurent Pernot, *La rhétorique dans l'Antiquité*, p. 301.

[184] Cicero, *Orator ad M. Brutum*.

[185] Cicero, *The Ideal Orator*, p. 41.

[186] Cicero, *Orator ad M. Brutum*.

[187] Cicero, *De Oratore*, propositions reported by Cicero.

[188] Cicero, *The Ideal Orator*, p. 43.

[189] Cicero, *The Ideal Orator*, p. 43.

[190] Quintilian, *Institutio Oratoria*, Book XI, Chapter II.

[191] Cicero, *On the Orator*, p. 59.

[192] Quintilian, *Institutio Oratoria*, Book XI, Chapter III. See also in this sense, *Techniques of Argumentation and the Art of Oratory*, p. 154.

[193] Quintilien, *Institution oratoire*.

[194] *Quintilien, Institution oratoire.*

[195] *Cicéron, L'orateur.*

[196] *Quintilian, Institution Oratoria, Book XI.*

[197] *Cicero, The Ideal Orator, p. 41.*

[198] *Quintilian, Institution Oratory, Book XI, Chapter II.*

[199] *Cicero, The Ideal Orator, p. 42.*

[200] *Cicero, De Oratore, p. 59.*

[201] *Cicero, The Ideal Orator, p. 47.*

[202] *Dictionnaire de l'Académie française, 2020.*

[203] *Michel Meyer, Rhetoric, Presses universitaires de France, p. 26.*

[204] *Michel Meyer, La rhétorique, p. 23.*

[205] *Cicero, The Ideal Orator, p. 58.*

[206] *Alessandro Traversi, Techniques of Argumentation and Rhetorical Art, p. 164.*

[207] *Fontanier, Les figures du discours, Paris, Flammarion, 1830.*

[208] *See in this regard Laurent Pernot who, in his book La rhétorique dans l'Antiquité p. 298, considers that the interrogation, the answer, the anticipation, the hesitation, the consultation, the element of surprise, the permission, frank speech, prosopopoeia, hypotyposis, irony, aposiopesis... are among the figures of thought.*

[209] *Laurent Pernot in La rhétorique dans l'Antiquité p. 299 continues on figures of words. He names, among others: pleonasm, periphrasis, additional clarification, flashback, antistrophe, and redoubling.*

[210] *Cicero, De Oratore.*

[211] *Laurent Pernot, La rhétorique dans l'Antiquité, p. 297.*

[212] *Cicero,* The Ideal Orator, *71.*

[213] *Laurent Pernot,* Rhetoric in Antiquity.

[214] *Laurent Pernot, in his work* Rhetoric in Antiquity, *on page 297, presents an interesting classification. One can note: "periphrasis (use of several words instead of one), enigma (use of a deliberately obscure expression), metalepsis (use of a word that, in another context, is a synonym), pleonasm (use*

of a redundant word), ellipsis (use of an incomplete word), hyperbaton (displacement of a word), anastrophe (inversion of the word order)."

[215] *It can be extended,* "in praesentia" *when both the compared and the comparison are present in the sentence, and* "in absentia" *when only the comparison is present in the sentence.*

[216] *Michel Meyer, La rhétorique, p. 73.*

[217] *Aristote, Poétique, chap. 21.*

[218] *Quintilien, Institution oratoire, liv. VIII.*

[219] *A beautiful example comes from Baudelaire and his work L'ennemi: "My youth was nothing but a dark storm."*

[220] *Cicero, On the Orator.*

[221] *Anonymous, The Song of Songs, IV, verses 1-3-5, cited by Traversi.*

[222] *Cicero, On the Orator, Book III.*

[223] *Kévin Labiausse, The Great Speeches in History, From Moses to George W. Bush.*

[224] *La Rochefoucauld, Maxims, p. 276.*

[225] *Psalms, 103, verses 15-16.*

[226] *Cicero, Defense of Lucius Morena (Pro Murena), cited by Traversi.*

[227] *Quintilian, Institutio Oratoria, Book VIII.*

[228] *Baudelaire,* Spleen - When the Low and Heavy Sky Weighs Like a Lid.

[229] *"A periphrasis is a phrase or a series of words used to designate something (or someone) that could have been designated with a single word. Example: The seventh art (cinema), the land of the rising sun (Japan), the author of* Les Rougon-Macquart *(Émile Zola),"* according to the Office québécois de la langue française.

[230] *According to Laurent Pernot in* Rhetoric in Antiquity, *this is: "the use of a redundant word."*

[231] *"Reversal of the word order," according to Laurent Pernot.*

[232] *Office québécois de la langue française, 2020.*

[233] *Also see in this sense, Alessandro Traversi,* Techniques of Argumentation and Oratory, *p. 170.*

²³⁴ *"A neologism is a new word, either in form or meaning." See in this sense the Office québécois de la langue française.*

²³⁵ *See in this regard, the Office québécois de la langue française.*

²³⁶ *"Accessory follows the principal." See in this regard the Latin expressions used in Quebec positive law.*

²³⁷ *According to the Larousse Dictionary, in the context of sub-Saharan Africa, it refers to a member of a caste of wandering poets and musicians, custodians of oral culture, and reputed to be in communication with spirits.*

²³⁸ *Marcien Towa, Essays on the Philosophical Problem in Contemporary Africa, CLE Editions, Yaoundé, 1971.*

²³⁹ *Victor Hugo, La légende des siècles, "Booz endormi."*

²⁴⁰ *Jean Racine, Andromaque.*

²⁴¹ *How could one ignore Émile Verhaeren, who in Les villages illusoires (1895), features stanzas full of alliterations: "On the heath, infinitely, here is the wind, which tears and dismembers, in heavy gusts, beating the towns, here is the wind, the wild wind of November.*

²⁴² *Alessandro Traversi, Criminal Defense, p. 178.*

²⁴³ *Literary study.*

²⁴⁴ *Paul Verlaine, "My Familiar Dream" in Saturnian Poems.*

²⁴⁵ *Édouard Herriot.*

²⁴⁶ *Larousse Dictionary.*

²⁴⁷ *Aristotle, Rhetoric, Book II.*

²⁴⁸ *French proverb.*

²⁴⁹ *French proverb.*

²⁵⁰ *French proverb.*

²⁵¹ *"Every society has its law."*

²⁵² *"He who prepares for war prepares for peace."*

²⁵³ *"To each country its own religion."*

²⁵⁴ *"Fraud renders null and void any act performed under its cover."*

²⁵⁵ *African wisdom.*

²⁵⁶ *African wisdom.*

²⁵⁷ *African wisdom.*

[258] *African wisdom.*

[259] *African wisdom.*

[260] *Francophone Debate Federation.*

[261] *Hélène Tronc, L'art du discours, p. 60.*

[262] *Longin (pseudo), Du sublime, cited by Traversi.*

[263] *Quintilian, Institutio Oratoria, Book VIII.*

[264] *Alessandro Traversi, La défense pénale, techniques de l'argumentation et de l'art oratoire, p. 106.*

[265] *According to the Larousse dictionary: "repetition after an interval of one or several words. Example: (... A flood of lugubrious stories! A deep flood of mothers on their knees)". From the Latin verb geminare, meaning "to double," it consists, according to Mortara Gravelli, of repeating a word at the beginning, middle, or end of the same segment of text.*

[266] *C. Perelman and L. Olbrechts-Tyteca, Treatise on Argumentation, the New Rhetoric, Paris, PUF, 1958.*

[267] *Paul Claudel, The Satin Slipper, Scene 2.*

[268] *Cicero, Rhetoric to Herennius, Book IV.*

[269] *The Catilinarian Orations (In Catilinam in Latin) refers to a series of four famous speeches delivered by Cicero in 63 BC when he was consul, accusing Catiline of conspiring against the Roman Republic. These speeches later became an example of eloquence and rhetoric.*

[270] *Cicero, Catilinarian Orations, speech delivered against Catiline when he was caught conspiring against the Roman Republic. See also The Criminal Defense, Techniques of Argumentation and Oratory, p. 199.*

[271] *Cicero, Rhetorica ad Herennium.*

[272] *Charles de Gaulle, excerpt from the speech on August 25, 1944, on the occasion of the liberation of Paris.*

[273] *François Hollande, excerpt from his speech on May 2, 2012, during the debate against Nicolas Sarkozy, on the sidelines of the French presidential election campaign.*

[274] *Excerpt from Nicolas Sarkozy's speech in Marseille on February 19, 2012, during the French presidential election campaign. The same excerpt was*

analyzed by Clément Viktorovitch in his show Le Choix des Armes, evaluating the cross-rhetoric between François Hollande and Nicolas Sarkozy.

[275] *Clément Viktorovitch, Cross-rhetoric Hollande/Sarkozy.*

[276] *Excerpt from Sarkozy's speech, during the 2012 presidential campaign in Le choix des armes. The candidate draws his audience's attention to the two months remaining before the crucial presidential campaign deadline, showing that everything is still possible. By evoking historical figures from France's history, he aims to present himself as part of a noble struggle, similar to what they fought for in their time for the republic. Hence, the necessity now more than ever to help him win the said election.*

[277] *Emmanuel Macron, Speech in Marseille on the sidelines of the 2017 presidential election, April 1, 2017.*

[278] *Cicero, Rhetorica ad Herennium. Also cited by Traversi in Techniques de l'argumentation et de l'art oratoire.*

[279] *Manuel Valls, Declaration of candidacy for the 2017 presidential election, Évry, December 5, 2016.*

[280] *Jean Racine, Iphigénie, Act 1, Scene 1.*

[281] *Cicero, Rhetorica ad Herennium, Book IV, quoted by Traversi.*

[282] *Jean-Jacques Rousseau, The Social Contract.*

[283] *Cicero, La rhétorique à Herennuis, Book IV.*

[284] *Cicero, First speech against Catiline delivered in the Senate, nineteenth speech.*

[285] *According to Laurent Pernot, it consists of reversing the order of words. Such a technique would make the speech more digestible and more capable of persuading effectively.*

[286] *"From the Latin transgressio, it consists of moving a word," Laurent Pernot, La rhétorique dans l'Antiquité, p. 298.*

[287] *"The oxymoron is a figure of opposition that involves combining terms of contrary meanings within the same group of words." www.etudes-literaires.com/figures-de-style/oxymore, February 5, 2020. With this figure, the speaker aims to create a surprise effect that enchants their audience.*

[288] *"From the Latin interrogatio, commonly known as the 'rhetorical question,'" Laurent Pernot, La rhétorique dans l'Antiquité, p. 298. The interrogation adds a boost to the tone of the speech while playing an emotional*

and persuasive role. Cicero's first speech against Catiline in the Senate, too well-known to be fully developed here, highlights the emotional and persuasive power of interrogation.

[289] *Grégoire Schmitsberger and Arnaud Sorosina, Les pouvoirs de la parole, p. 219.*

[290] *C. Perelman and L. Olbrechts-Tyteca, Traité de l'argumentation, la nouvelle rhétorique, p. 306.*

[291] *Quintilian, Institutio Oratoria, Book VIII.*

[292] *Unknown source.*

[293] *Victor Hugo, Les Misérables.*

[294] *Alfred De Musset, La nuit de mai.*

[295] *François Fillon, Speech from March 1, 2017, in which he mentions being summoned on March 15, 2017, by investigating judges to be indicted. He thus denounces a political assassination against him and the presidential election itself.*

[296] *Grégoire Schmitzberger and Arnaud Sorosina, The Powers of Speech, p. 219.*

[297] *Adrian, Gradation, simple definition and example.*

[298] *Cicero, Second Speech Against Catiline in the Senate.*

[299] *Alphonse de Lamartine, The Oak.*

[300] *Charles Baudelaire, The Bottle.*

[301] *François Hollande, Speech at the Bourget, January 22, 2012.*

[302] *François Hollande, Speech at the Bourget, January 22, 2012.*

[303] *François Hollande, Speech in Rouen, February 15, 2012.*

[304] *Cicéron, The Ideal Orator.*

[305] *"He is severe, he is virtuous. He is a member, with good carpets under his feet in December, of the great party of order and honest people," says Victor Hugo in Les quatre vents de l'esprit in 1881.*

[306] *Longinus (Pseudo), On the Sublime, Chapter XII.*

[307] *Cicero.*

[308] *Cicero, De Oratore ad Quintum fratem, Book II.*

[309] *As defined by Mortara Garavelli in Manuale di retorica: "the sudden shift in speech, where the speaker addresses someone different from the natural or conventional recipient of the speech itself." From the Latin personae fictio. It allows the orator to animate what is inanimate in a speech, making present what is absent. Quintilian in Institutio Oratoria states that "it is permissible to bring gods down from the heavens, to raise the dead from their graves, and even to give voice to cities and peoples."*

[310] *From the Latin personae fictio. It allows the orator to animate what is inanimate in a speech, making present what is absent. Quintilian in Institutio Oratoria states that "it is permissible to bring gods down from the heavens, to raise the dead from their graves, and even to give voice to cities and peoples."*

[311] *Alessandro Traversi, La défense pénale, techniques de l'argumentation et de l'art oratoire, p. 219.*

[312] *Francophone Debate Federation.*

[313] *Michel Meyer, La rhétorique, PUF, p. 16-17.*

[314] *Assemblée nationale du Québec, www.assnat.qc.ca/en/patrimoine/lexique/débatparlementaires.html, 14 February 2020.*

[315] *John Locke, Two Treatises of Government, 1690.*

[316] *Charles De Montesquieu, The Spirit of the Laws, Book XI, (1748), p. 48.*

[317] *Ministry of Europe and Foreign Affairs of the French Republic.*

[318] *Amadou Hampâté Ba, during a heartfelt tribute to African culture and an advocacy for African oral traditions during a mission with his country, Mali, at UNESCO in 1960.*

[319] *Ahmadou Kourouma, Soleil des indépendances is a classic of African literature.*

[320] *Louise Bélanger-Hardy and Aline Grenon, Elements of Common Law and Comparative Overview of Quebec Civil Law, p. 51.*

[321] *Frantz Fanon, The Wretched of the Earth, 1961.*

[322] *According to Les pouvoirs de la parole, edited by Grégoire Schmitsberger and Arnaud Sorosina, it refers to "the moral credibility of the speaker and the trust they inspire, often depending on the closeness they manage to create and maintain with their audience."*

[323] "Pathos, in Greek, refers to the experience of suffering, and in Aristotle's rhetoric, it refers to the speaker's ability to express emotions and make the audience feel them through the evocative power of their speech." See Les pouvoirs de la parole, previously cited on page 220.

[324] Physical or verbal assaults, as well as attempts to ridicule a debater based on racist, sexist, homophobic, ethnic, or religious grounds, are not tolerated. We will revisit this issue in depth regarding the speaker's responsibility towards the ethics of discourse and multiculturalism.

[325] Judith Wyatt, How to Prepare for a Debate, in Canadian Federation of Student Debates, 1980.

[326] Alessandro Traversi, Techniques of Argumentation and Oratory, p. 124.

[327] According to Philippe Lemay from the Canadian Interuniversity and Intercollegiate Debate Society, refutation "aims to destroy the opponent's argument and, by doing so, nullify its weight in the final judgment of the debate."

[328] The crystallization of the debate is the final intervention of the debater. It must focus on the key themes that emerge from the debate. In this last opportunity, the orator must show how their thesis still holds up against an opponent who relies on weak arguments that more than ever need crutches to stand.

[329] In honor of Sir Wilfrid Laurier, a graduate of McGill Law School in 1864 and the first Francophone Prime Minister of Canada, the Laurier Cup is an initiative by the McGill Debating Union bringing together debaters from Quebec.

[330] "Les faucons" refers to the legendary name attributed to the debate team of the University of Montreal: "Faucon wins," that was our credo.

[331] See in this regard, Canadian Intercollegiate Debating Society, Judge's Guide, p. 8.

[332] Denzel Washington, The Great Debaters.

[333] Cicero, The Ideal Orator, an epistolary treatise composed at the request of the famous Brutus in 46 BC.

[334] See in this regard sedfuo.blogspot.com.

[335] The heckling should be brief and comedic, and used in exceptional circumstances to maximize the desired effects. Such a maneuver, often used, can

cause the debater to lose the sympathy of the audience, making them appear rather detrimental. In such a context, the debater risks becoming the victim of their own actions, much like the "sprayer getting sprayed."

336 According to the website of the Quebec National Assembly, these are "words prohibited by the Assembly's rules because they are considered offensive or inappropriate for the decency that should prevail in parliamentary deliberations." This same principle applies in parliamentary debate and can lead to a point of order.

337 Honorable Prime Minister, Honorable Minister of the Crown, Honorable Member of the Opposition, Honorable Leader of the Opposition, are the official titles of the speakers. It is forbidden to use their personal names or nicknames, according to the customs of parliamentary debate.

338 Judith Wyatt and Jocelyne Tessier, How to Prepare for a Debate in the Canadian Federation of Student Debates.

339 See in this sense, Judith Wyatt and Jocelyne Tessier, in How to Prepare for a Debate on the website of the Canadian Federation of Student Debates.

340 See in this regard the guide How to Prepare for a Debate by the Canadian Federation of Student Debating.

341 Jocelyne Tessier and Judith Wyatt, Canadian Federation of Student Debating.

342 Denzel Washington, Nate Parker, Jurnee Smolet, The Great Debater.

343 L. Lanza, "Il percorso della decisione," in Il processo invisibile, Venice, 1997, p. 39 and following, cited by Alessandro Traversi in La défense pénale, techniques de l'argumentation et de l'art oratoire, p. 242.

344 We have often seen, notably once during the Édouard Montpetit Cup at the University of Montreal, judges exercising excessive power, using non-verbal language and sometimes condescending tones in their comments to the debaters. After analyzing the situation, we concluded that this is what naturally happens when a judge has the privilege of judging speakers of a level they still aspire to reach. The amateurism of some judges is certainly one of the stumbling blocks in Canadian parliamentary debate; at least, based on the experiences lived as both an actor and a spectator.

345 See in this regard Le débationnaire by the French Debate Society of the University of Ottawa: "A good argument, a good title," August 9, 2011.

[346] *Le débationnaire, trucs et astuces pour un débat réussi : un argument est plus qu'un énoncé*, March 2011, French Debate Society of the University of Ottawa.

[347] According to the Robert Dictionary, crystallization is the act of "gathering scattered elements into a coherent whole."

[348] *The Debater: Crystallization: The Importance of Synthesis*

[349] See the result sheet from the Canadian Intercollegiate Debating Society.

[350] See in this sense the result sheet of the Canadian Intercollegiate Debating Society.

[351] Cicero, *The Ideal Orator.*

[352] Cicerón, *De inventione, escrito entre el 80-84 a.C.*

[353] Francophone Debate Federation.

[354] Denis Diderot, "Political Authority," excerpt from *The Encyclopedia 1751.*

[355] It must be acknowledged, however, that here the questions can be more aggressive. We have seen orators disturb their opponent by the necessity of absolutely asking questions. We have seen teams simultaneously request the floor with the aim of destabilizing. While we were facing orators from the University of Lausanne, Switzerland, and the University of ex-Marseille in the final of the World Debate Championships, we observed the fervor that animated them all. They all stood up at the same time to request a question while we were in the middle of my argument. This maneuver, it seems to us, is more about destabilizing the beautiful rhetorical momentum initiated by an opponent than genuinely wanting to ask a question. The best approach is to release the pressure by calling on one of them for their question at the moment they least expect it. They may have forgotten about it, which would work to our advantage.

[356] These were the names of societies like "Révolte-toi Sorbonne," "Révolte-toi Assas," "Révolte-toi Sciences Po," "Révolte-toi Nanterre," "Révolte-toi Évry," and others.

[357] Following the French Revolution of 1789 and its Declaration of the Rights of Man and Citizen, revolutionary winds spread across the West in the 19th century. In the Americas, several Spanish colonies gained independence. Even today, the constitutions of several states carry the revolutionary spirit of 1789 within them.

287

[358] *The Louis Liard amphitheater is a true temple of speech, where debate and rhetoric are given a sacred dimension. The portraits of great thinkers and revolutionaries from the Enlightenment testify to the spirit that animates this majestic space, reserved for distinguished orators.*

[359] *Aristotle, Rhetoric, Book III.*

[360] *Alessandro Traversi, Techniques of Argumentation and Oratory, Chapter VI.*

[361] *Aristotle, Rhetoric, Book III.*

[362] *Protected time is a period during which the speaker cannot take questions.*

[363] *Francophone Debating Federation.*

[364] *Alphonse de Lamartine, 1790-1869, Le Lac.*

[365] *See in this sense Bertrand Périer, La parole est un sport de combat.*

[366] *Denzel Washington, The Great Debaters.*

[367] *Cicero, The Ideal Orator.*

[368] *Cicero, The Ideal Orator, an epistolary treatise composed at the request of the famous Brutus in 46 BCE. In it, Cicero highlights the various elements of eloquence through the figure of an ideal orator.*

[369] *"Docere, delectare, movere" (to instruct, to charm, to move).*

[370] *Alessandro Traversi, La défense pénale, techniques de l'argumentation et de l'art oratoire, p. 87.*

[371] *Master Bertrand Périer, Speech is a Combat Sport, October 2017, Éditions Lattès.*

[372] *Paul Stéphane Nicolas Sarkozy De Nagy Bosca was a lawyer, Minister of the Interior, and President of the French Republic from 2007 to 2012. In his speeches, he excels in his ability to use with brilliance an amplification figure analyzed earlier: anaphora.*

[373] *Cicero, The Ideal Orator.*

[374] *"My wife always tells me, don't make political statements, you're in France, remember that almost all of them are left-wing... And so, I don't make political statements... after this rhetorical precaution, I'll return to my critique," Marc Bonnant humorously stated in the context of the historical Fleurs du mal trial.*

[375] *Marc Bonnant: "Trial of Les Fleurs du mal", March 14, 2013, in the first chamber of the Paris Court of Appeal.*

[376] *Jacques Amyot was an advisor to King Henry III.*

[377] *Jacques Amyot, Projet d'éloquence royale, Éditions Les Belles Lettres, 1992.*

[378] *Cicéron, L'orateur idéal, p. 46-47, translated from Latin, with a preface and annotations by Nicolas Waquet.*

[379] *The Société des ambianceurs et des personnes élégantes is a movement that emphasizes appearance and the art of coordinating colors. This distinguished aspect was notably observed among the orators from the University of Paris Nanterre, who found in rhetoric an entire art of being. Beyond savoring the scent of words, being an orator for them is an attitude that requires a sense of leadership.*

[380] *During the final of the World Debate Championship at the Sorbonne, Nathalie Kosciuszko-Morizet (NKM), former Minister of Ecology and President of the jury, decided to change the rules of the debate by reversing the positions. The government became the opposition, and the opposition became the government. The speaker from the University of Lausanne, in a spectacle-worthy moment akin to Hollywood, suddenly removed his jacket, as if to show his change of position. After this theatrical effect, he said: "French people, I have deceived you..." It was a magical moment in the debate, which undoubtedly contributed to him earning the ultimate glory of the debate. This shows that oratory action, just like the argument itself, can help win a cause.*

[381] *"Literally, it is the art of discussion. In Aristotle's Rhetoric, the term refers to all the deductions we draw from opinions that are uncertain. In Plato, a disciple of Socrates, the term refers to the movement of thought that operates through discourse, viewed as a dialogue of the soul with itself," definition taken from The Powers of Speech, Flammarion, p. 218.*

[382] *Amadou Ampathé Ba, Malian writer.*

[383] *In ancient Africa, the griot is an official and traditional communicator who, depending on the circumstances, may be a musician, poet, historian, journalist, or diplomat. Through verbal magic, they contribute to the construction of the empire.*

[384] *Unlike an artist, not everyone can become a griot. It is a matter of lineage, passed down from father to son or mother to daughter. While the griot*

certainly has artistic talent, as a musician or poet, their role goes beyond that of an artist.

[385] *The kora refers to a musical instrument originating from Mali, found in West Africa.*

[386] *Doumouya Salia, Kassa Le messager – Kassa au pays du balafon.*

[387] *Marcien Towa, Essais sur la problématique philosophique dans l'Afrique actuelle, Éditions clé, Yaoundé, 1971.*

[388] *Ahmadou Kourouma, Soleil des indépendances, Presses de l'Université de Montréal, 1968.*

[389] *The "years of embers" in the African context refer to various civil society organizations' demands for the necessary democratic openness for public debate.*

[390] *This can be seen in this excerpt from his 1990 speech, where Mobutu announces, with tears in his eyes, the country's transition to multipartism: "... What becomes of the leader in all of this (Mobutu asks in a martial tone)? I announce that, from this day, I take leave from the Popular Movement of the Revolution to allow it to choose a new leader to guide... (there was a brief silence from the strongman followed by a now-legendary phrase)... understand my emotion."*

[391] *MARIUS YANNICK BINYOU-BI-HOMB, Pratique orale et médiaculture en Afrique contemporaine, Master's thesis presented at the Senghor University of Alexandria.*

[392] *Frantz Fanon, The Wretched of the Earth, 1961.*

[393] *African proverb*

[394] *"Les débats oratoires' is an institution in Burkina Faso aimed at promoting the art of oratory, structured debate, and democratic culture.*

[395] *Francophone debating federation.*

[396] *The hypothetical case is the imaginary story that raises legal issues on which the student must plead both as the claimant on one hand, and as the defendant on the other.*

[397] *The jury here is very prestigious. It consists of professors and experts in international law, judges from national and international courts.*

[398] *See in this regard, Center for Human Rights, University of Pretoria: African Moot Court Competition on YouTube.*

399 *Nelson Mandela.*

400 *Antoine de Saint-Exupéry in his book Terre des hommes.*

401 *Stephen E. Lucas, The art of public speaking.*

402 *This refers to the genocide or the attempted extermination of Jews by the Nazis during World War II.*

403 *Cicero, On the Art of Oratory, Book One.*

404 *Council of Europe, Committee of Ministers, Recommendation No. (97) 20. See also Connexion, Manual for Combating Hate Speech Online through Human Rights Education.*

405 *Thorbjorn Jagland, Secretary General of the Council of Europe.*

406 *See in this regard, Pavel Ivanov v. Russia before the European Court of Human Rights, and W.P. and Others v. Poland.*

407 *The European Court of Human Rights has ruled on the issue of racial hatred in several cases, notably: Glimmerveen and Hagenbeek v. Netherlands.*

408 *See in this regard, Norwood v. United Kingdom, Belkacem v. Belgium.*

409 *The Court made a ruling on the issue in the case Roj TV A/S v. Denmark.*

410 *See the Court's decision in the case Communist Party of Germany v. Federal Republic of Germany.*

411 *European Court of Human Rights/Press Unit.*

412 *Patrice Émery Lumumba, Speech of June 30, 1960, Independence Day of Congo.*

413 *Patrice Émery Lumumba, Speech of June 30, 1960, Independence Day of Congo.*

414 *"My dear companion, I write these words without knowing whether they will reach you, when they will reach you, and if I will be alive when you read them. Throughout my struggle (...) I have never doubted for a single moment the final triumph of the sacred cause to which my companions and I have devoted our entire lives (...) Whether dead, alive, free, or in prison (...) It is not my person that matters. It is Congo (...) No brutality, no abuse, no torture has ever led me to ask for mercy, for I prefer to die with my head held high, unwavering faith, and deep trust in the destiny of my country, rather than live in submission to sacred principles (...) Africa will write its own history, and it will be, from north to south of the Sahara, a history of glory and dignity. Do not*

cry, my companion. I know that my country, which suffers so much, will defend its independence and its freedom."

[415] *Ad verecundiam.*

[416] *European Court of Human Rights/Press Unit.*

[417] *See in this regard Barthes and his book The Ancient Rhetoric.*

[418] *Quintilian, Institutio oratoria, Book III.*

[419] *Council of Europe, Committee of Ministers, Recommendation (97) 20.*

[420] *In Latin (Bonitas), see Cicero in De Oratore to M. Brutum.*

[421] *Barack Obama, Yes We Can, 2008.*

[422] *Barack Obama, Speech on the 50th Anniversary of the Selma March, 2015.*

[423] *"It is said that the first sentence of a speech is always difficult..." this is how the Polish poet Wisława Szymborska expressed herself at the opening of her speech upon receiving the Nobel Prize in Literature. The speaker, with a pointed sense of humor, thus makes it clear that she is not a specialist in speeches. This is actually a common technique since antiquity, allowing the orator to gain the favor of the audience by apologizing for their perceived inadequacy.*

[424] *To win the goodwill of the audience.*

[425] *Aristotle, Rhetoric, Book III, Chapter 4.*

[426] *"In This Act, 'prohibited act' means any conduct or communication by a person that has as its purpose interference with the civil rights of a person or class of persons by promoting: a) hatred or contempt of a person or class of persons, or b) the superiority or inferiority of a person or class of persons in comparison with another or others, on the basis of color, race, religion, ethnic origin, or place of origin..."*

[427] *"Milo, after having been at the Senate until the session ended, returned home, changed his shoes and clothes. He waited a bit while his wife... it's always the same story! was getting ready, so he left at a time such that, if Clodius truly intended to return to Rome, he could have. Clodius approaches, unbothered, on horseback, without luggage, without even his cohort of Greeks, without his wife, which almost never happened, while Milo, the aggressor, who had organized this trip solely to commit a murder, left in a carriage with his family dressed in traveling clothes, with his entourage fed and intrusive, perfumed and graceful with servants and young men!"*

[428] *Martin Luther King, I Have A Dream.*

[429] *Ibid.*

[430] *Martin Luther King, I Have A Dream.*

[431] *Étonnantes classiques, Les pouvoirs de la parole, p. 129.*

[432] *Cicero, For Caelius (Pro Caelio), is a speech delivered by Cicero on April 4, 56 BC. From ancient times, it was considered a masterpiece of judicial eloquence.*

[433] *Cicero, De l'invention oratoire, Book I, p. 7.*

[434] *Cicero, De l'invention oratoire, Book I.*

[435] *Cicero, The Ideal Orator.*

[436] *"The art of speaking well, deliberating, and persuading." See in this sense The Powers of Speech, p. 218.*

[437] *Public speaking coach.*

[438] *Les Échos START, "Eloquence, a skill that makes a difference in professional life."*

[439] *MC Solaar.*

www.ingramcontent.com/pod-product-compliance
Lightning Source LLC
Chambersburg PA
CBHW052109030426

42335CB00025B/2903